Praise for
Running *with the* Kenyans

"Every book, like every life, is a pilgrimage with one central question: Is this about the journey or the destination? The subtitle of Adharanand Finn's *Running with the Kenyans* promises . . . 'the secrets of the fastest people on Earth.' Are we going to too? Yup."

"A hymn to the spirit, t⋯⋯⋯⋯⋯⋯⋯⋯⋯⋯⋯y, to the joy of movement."

"Finn's account of his journey to running Nirvana feels completely satisfying, as well-paced and exhilarating as a good run."
—*The Boston Globe*

"Part scientific study, travel memoir, and tale of self-discovery, Finn's journey makes for a smart and entertaining read."
—*Publishers Weekly*

"[*Running with the Kenyans*] strikes a balance between memoir and applicable lessons for those interested in learning the reasons for the success of Kenyan runners. Finn's writing is accessible, and he threads entertaining familial vignettes through the book. Recommended for runners as well as the sport's fans."
—*Kirkus Reviews*

"Anybody with an interest in sports will find it exciting."
—*Kansas City Star*

"Finn is a generous and insightful storyteller, expertly weaving in stories of the many remarkable runners. . . . A well-crafted story about pursuing a dream and experiencing life from a new perspective that runners and nonrunners alike will enjoy."
—*Booklist*

"I've seldom read a better account of the exhilaration of running—the sense of testing oneself to the limit, the constant blur of impressions, the 'stirring of something primeval in the depths of our bellies.' . . . What gives *Running with the Kenyans* its special appeal is Finn's charm."
—*London Evening Standard*

"Finn's story is escapist and colorfully evocative . . . populated with engagingly drawn characters and towards the end, Finn's quest—the burning need to attain a certain marathon time—is gripping."
—*The Telegraph* (four-star review)

"Equal parts cultural examination, cult-of-running treatise and poignant memoir, *Running with the Kenyans* thrives on a variety of levels. Like the skilled distance runner he is, Finn paces his story marvelously and then saves the best for the final kick. This book packs all the pleasure and satisfaction—and none of the ancillary pain—of a long training run."
—L. JON WERTHEIM, senior editor,
Sports Illustrated, and co-author of the
New York Times bestseller *Scorecasting*

"Not everyone gets to heaven in their lifetime. Finn tried to run there, and succeeded. *Running with the Kenyans* is a great read."
—BERND HEINRICH, author of *Why We Run*

"If you want to know the secrets of Kenyan runners, and have a rollicking adventure along the way, join Finn in his fascinating tale of what it is to go stride for stride with the fastest people on Earth."
—NEAL BASCOMB, author of *The Perfect Mile*

"An extremely good book . . . If *Born to Run* taught us what to wear (or not to wear) when running, Finn's fascinating *Running with the Kenyans* teaches us how to run and should be required reading for anyone planning their first fun run or marathon."
—ROBIN HARVIE, author of
The Lure of Long Distances

"If you have ever wondered what it is like to train with the Kenyans, as I have, I strongly recommend this book. You will feel like you are pounding out hard runs on the dirt roads as you turn each page. You will also learn many of the secrets behind one of the greatest running cultures of all time. A must-read!"
—RYAN HALL, member of the
U.S. Olympic marathon team

Running

◄ *with the* ►

Kenyans

Running

◄ *with the* ►

Kenyans

———

Discovering

the Secrets of the

Fastest People on Earth

———

Adharanand Finn

BALLANTINE BOOKS TRADE PAPERBACKS

New York

LIBRARY OF CONGRESS CATALOGING-IN-PUBLICATION DATA
Finn, Adharanand.
Running with the Kenyans : discovering the secrets of the
fastest people on earth / Adharanand Finn.
p. cm.
ISBN 978-0-345-52880-3 (trade paperback) — ISBN 978-0-345-53352-4 (ebook)
1. Runners (Sports)—Kenya. 2. Running—Social aspects—Kenya.
3. Track and field—Social aspects—Kenya. 4. National characteristics,
Kenyan. \I. Title.
GV1061.23.K4F56 2012
796.424096762—dc23   2012009641

To my fellow collaborators
Marietta, Lila, Uma, and Ossian

When the divine is looking for you,
that's a pretty powerful force.

—PREM RAWAT

Prologue

On your marks . . .

hear someone else's alarm go first. I've been waiting for it, in my half-sleep. A shallow, impatient slumber under the thin sheet, the name of the hotel stamped across it in green ink: BOMEN. The light from the hallway makes the room visible: bare walls; a dark, pink color in this light, but in the day an intoxicating bright peach. An energy-saving lightbulb hangs from its wire above my head.

A phone rings. Godfrey, in the other bed a few feet away, answers it immediately, as though he's been waiting for it to ring. He speaks in calm, wakeful Kalenjin, and then hangs up.

"Chris," he says in the darkness. He knows I'm awake. "He wants to go down for breakfast."

My alarm goes off, buzzing meekly on the bedside table. I reach over and turn it off: 4:00 A.M. Time to get up.

◄►

The hotel is a clatter of pots and pans and people talking. Some of the guests must be turning over in their beds and wondering what is going on, checking their watches. I head out along the corridor. The leaves of a palm tree bristle at one end. At the top of the stairs I meet Beatrice, standing in the shadows, unsure whether to go down. She smiles, her teeth white against her black skin.

"Let's go," I say.

Without replying, she follows me down.

In the dining room the waiters are ready. They've been pulled out of their beds in the middle of the night and pressed into their waiting suits. They don't look pleased.

"Tea? Coffee?" asks the headwaiter, holding a tray of pots and cups. We both shake our heads. I sit down at the table. Beatrice follows, sitting down opposite me. Outside, the street is silent.

I look at Beatrice. "Ready?" I ask her.

She smiles. "I will make it," she says, nodding.

Japhet and Shadrack walk into the room. Two young men in their early twenties. Neither of them has ever been this far from home. Japhet is all big, toothy smiles, excited; while Shadrack, his eyes staring straight ahead, looks permanently as though he has just seen something both shocking and incredible.

The waiter is back at the table with his tray. "Tea? Coffee?"

"Chai," says Shadrack so quietly he has to repeat it twice before the waiter understands. Japhet just nods. The waiter pours out the tea.

"You both feeling ready?" I ask.

Shadrack looks at me confused, as though I've just asked him if he has ever been in love.

"We're ready, yes," says Japhet, grinning.

The waiter, on a roll now, brings us all a plate of fruit. Shadrack pokes his watermelon nervously with a fork and offers it to Beatrice. Then the waiter brings plates of bread and fried eggs for everyone.

"Whatever you do," Godfrey told us the night before, "don't eat eggs for breakfast." I look at the others.

"You like eggs before a race?" I ask them. But they're already tucking in. I decide not to make a fuss, but I leave mine untouched. Two slices of bread and butter is enough. I eat quickly and return to my room.

I had planned to go back to sleep after breakfast, but I'm too awake, so I pack up my bags and sit on the bed. My foot feels fine. I rub it to make sure it's all right, pressing my thumb into the sole where the injury was. I pull out a bottle of Menthol Plus, a balm from the pharmacy back in Iten. I rub it on my foot, then pull my socks on and sit back on the bed. Slow, deep breaths. An hour later, it's time to go.

◄ ►

The dawn is casting a faint light across the parking lot as we all stand around beside the minibus, waiting for Godfrey. I left him combing his hair in the bedroom. He has a grade-one crew cut, but still he spends five minutes combing it each morning. The others stand quietly, patient. Finally he turns up.

"Sorry, guys," he says, sliding open the minibus doors. The junior members of the team, Japhet, Shadrack, and Beatrice, climb in to the back of the bus. Chris, Paul, and Philip, all veteran runners, take the middle row. As the sole *mzungu*, white man, I'm given the front seat next to Godfrey, our trainer and driver.

We bump our way out of the drive and along the dirt street to the main paved road. People are up walking around, herding goats, carrying large sacks across their shoulders. Crowded *matatus*, small buses, pull over and more people squeeze in. The day is already under way.

Inside our bus nobody speaks. Godfrey fiddles with the radio, but he already knows it doesn't work. He drives on, the road straight, rising up along the edge of the savannah, which spreads out vast and empty on one side. On the other side are makeshift houses, small fields of maize, kiosks painted in bright colors advertising phone companies.

After about twenty minutes we reach the main entrance gate to Lewa, a 55,000-acre wildlife conservancy 170 miles north of Nairobi. A long line of 4x4 cars is filing through. People are walking beside the road. We join in the line of traffic. The savannah spreads out on both sides now, filling the world. This is the classic African landscape. Dry, grassy plains dotted with spiky acacia trees.

In the back, they're all getting excited suddenly, pointing out the window.

"What is it?" I ask.

"Look," says Godfrey, pointing to one side, where an elephant is standing, as still as a statue, just a few feet away.

"Is it real?" Philip asks, craning over my shoulder to see.

We bump on through the clouds of dust from the other cars. The elephant has lightened the mood in the bus. Godfrey starts out on his pep talk.

"Okay, guys. Here we are. I know we have a winner in this car. You've all done the training, now it's time to run. Remember that this is a marathon. You mustn't go too fast at the beginning. But you need to stay in touch with the leaders. You know you can do it."

Godfrey pulls the bus to a halt. Even though it's still barely past 6:00 A.M., hundreds of people stand lined up behind a rope, being pushed back by security guards. Runners in shorts and vests, numbers pinned to their chests, are streaming along the track toward the start. Before I know it, everyone is off the bus and has disappeared.

"They've gone straight to the start," says Godfrey. "You go, I'll meet you there."

It's already warm, so I strip off my tracksuit and throw it in the bus. I'm wearing my yellow vest. My number, 22, is pinned to the front. Along the back are the words: ITEN TOWN HARRIERS.

The start is buzzing with over a thousand runners. Among the melee I spot a group of yellow vests, the rest of the team. They're with my wife, Marietta, and my two-year-old son, Ossian. My two daughters are somewhere watching from the sidelines. Marietta's waiting for me so she can take a group photograph.

We huddle together. Godfrey doesn't want to be in the picture, but we haul him over. We couldn't have done this without him. He stands at the back, his face lost under the shadow of his hat.

"Okay, thank you," says Marietta, releasing us from our pose. "Good luck." And with that we're lining up. We all shake hands, but there's nothing left to say. This is it. Months of training on the line. The wild plains of Africa lying before us. Waiting. Still. Helicopters hover overhead. The man with the microphone doesn't say it but we're waiting for some lions to move off the course. The helicopters are swooping low over them, trying to force them on. It seems a long time to stand there. I stretch my arms. Twenty-six miles; forty-two kilometers. But they are just numbers. One step at a time. One breath at a time. The morning heat rises from the spiky grass. My children, with big smiley faces, are waving at me from the side. And then we're counting. Five. I feel my breath filling me with life. Four. People hold their watches, crouching. Three. Two. This is it. One. Go.

Running
◀ *with the* ▶
Kenyans

One

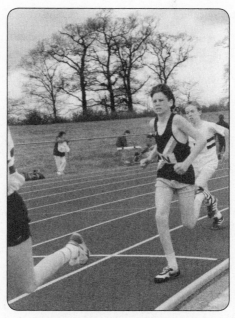

*Running in the Northamptonshire County
Championships, 1988*

We're running across long, wavy grass, racing for the first corner. I'm right at the front, being pushed on by the charge of legs all around me, the quick breathing of my schoolmates. We run under the goalposts and swing down close beside the stone wall along the far edge of the field. It's quieter now. I look around. One other boy is just behind me, but the others have all dropped back. Up ahead I can see the fluttering tape marking the next corner. I run on, the cold air in my lungs, the tall poplar trees shivering above my head.

We go out of the school grounds, along a gravel path that is normally out of bounds. My feet crunch along, the only sound. An old man pushing a bicycle stands to one side as I go by. I follow the tape, back down a steep slope on to the playing fields, back to the finish. I get there long before anyone else and stand waiting in the cold as the other runners come in, collapsing one after the other across the line. I watch them, rolling on their backs, kneeling on the ground, their faces red. I feel strangely elated. It's the first PE class in my new school and we've all been sent out on a cross-country run. I've never tried running farther than the length of a football field before, so I'm surprised by how easy I find it.

"He's not even breathing hard," the teacher says, holding me up as an example to the others. He tells me to put my hands under my armpits to keep them warm as the other children continue to trail in.

◄ ►

A few years later, at age twelve, I break the 800 meters school record on sports day, despite a few of the other boys attempting to bundle me over at the start in an effort to help their friend win. Five minutes later, I run the 1,500 meters and win that, too. When we get home, my dad, sensing some potential talent, suggests that I join the local running club and looks up the number in the telephone directory. I hear him talking to someone on the phone, asking directions. From that point on, a course is set: I am to be a runner.

It all begins rather inauspiciously one night a few weeks later. I put on my shorts and tracksuit and walk across the bridge to the shopping mall next to our suburban housing estate in Northampton, England, a town of 200,000 people sixty-five miles north of

London. The precinct is half deserted, save for a few late shoppers coming out of the giant Tesco supermarket. I head down the escalator to the car park, and then across the road to the unmarked dirt track where the Northampton Phoenix running club meets. It's a cold night and all the runners are crammed into a small doorway in the side of a huge redbrick wall. Inside, the corridor walls are painted blood-red and covered in lewd graffiti. Down the hall are the changing rooms, where men can be heard laughing loudly above the fizz of the showers. I give my name to a lady sitting at a small table.

Rather than head out onto the track, as I had imagined, I'm taken back across the road with a group of children my age, to the shopping mall's delivery area, a stretch of covered road with shuttered loading bays all along one side. The road itself is thick with discharged oil. A man in tights and a yellow running jacket gets us to run from one side of the road to the other, touching the curb each time. Between each sprint he makes us do exercises such as pushups or jumping jacks. I begin thinking, as I lie back on the cold, hard concrete ready to do some sit-ups, that I've come to the wrong place. This isn't running. I had imagined groups of lithe athletes hurtling around a track. My dad must have gotten confused and called the wrong club.

◅ ▻

I'm so convinced this isn't the running club that I don't return for another year. When I do, they ask me if I'd like to train in "the tunnel"—which I take to mean the shopping mall loading bays—or head out for a long run. I opt for the long run and am directed over to a group of about forty people. This is more like it. As we set off along the gravel pathways that wind around the council estates of east Northampton, I feel for the first time the sensation of running in the middle of a group of people. The easy flow of our legs moving below us, the trees, houses, lakes floating by, the people stepping aside, letting us go. Although most of the other runners are older and constantly making jokes, as I drift quietly along, I feel a vague sense of belonging.

I spend the next six years or so as a committed member of the club, running track or cross-country races most weekends, and training at least twice a week. Much of my formative years I spend out pounding the roads. Even when I grow my hair long and start playing the guitar in a band, I keep on training. The other runners nickname me Bono. One night, when I'm about eighteen, I pass a bunch of my school friends coming back from the pub. We are going at full pace in the last mile of a long run. My school friends stare at me open mouthed as I charge by, one shouting, incredulously: "What are you doing?" as I disappear into the distance.

◄ ►

I first become aware of Kenyan runners sometime in the mid-1980s, around the time I join the running club. They seem to emerge suddenly in large numbers into a running world dominated, in my eyes, by Britain's Steve Cram and the Moroccan Said Aouita. I'm a big fan of both of these great rivals. Cram, with his high-stepping, majestic style; and the smaller Aouita, with his grimacing face and rocking shoulders, who is brilliant at every distance—from the short, fast 800 meters right up to the 10,000 meters.

But by the 1988 Olympics in Seoul, it is all Kenyans, winning every men's middle-distance and long-distance track gold medal except one. What impresses me most about them is the way they run. The conventional wisdom is that the most efficient method, particularly in the longer distances, is to run at an even pace, and most races are run that way. The Kenyans, however, take a more maverick approach. They are always surging ahead, only to slow down suddenly, or sprinting off at a crazy pace right from the start. I love the way it befuddles the TV commentators, who are constantly predicting that a Kenyan athlete is going too fast, only to then see him go suddenly even faster.

I remember watching the 1993 world championship 5,000 meters final on a warm mid-August evening in our living room in Northampton. My mum keeps coming in and out, suggesting I go and sit outside in the garden. It's a lovely evening, but I'm glued to the TV. The television cameras are focused on the prerace favorite, the Olympic champion from Morocco, Khalid Skah, and also on a young Ethiopian named Haile Gebrselassie, who won both the 5,000 meters and the 10,000 meters at the world junior championships the year before. The athletes stand side by side at the start line, looking back into the camera. They smile nervously when their names are announced, and give the odd directionless wave.

The race sets off at a blistering pace, with a succession of African athletes streaking ahead one after the other at the front. Skah, who has taken on and beaten the Kenyans many times before, tracks their every move, always sitting on the shoulder of the leader. Britain's only runner in the race, Rob Denmark, soon finds himself trailing far behind.

With seven laps still to go, the BBC television commentator Brendan Foster is feeling the strain just watching. "It's a vicious race out there," he says. Right on queue, a young Kenyan, Ismael Kirui, surges to the front and, within a lap, opens up a huge gap of more than 150 feet on everyone else. It's a suicidal move, Foster declares. "He's only eighteen and has no real international experience. I think he's got a little carried away." I sit riveted, screaming at the TV as the coverage cuts away to the javelin for a few moments.

When it switches back, Kirui is still leading. Lap after lap, Skah and a group of three Ethiopians track him, but they aren't getting any closer. The camera zooms in on Kirui's eyes, staring ahead, wild like a hunted animal as he keeps piling on the pace. "This is one savage race," says Foster.

Kirui is still clear as the bell sounds for the last lap. Down the back straight he sprints for his life, but the three Ethiopians are flying now, closing the gap. With just over 100 meters left, Kirui glances over his shoulder and sees the figure of Gebrselassie closing in on him. For a brief second everything seems to stop. This is the moment, the kill is about to happen. Startled, frantic, Kirui turns back toward the front and urges his exhausted body on again, his tired legs somehow sprinting away down the finishing straight. He crosses the line less than half a second ahead of Gebrselassie, but he has done it. He has won. Battered and bewildered, he sets off on his lap of honor, the Kenyan flag, once again, held aloft in triumph.

That evening I head down to the track for a training session with my running club. I try to run like Kirui, staring straight ahead, going as fast as I can right from the start. It's one of the best training sessions I ever have. Usually, if you run too hard at the beginning, you worry about how you'll feel later. You can feel it in your body, the anticipation of the pain to come. Usually it makes you slow down. It's called pacing yourself. But that night I don't care. I want to unshackle myself and run free like a Kenyan.

◄ ►

The night I spend hurtling wide-eyed around the track after watching Ismael Kirui turns out to be one of the last sessions I ever have with my running club. Just over a month later I pack my belongings into my parents' car and drive up to Liverpool to begin college. Although I join the college running team, my focus on training is soon lost amid the whirlwind of university life. Like most teenage students, I'm unleashed into a new world in which anything seems possible. Running seems to belong in a previous life, although I never completely let go of it.

The extent to which my training peters out becomes clear by the time the British University cross-country championships come around the following March. The night before the race, I take off on a spontaneous road trip to Wales with three friends, clambering onto the team bus the next morning ready for little else other than sleep. It's a miracle I make it at all.

A hundred miles away, in the small northern town of Durham, it's a cold, blustery day. I lace up my spikes and go through the familiar routine of jogging and stretching, but once the race starts, my legs, sucked down by the thick mud, give up without a fight. I jog around, unable to rouse myself to run any faster. I finish in 280th position. My good friend and rival from my running days in Northampton, Ciaran Maguire, comes second. Just a few years earlier we battled neck and neck all the way in the county cross-country championships, until he edged past me on the line to win. And now here we are separated by almost three hundred people. I see him after the race. "All you need is to give yourself one good year of training," he says consolingly. I nod, but deep down I know it is not going to happen.

Over the years, I've met others like me: former runners who still, every now and then, dig out their old sneakers and start lapping the local park in the vague hope of remembering what it felt like. We sign up to a local 10K or half marathon, determined to get back in shape. But something—life, an injury, a lack of dedication—

always gets in the way, and we stop training. But the embers refuse to die, and we refuse to chuck our moldy old sneakers away. We know we might need them again, that the urge to run will return.

After I have children, it becomes even harder to find the time to train, that is, until I manage to land a freelance job writing race reports for *Runner's World* magazine. Although it doesn't pay much, it makes the running feel less self-indulgent. It isn't just me doing something for myself in an effort to revive some lost childhood fervor. It is now work.

With regular assignments from *Runner's World*, I start training more frequently over the next few years, although with young children it's still hard to get out more than twice a week. I descend the stairs from my office to find Marietta with little Ossian hanging off her hip, struggling to get lunch ready, as my two daughters, Lila and Uma, are screeching at each other and tussling over a book. The yard is overgrown, the trash needs to be taken out, and the phone is ringing. It's not easy to say, *I'm just popping out for a long run. See you in an hour or so.* So even though I start racing regularly, my times barely improve. I run my first half marathon when I'm twenty-nine, in 1 hour 30 minutes. Seven years later I've run three more in exactly the same time.

I keep telling myself that one day I will train hard and run really fast. I'm not sure what that would mean exactly—an under-three-hour marathon, perhaps? But the years are slipping away. Every time an athlete over thirty-five wins a big race on television, I tell myself that there is still hope. It isn't that I want to achieve any specific goal; I just don't want to look back one day and regret that I never gave myself a decent chance to see what I could do.

Two

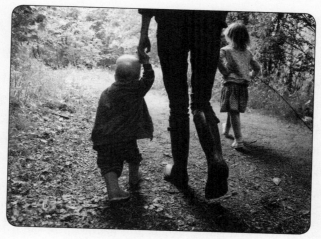

"I think it's a brilliant idea."

I sit looking out of the car window on the way to a 10K charity race near our home in Devon. It's a blustery September morning and I'm not feeling well. If I wasn't writing about it for *Runner's World,* I probably wouldn't run. I make myself feel better by resolving to start at a slow pace and to just enjoy the scenery. The course loops around the grounds of the lovely Powderham Castle, past deer and along the Exe Estuary. It will be nice to take in my surroundings as I run for a change. As we park the car, I have no idea that something is about to happen that will make me rethink my whole approach to running.

Once I get to the start line, I seem to forget about my illness, instinctively snaking my way to the front. I can't let myself start behind with all the fun runners, no matter how bad I feel. There are almost one thousand people in the race, but most of them are here purely for the fun of the event or to raise money for charity. The actual running is just an excuse. For many, it's the chatter of friends, the picnics on the grass, and the general sense of the occasion that brings them out.

It occurs to me afterward, though, when we've all finished, that perhaps, secretly, it's the other way around. Afterward, the race is all anyone wants to talk about. *What time did you do? I couldn't get going. I went off too fast.* People beam as they tell each other how tired they feel, their faces flushed, their bodies tingling blissfully as they pull their tracksuits back on. Perhaps, really, all the other stuff is the excuse. If it comes disguised as a charity event, with team T-shirts and picnics, people will have a good excuse to run. In fact, they'll come flocking. A thousand people, and nearly all of them feeling better for it afterward. One woman tells me, as we sit on the grass, that she thinks running is like getting drunk in reverse. With drinking, it feels great at first, but then you start feeling awful. With running, you feel awful at first, but then, after you finish, you feel great. That sounds like a much better deal.

◄ ►

As the starting gun fires, we surge forward across the grass. I'm near the front as we come to the first corner. A sharp bend leads us on to the gravel drive up toward the castle. As we run, a man beside me asks me what my personal best time is. "I don't know," I say. I did run a 10K a few years before, in forty-seven minutes, but I'm sure I'm faster now.

We clatter in under the arched entrance to the castle and across a small courtyard. My daughters are standing there with my mother-in-law, Granny Bee. "Here he is," she tells them, pointing me out among the sea of charity T-shirts. "Come on, Dhar," she shouts. My daughters just stare at me as I run by. I smile at them, to reassure them it's okay, it's still me. And with that, we head out under the arch and off into the countryside.

The course dinks down a short hill and then along by the Exe Estuary, the sailing boats bobbing and clinking out on the water. I'm still near the front, and decide to stretch my legs to make use of the wind blowing behind us. No one else seems to have the same plan, and they let me go, racing off at the front, blown like tinder along the path. The two-kilometer marker seems to appear almost instantly. Surely they've put it in the wrong place—we haven't run that far already, have we? I look back. I'm now a good 40 meters clear at the front. If I keep this up, I think, I could finish in the top ten. In my mind I'm already rehearsing how I'm going to tell the story afterward. *I was still in the lead at three kilometers.*

As the three-kilometer marker comes and goes, I revise my story. *I was still in the lead at four kilometers. And five kilometers.*

I keep expecting a stream of runners to pass me at any moment. Where are they? What is going on? It's strange being out on my own. It's almost as though I'm not in a race at all, but on a solitary training run, except for the fact that there are a thousand unseen runners massing behind me, chasing me. Like some fugitive, each time I feel my legs slowing I force myself on, bursting up hills, tumbling down grassy banks. I'm running more on some primal survival instinct than any fierce desire to win.

In the end, I finish well clear of the field in a huge personal best time of 38 minutes 35 seconds. My daughters run over as I cross the line and give me a big hug. A reporter from the local newspaper comes up and starts asking me questions. I feel like I've won the Olympics.

As I sit in Granny Bee's car on the way home, I wonder again, for the millionth time since I left school, what would happen if I trained properly. If I did what Ciaran said, and gave myself one year of real training. But how could I fit it in? As the car purrs along, the wipers swishing back and forth, the girls quiet in the back, tired from a morning of running around outside, I begin devising a crazy plan.

A few months earlier, Marietta's sister, Jophie, suggested I come to Kenya, where she lives, to run the Lewa Marathon. Famous as one of the toughest marathons in the world, the race is run across a wildlife conservancy. "There are lions roaming around," she said, as if that somehow made it more tempting. "But there are helicopters in the sky to make sure they don't come too close." I wasn't really listening. I wasn't ready to run a marathon, and besides, I couldn't travel all the way to Kenya just for a race. Life doesn't work like that. Right? But now, sitting here weaving our way along the A379 back to Exeter, it seems like a great idea.

◄ ►

For years I've been telling people the story of Annemari Sandell. In 1995, when she was a talented junior athlete in Finland, she traveled to Kenya and spent six weeks training in the Rift Valley in the lead-up to the world cross-country championships, which were held in Durham, England. I was there, on a cold, rain-drenched afternoon, watching as the sixteen-year-old Sandell ran away from the Kenyans and Ethiopians to win the title. What had happened to her out there in Kenya? What did she find that had turned her into a world champion? Could I find it, too?

The Kenyans are, quite simply, the greatest runners on Earth. Considering that running, and in particular long-distance running, is the most universal, accessible, and widely practiced sport in the world, it is remarkable that one tiny corner of the planet can dominate it so thoroughly. In virtually any elite road race anywhere in the world, a group of Kenyans will break away within minutes at the front of the field.

The facts and figures attesting to their running dominance are incredible. In 2011 the top twenty fastest marathons of the year were *all* run by Kenyans. And of the top twenty fastest marathons of all time, seventeen were run by Kenyans. (The other three, incidentally, were run by athletes from Kenya's east African neighbor, Ethiopia.)

From 1991, at the world athletics championships in Tokyo, to 2009, at the world championships in Berlin, Kenyan men won a total of ninety-three world and Olympic medals at middle- and long-distance running events. Thirty-two of those medals were gold. In that same eighteen-year period, spanning ten world championships and five Olympic games, Britain won precisely zero medals.* Even the United States managed only three gold medals, and two of those were won in Osaka in 2007 by a man who became a U.S. citizen at the age of twenty, having been born and raised and developed as an athlete in . . . you guessed it, Kenya.

◁ ▷

As a teenager I used to imagine I was running across the plains of Africa, as I skirted around the edges of the Northampton housing estates. I used to love to run on hot days, when the heat would visibly shimmer across the road, because it was how I imagined Kenya

---

*In the 2011 world championships in Daegu, Somali-born Mo Farah won Britain's first medals in the middle- and long-distance events in over twenty years, with gold in the 5,000 meters and silver in the 10,000 meters. Kenya, despite no medals in either of these two races, ended the championships with seventeen medals, its biggest medal haul ever.

to be. Of course I had no idea. I was just daydreaming. But the thought of doing it for real is intoxicating. Not just running the Lewa Marathon, but going and training with the Kenyans, too. To discover their secret, as Annemari Sandell did. But first I'll have to sell the idea to Marietta. If I'm going to go, I want her and the children to come, too.

I first met Marietta in college in Liverpool. Her hair was cut in a boyish crop, she ate a diet of nothing but rice and seeds, and she liked techno music. I could have never guessed she was from an aristocratic Devonshire family. She had a self-contained air that intrigued me, and we ended up becoming good friends, before I finally realized I had fallen for her. It took one of my friends to point it out.

"I think you're in love with Marietta," he said in a bar one night.

"What?" I said. "Are you mad?" But he was right.

Breaking the news to her was awkward, since we were both living in the same shared house with three other friends, and she had a boyfriend. At first she wasn't keen, but I was consumed with teenage love, staring forlornly out of rain-splattered windows, sitting up late at night writing poetry. For about a month I couldn't get her out of my head, I was thinking about her constantly. And then, suddenly, it was gone.

I felt relieved, like a weight had been lifted from me. I walked inside the house one afternoon and saw her standing in the kitchen. *It's okay,* I wanted to tell her, *I'm cured.* But she ran over and kissed me. Eight years later, Lila, our eldest daughter, was born.

Ever since we had children, Marietta and I have wanted to take them traveling, to give them an adventure, open their eyes to the immensity of the world. When I first met Marietta, she had just come back from traveling around South America for a year. I was impressed. I'd never been outside the British Isles.

After we got together, we took time out from school to travel to Venezuela together, and a few years later we both went back there again. So we figured South America was our stomping ground. Marietta was always suggesting we take the children there. "You mean for a holiday?" I'd ask. "No, for longer. Six months. A year. Imagine it, they'd learn to speak Spanish, it would be an incredible education for them." I was always the one coming up with the excuses, afraid to leave the safety of my job, our little house, our families.

So I don't think Marietta will be fazed by the idea of an extended trip. And why not Africa? Her brother lives in Tanzania. Her sister lives in Kenya. In some ways our visit is well overdue. The only snag may be when I tell her I want to go there to run. Marietta has no interest in running. In our last year at school I tried to get her enthused about it. We lived beside a park, which was about two miles around on the outside. I used to take her out every few nights, at a slow jog, and by the end of a few grueling weeks we made it the whole way around without stopping. That night Marietta developed a huge migraine and lay in bed cursing me and my training regime. Her running career, it seemed, was over.

Years later I decided that perhaps she would be better at middle distances, such as the 800 meters. Perhaps the lap around the park was just too far. By then we were living in London, so I somehow managed to convince her to come to the local track for a 400-meter time trial. If she could run it in under ninety seconds, I thought, we'd have something to work on. She obviously thought I was mad as I took her through the warm-up routine and got her to stand with her toes just behind the start line. I held the watch up. Ready? Go.

We started off, jogging. "It's only one lap," I said. "Can you go any faster?" She looked like she was going to punch me.

No, running is not for her. Sometimes we sit across from each other at the table in the evening and I find myself recounting some new world record and telling her how the athletes were lapping in under sixty seconds, or how the winner ran a fifty-two-second last lap, and I see her eyes glazing over. So I'm not sure what she's going to make of my plan to move us all out to the land of runners.

◄ ►

One night, after the children are in bed, I put forward my idea. Six months in Kenya. We'll have an adventure. She'll get to visit her sister. We'll see elephants, zebras, go riding across the bush in the back of a jeep—the kids will love it. And I'll get to run. Really run. With the greatest runners on earth. And if I find their secret, I can bottle it and make a fortune.

She looks at me across the table. "Are you serious?"

"Yes," I say. "What do you think?"

"I think it's a brilliant idea."

Three

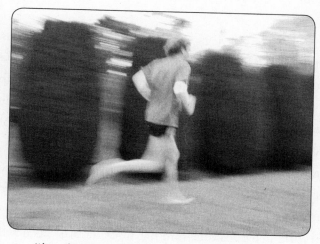

It's as though my feet are afraid to touch the ground.

"You're brave," says a neighbor in our village when she hears we're off to Kenya. "But then, you lot are like that." She's trying to be nice, saying brave, but she means mad. We get quizzical looks from people whenever we mention our plan. But we're pressing on with the preparations. The children, of course, take it all in their stride. One evening, as I'm putting them to bed, I conduct a mock television interview with Lila and Uma, pretending that they're famous explorers. Ossian, picking up on the general sense of excitement, is running around in his pajamas yelling like a lion and laughing. I ask Uma what she thinks it will be like in Africa.

"Hot," she says.

"And what else?" I probe.

She pulls a thoughtful face, looking up at the ceiling. "And not cold."

Right now, that's about as much as any of us know.

◄ ► ►

As well as making all the travel arrangements, I need to get as fit as I can if I'm going to stand a chance of keeping up with the Kenyan athletes. One evening I read an article in the newspaper about a group of Kenyan runners who live and train in Teddington, in southwest London. I decide to look them up. Perhaps they can give me a few insights before I head out to Kenya.

So a few days later, at eight o'clock on a Tuesday morning, I find myself standing outside a small suburban house. I check the details again. It's definitely number eighteen, opposite the Tesco super-market parking lot. An unassuming 1960s terrace house with gray blinds. Weeds are coming up through cracks in the concrete park-ing spot in front of the house.

The front door is set back into the wall, so I have to venture into the dimness of the brick doorway to ring the bell. I wait for a few minutes, stepping back outside onto the quiet street, but there is no answer. The athletes' manager, an Irishman named Ricky Simms, told me that they would be expecting me. He even said that they'd take me for a run. I try the bell again. After another few minutes, the door opens slowly. A slim man in a tracksuit opens it and looks at me with sleepy eyes. I explain who I am. He nods and lets me in.

Inside, he takes me upstairs to an untidy living room and spends about five minutes absently pointing the remote control at the TV before it finally turns on. He doesn't say anything other than that his name is Micah. Once the TV is on, he turns and leaves the room.

Micah, it turns out, is Micah Kogo, the 10K world record holder and bronze medalist at the Beijing Olympics. He has gone to get changed.

Heads appear intermittently in the doorway behind me as I sit there watching the news. There are six Kenyan athletes living in the house, and they seem to be finding my presence amusing. I can hear them talking to one another in the landing. Eventually Enda, another Irishman who works for the manager, turns up and introduces me to everyone. They offer me limp handshakes and smile at one another as I'm told who has broken which world record, or won which world championship medal.

"Are you going for a run with them?" Enda asks me.

I nod, unsure whether it's a wise thing to do. "You think that's okay?"

"Sure," he says. "If you want."

I try to act calm as we head out through the small backyard of the house, a couple of bikes leaning up against the fence, an old bulldog in the next-door garden barking at us hoarsely. We walk to the end of a small cul-de-sac and then on to the main road. The athletes talk and joke with Enda about their recent races. Nobody seems to be in a hurry to actually start running. One of the athletes explains to me that they don't like to run on concrete, so they walk until they get to the grass. In Kenya, he says, they run only on dirt roads.

The nearby Bushy Park is a large expanse of flat grassland, complete with deer and a maze of gravel pathways and tracks perfect for running. It's one of the reasons the Kenyans use this corner of London for their base while they're away from home. Once we get inside the park gates, there's a lot of standing around and talking, and some halfhearted stretching. And then, without warning, we're off. The pace is surprisingly easy, and, initially at least, I can keep up without too much trouble. Because they're all in between competitions, they're doing only easy running. I'm secretly hoping that people will stare at us in wonder as we run past. *Wow, look, Kenyans! And did you see that white guy? He must be some runner.* But the park is virtually empty, save for a few dog walkers who don't even give us a second glance.

After about two miles, Mike Kigen (a former Kenyan 5,000 meters champion), Micah Kogo, and Vivian Cheruiyot (the women's world 5,000 meters champion)* all suddenly speed up. None of them says anything, it just seems to happen. Within seconds, like startled animals they're gone, their heads bobbing away into the distance. The rest of us keep the easy pace (at least for the Kenyans it's easy), running in a pack, until we get back to where we started. I'm blowing hard but I just about manage to keep up.

◄ ►

Back at the house, Micah cooks up some *ugali* and green vegetables for everyone's lunch. *Ugali* is the runners' favorite food. It's basically maize flour and water boiled up to make a white, sticky dough. Micah cuts me a huge slab with a knife and lays it on the plate on top of the vegetables. It has a soft, moist texture but doesn't taste of much. The athletes, however, love it. They tell me, only half-joking, that it's the secret to Kenya's running success. Packets of maize flour brought over from Kenya are piled up on the floor in a corner of the kitchen.

Micah tells me, as we eat, about the day he broke the world 10K record. He says he remembers warming up and feeling light but strong. "So light, but so strong," he says, almost reverential of the memory. All the athletes perk up when they talk about running.

---

* In 2011, Vivian Cheruiyot retained her world 5,000 meters title, as well as winning the 10,000 meters gold medal and the world cross-country championships.

Vivian, a tiny woman who can't weigh more than eighty-five pounds, tells me about the day she won the world championships, beating the supposedly unbeatable Ethiopians. "It was so much fun," she says, grinning.

Later that afternoon, after they've all slept and had a massage, Richard Kiplagat, an 800 meters specialist, and Vivian head out for another easy run. I decide to join them again. Afterward, as we stand in the park stretching, a man in his mid-forties, slightly overweight and drenched in sweat, jogs past.

"In Kenya, do you have runners like that?" I ask, pointing at the jogger. "People who are just running to get fit?" I assume that's what he's doing. Hoping to lose some weight, too, no doubt. He doesn't look like he's running for the pure joy of it. And he certainly isn't hoping to make a living from it.

Richard, who will go on to win a silver medal in the Commonwealth Games a few months later, grins at me and shakes his head. "No," he says definitely.

"In Kenya," says Vivian, "there are only athletes." It isn't a boast, but merely a statement of fact. In Kenya, it would seem, if you are an athlete, you run. If you aren't, you don't.

"Maybe in some areas in the big cities," says Richard, wanting to be clear, "where rich people live, you may see a runner like that. But not in the rest of the country."

It is to the rest of the country I'm headed. When I made my plan, I had imagined running hard across the plains in the midst of a group of Kenyans, the pounding of our feet shaking the dry earth. But seriously, who am I kidding?

"How fast is the slowest athlete in Kenya?" I ask, looking to find a crumb of hope. Maybe I am an athlete. I won the Powderham Castle 10K race. My time was 38 minutes 35 seconds. "For the 10K, for example, what would be the slowest time?"

They look at each other. This is obviously a tricky question. "Are we including juniors?" Richard asks me. That's eighteen- and nineteen-year-olds. I nod. I could train with juniors, why not. Perhaps that's the solution. "And girls?" I nod again. The more the merrier. "About thirty-five minutes," he says.

So I'm three and a half minutes slower over 10K than the slowest junior girl in Kenya. I've got less than six months to go before I get there. I've got some work to do.

◅ ▻

Things start off well when, a few months later, I manage to finally lower my half-marathon time to under 1 hour 30 minutes with a barnstorming 1 hour 26 minutes in a hilly race in Dartmoor in Devon. But just as my fitness is improving, I set myself back by embarking on an experiment.

It all begins, as it does for many people, when I read Christopher McDougall's book *Born to Run*, about a race in the Copper Canyons in Mexico with a tribe of ultra-runners called the Tarahumara. It's a fascinating tale, but the most intriguing part of the book, and the thing that has catapulted it onto bestseller lists across the world, is its revelation of the concept of barefoot running.

McDougall talks about a theory developed by Harvard scientists that humans evolved in the way we did partly because we hunted by running animals into the ground. While we are painfully slow at sprinting compared to most four-legged creatures—say, the cheetah, horse, rabbit, or a thousand others—when it comes to long-distance running, we are the Olympic champions of the animal kingdom. Our key advantage is our ability to shed most of our heat through sweating. This means we can cool ourselves down on the move, while most other animals need to stop when they get too hot in order to pant their heat away. Our ancestors could chase even the swiftest runners like antelope until they literally dropped dead from overheating, and McDougall's book recounts a story about bushmen in the Kalahari Desert in Namibia who still do this today.

The scientists claim, in effect, that humans are born to run long distances, that our bodies are designed specifically for the purpose. It's why we have Achilles tendons, arched feet, big bums—to help keep us balanced when we run—and a nuchal ligament at the back of our necks (to keep our heads still). And we are designed to run, they say, in bare feet. Running shoes only mess things up.

A few weeks before reading all this, I had bought myself a new pair of sneakers. The shop in London was equipped with a hi-tech system for assessing your running gait. I was asked to put on some sneakers and hop on a treadmill. The man in the shop then filmed my feet and played the footage back to me. I was, like 80 percent of runners, he told me, landing heel first. This made my legs pronate, which meant that they were basically buckling under me with each step. To remedy this, he told me, I needed running shoes with added support on one side.

I thanked him for his useful advice and bought a pair of shoes with added stability, as he suggested. A week later I broke my half-marathon best time. Unfortunately, I also developed a slight injury at the top of my left calf muscle. Injuries are a common part of being a runner, so I didn't panic. Depending on which study you read, somewhere between 60 and 80 percent of runners get injured at least once a year. So I'd have to be very lucky never to get injured. A small muscle strain was getting off quite lightly.

McDougall, however, disagrees. The reason runners get injured so often, he says, is because they land heel first. And the reason they land heel first is because they wear stability trainers. It sounds like a catch-22, but according to both McDougall and the Harvard scientists there is a simple way out: Take off the shoes. Our body is the perfect running machine, they say, developed over millions of years of product testing and fine tuning. We don't need the modern invention of running shoes to do something we've been doing perfectly well for millennia.

Like most people, at first I think this is an interesting theory, but really, you can't go around running in bare feet. What about broken glass? What about dog poo? But then I read something that makes me prick up my ears: One of the key scientists cited by McDougall, Daniel Liebermann, developed his ideas through studying Kenyan runners.

Because they grow up running barefoot, Kenyans have a completely different style of running. Rather than landing heel first, they land forefoot first. Not only does this reduce the risk of injury, but it is a more efficient way of running. In effect, by landing heel first, most Western runners are braking with every stride. No wonder we can't keep up.

I decide to try barefoot running in the local park one evening. I run there in my shoes, but once I get to a clear, grassy patch, I take them off, hide them in some bushes, and then set off around a field of football pitches. My running style instantly changes to a shorter, faster stride pattern, as though my feet are afraid to touch the ground. I go for about ten minutes, before deciding I've done enough. It's fun, but afterward it's nice to put my shoes back on. They feel warm and comforting, like big soft pillows.

But I need to find out more. I decide to track down biomechanics expert Lee Saxby. He's one of the men who taught McDougall to run barefoot. Can he teach me to run like a Kenyan? I wonder. Lee works out of a boxing gym by the railway tracks in north London. I struggle to find it at first, walking up and down the road, evening commuters dashing around me to catch their trains home. I turn my map up the other way, but it still doesn't make sense. Then I realize his place is tucked down a back alley between two tall, four-story houses. I walk down a narrow passage and find a black, unmarked door. This must be it. I ring the buzzer and the door opens automatically. I step inside a huge room with an empty boxing ring in the middle. High up on a small balcony along one wall I spot a man looking down. He gives me a nod and points to another door at the side of the gym. I walk over and a skinny boy opens it.

"I'm here to see Lee," I say. He nods and points up some stairs.

At the top is Lee's office. Lee stands at the door, smiling. "Come in," he says.

I enter, full of questions. I leave, a few hours later, convinced I have discovered the secret of Kenyan running.

"With any other sport, to get good you need to learn about technique," he says. "But with running, people think they can't change their style. Well that's rubbish."

He has a certainty that is hard to argue with. Why don't the top African runners actually run barefoot in races? I ask. "A top runner can't afford to hurt himself stepping on a sharp stone," he says. "But they wear racing flats. There is no stability or cushioning on running flats. They allow you to run in a barefoot style. They don't force you to land heel first like most running shoes."

He has a mischievous twinkle in his eye. "Sometimes I feel like the Che Guevera of running," he says. "I'll show you." He tells me to hop up on his running machine. First he films me running in my normal style. Then he tells me to take off my shoes and films me again. I immediately and instinctively start landing forefoot first.

"Your body won't let you run heel first if you're barefoot," he says. "It would be too painful." With shoes on we have a false sense of security, and feel that we can hammer the road as hard as we want. But the impact from landing heel first is still shooting up the leg, juddering the knees, the hips, the back, regardless of how much cushioning you put under your feet (McDougall describes it as akin to putting an oven mitten over an egg before hitting it with a hammer). In fact, because you can't feel the ground when you're wearing shoes, you're forced to land even harder as your body instinctively looks for stability and a harder surface. Without shoes, however, you're forced to tread lightly, skipping gently over the ground. Your body just does it naturally.

According to Lee, however, it's not only about the forefoot strike. He tells me to keep my head up, lead with my chest, and pull my legs through, as though I'm on a unicycle. If that isn't enough to think about, he starts a metronome going at a rapid-fire *tack tack tack*. I have to match it stride for *tack*, as he films me. Then he plays the three films back to me.

It is quite shocking to watch. With my sneakers on I look like an overweight office worker out for a slow jog. (Admittedly, that's perhaps what I am, but it isn't how I imagine I look when I'm running.) I seem to be sinking backward at the waist, as though I'm half-slouched into an invisible armchair. With the shoes off it looks a bit better; and after Lee's lesson I look like a proper runner. "You look like a Kenyan," he says, though that may be pushing it.

Outside, the evening commuter trains are rattling in and out of London. Do I even need to go to Kenya? Have I found the secret right here in this West Hampstead gym? Part of me is mad that I didn't discover this years ago, when I was still young enough to put it to good use. In that moment, watching the videos, I have no doubt that this is the key reason the Kenyans are so good at running. It makes complete sense.

◄ ►

In the following weeks, as the initial excitement of my discovery begins to die down, I realize that the proof will be in the running. The whole notion of barefoot running appeals to me. I love it when, after years of research, we realize that the most natural and primitive way to do something—the way we always did it before scientists and corporations got their hands on it—was actually the best way after all. I love the fact that despite all our technological advancements, poor Kenyans running barefoot have the edge over us. As a notion, it's brilliant. But as a reality? The only way to find out is to try it.

One of the reasons so few athletes have tried to change their style, according to Lee, is because it involves relearning how to run from scratch. Since barefoot running uses different muscles, you need to start with short one-mile runs. Once you can do that without hurting the next day, you can start to increase the distance slowly.

I had hoped to combine barefoot running with my usual style, to hedge my bets and to avoid getting out of shape. But that's not an option, according to Lee. "It's all or nothing," he says. "Your mind will slip into the style it's most used to. If you're running heel first most of the time, your body will do that automatically."

Before I leave, Lee promises to send me a pair of barefoot shoes to run in. It may sound like an oxymoron, but the barefoot style of running is less about actually being barefoot and more about the way you run. Barefoot shoes have minimal cushioning or support, but they have a firm under sole to protect your feet from the glass and dog poo. Once I get used to my new style, I decide, I'll switch to running flats, just like the Kenyans. These have a little more support than barefoot shoes, but none of the bulk and weight of the conventional sneakers usually worn by Western runners.

So for the next six weeks I start learning how to run again. Running short distances has its advantages. The runs take a fraction of the time they used to, which means I can fit them in more easily. "Don't worry," I tell Marietta as I head out the door, "I'll be back in ten minutes." Lunchtime runs at work are also less of a mad panic to get back to my desk within the regimented hour.

As Lee predicted, my legs feel sore after the first few runs, but the more I do it, the farther I can run, and the more natural it begins to feel. I even find myself spontaneously running around the street in my new style. Whereas before I used to feel wary about breaking into a trot without my running shoes on, I'm now happy to run in any footwear. In fact, running shoes seem to be the singularly worst possible shoes to run in. My normal office shoes have very little heel, and I find I can run barefoot style in them quite easily. And the more I do it, the zippier it feels.

The only problem with embarking on this experiment is that by the time we've packed our bags and we're ready to go to the airport, I'm still only up to three-mile runs. I'm hardly in shape to keep up with the Kenyans, but the experiment has to go on. If it really is the secret to their success, I'll soon catch up to where I was, and then, well, who knows where I'll end up.

Four

A zebra wanders past the mess tent

Our plane touches down in Nairobi on a bright, late-December morning. As we unfold ourselves out of the cramped cabin, the warm, African air feels soft on our frazzled skin. It's been almost twenty-four hours since we drove away from our cottage in Devon, leaving the garden and surrounding fields covered in a thick blanket of snow.

We plan to spend most of our time in Kenya up in the Rift Valley, in a town called Iten. I've read so much about Iten that it has become an almost mythical place in my mind. Before we left England, I watched a local news report on the Internet in which the town's taxi drivers were complaining that they couldn't do their job properly because the roads were so clogged up with runners. It's only a small town, with about four thousand residents, but I've read that at any one time you can find around one thousand top athletes living and training there.

But before we get to Iten, we head off to spend a week with Marietta's sister, Jophie, in Lewa, where I will run my first ever marathon at the end of the trip. Jophie first came to Kenya in 2004 to do some volunteer work on a monkey conservation project. One night, in a bar on the coast, she met Alastair. Of Scottish ancestry, but born and bred in Africa, Alastair is a tough man. Marietta's brothers joke that he is like Crocodile Dundee, at one in the wildness of the bush. In Kenya they call them KCs, or Kenyan Cowboys. Big, strong men in leather boots and denim shorts who sit around drinking Tusker beer and talking in slow, deliberate voices about things like boreholes, hunting, and motorbikes. But even among the KCs, Alastair is tough.

Jophie and Alastair have two small daughters and live in a tented camp in the middle of the bush. On New Year's Eve, after the children are asleep, the four of us sit around the fire drinking Tusker. The trunk of a tree lies across the flames, burning in the middle. Alastair said he was going to look for firewood, and he came back with an entire tree across his shoulders. He is sitting there silent, with that wild, quizzical look he gets in his eyes after he has had a few beers. "So those guys up there, they can really run, you know," he says, talking about the athletes in Iten.

"I know," I say.

"How are you going to keep up? They're not messing around up there. Those guys can run."

I still haven't worked out how I'm going to keep up. At the moment I can barely walk after hurting my calf on a treadmill in a hotel in Nairobi. But after a few drinks, Alastair doesn't wait around for answers. His question has already drifted off into the darkness. He is telling a story about when he was a safari guide in Botswana.

"One time I went on this trip with a wealthy American couple. We're talking rich, man. Gold Rolex watches dripping from their wrists. The three of us were walking through the bush when, from nowhere, this bull elephant is charging at us. So I push them both to the ground." He almost falls out of his camp chair demonstrating how he pushed them. "I pushed them and then I turned and I charged at the elephant."

I look over at Jophie. She isn't telling him to shut up.

"What happened?" I ask.

"If you have a bull elephant charging at you, your best hope is to charge back. I had my arms waving around in the air and I was roaring as loud as I could."

He stops to take a sip of his beer. The fire crackles in the night. The stars spill across the sky above us.

"It stopped," he says. "Turned on its heels and ran."

◄ ►

The next evening, we get our own close encounter. At night in the camp you have to walk quickly from tent to tent, using a flashlight to look out for snakes or other wild animals. However, our cheap windup flashlights can barely light up the ground in front of us, let alone pick out a lion from the engulfing blackness. "Look for the eyes," says Alastair, swinging his torch's huge light beam across the darkness. "There." A pair of staring eyes hovers unblinking in the beam less than thirty yards away. "Buffalo," he says.

Later, as we're walking to our tent to go to bed, we hear a terrible grunting sound. It starts off far away, but with each grunt it gets louder and fiercer. It sounds like something running at us. We rush for the tent and I throw Lila through the opening before Marietta and I both dive in and zip up. Uma and Ossian are already fast asleep in their beds.

"What was that?"

"A lion," says Marietta. She has heard the noise before on other nights, but from much farther away. It starts again. It sounds far away at the onset, but by the end of its roar you can almost feel the air vibrating. Lila is terrified, but she is trying not to cry.

"I'll get in your bed with you," I say, as if I could fight off a lion.

Alastair has told us that lions don't know the difference between a tent and a rock, and that we are quite safe once we're inside. But with all the ferocious grunting noises going on just outside, I start having doubts. Surely the lions can smell us. There are no people inside rocks. Then I remember that the zipper at the back of the tent is broken. The tent is actually open, partly, at the bottom. I try to forget I've just remembered that.

◄ ►

It's a ten-hour taxi ride from Lewa to Iten, so we decide to stop for the night in Nyahururu, another big running center. We book ourselves in at the town's most exclusive hotel, the Thomson's Falls Lodge, which employs a local athlete to take guests out running. His name is John Ndungu and he agrees to take me out for a run at 7:00 A.M. before we continue on our journey. I get the impression it's a little late for him, but he gives me a crooked smile and says it's fine.

So on a bright, crisp morning at 8,000 feet, I head out for my first run with athletes in Kenya. I find John waiting for me at the main entrance to the lodge with another man, a serious-faced eighteen-year-old from John's village called Lucas Ndungu. The two are not related, they tell me, surprised that I think they might be.

I need to go slow and not too far, I tell them. I'm not only worried about keeping up, but I'm concerned that my new barefoot-running style might give me an injury if I push it too far too soon. To give my calves some added protection, I decide to wear racing flats rather than my barefoot shoes. It also means that I won't have to feel embarrassed wearing new-fangled shoes designed to mimic the Kenyans' running without shoes. Somehow, now that I'm here, that seems an odd thing to want to do.

As we jog out along the hotel drive, two baboons ambling across the lawn turn to watch us briefly, before scuttling away. The security guard at the hotel gate gives us a salute. Once we're out of the hotel complex, we turn onto a dirt track and head up into town toward the main road.

The first thing I notice is that Lucas is wearing big, chunky running trainers and is landing heel first. John is wearing racing flats, a bit like mine, and is landing forefoot first. It's far too soon to be drawing any conclusions, of course, but Lucas's heel-first foot strike is unexpected.

As we run, we pass streams of other athletes coming in the opposite direction, and none of them are barefoot. Most of the runners are wearing normal training shoes with lots of support around the heel. It's hard to tell, running toward them, if they're landing heel first or not, but it looks like some of them might be. I'm confused. Where are all the barefoot runners?

The run in the end feels surprisingly gentle, considering the altitude. We run for thirty minutes, with the pace picking up slightly over the last mile or so. I'm just congratulating myself for keeping up with them when they tell me that they have already run six miles from their village to meet me, and they plan to train again a few hours later.

"You?" they ask.

I'm not planning on running again for a few days.

"I'm still adjusting to the altitude," I say. "I don't want to overdo it and get injured." My calves feel fine, however, even though it's the longest run I've done since I switched to my barefoot style.

After we cool down, Marietta and the children come out to find us. Lila and Uma are all sleepy smiles and sticking-up hair, shaking hands with the two men and showing off their dolls. John turns to me and tells me that I now have four children. I give him a confused look. "Me," he says, smiling. He's older than me.

Five

Our house in Iten

At the bottom of the Rift Valley the road to Iten crosses over a deep gorge. The driver stops for a rest and we all get out. Far down below, basking on a sandbank, their mouths fixed wide open, are four crocodiles. Ahead of us the road shimmers in the baking heat. On the roadside is a rickety honey stall, the bottles lined up in rows, glowing in the sun. In the distance the land rises up over four thousand feet to Iten, which sits perched on the edge of the Kerio escarpment.

"Dad, I'm thirsty," says Uma, standing in the shade of a withered tree. We've been on the road for about five hours, the children bumping around in the back, clambering over the seats, spilling their pens and sandwiches all over the floor. But we're nearly there.

From the bottom, the road winds up, twisting back and forth, twirling around cone-shaped foothills, the land changing color, turning greener the higher we rise. The driver keeps pointing at the thermometer gauge, which drops down another degree every few minutes. The cooler it gets, the more houses we see, and the more people sitting beside the road or walking along it. They glance over at us, the engine straining with the slope. At a sign for the Lelin Campsite, the car swings off the road onto a dirt track, bumping along, the underside scraping on the stones, until we come to a large, elaborate gate painted in blue and yellow, the word KARIBU (Welcome) in an arch above it.

Before we left England I tried to arrange somewhere for us to live in Iten, but finding a house to rent in a small Kenyan town from the other side of the world was not easy. Most people who travel to the town stay either at an upmarket athletics training camp run by Lornah Kiplagat, the holder of four world records, or at the Kerio View, a hotel perched on the edge of the escarpment overlooking the valley. However, both of these places are beyond our budget, so instead we've decided, rather apprehensively, to stay at the Lelin campsite about five miles down the side of the valley.

We arrive in the early afternoon. The campsite owner comes down from his house on a nearby hill to greet us. He shakes hands with everyone and shows us to our rooms. We have three rooms in his newly built cottages, two to sleep in and one to cook in. The kitchen room has a camping stove on the table and a few pots and plates on the bed. He is obviously delighted to have us stay, so I try not to look disappointed as he shows us around. The bedrooms are just big enough to fit the beds, the pillows are tatty bits of hard foam, the toilets have no seats, and there is no sink in the bathroom, just a tap on the wall. His smile drops when I ask him where the sink is. I mime brushing my teeth. Washing hands. He points to the tap.

"Oh, you use that?" I say. "Of course. Perfect."

Although I didn't manage to find a house, I did get ahold of a contact in Iten, a former athlete named Godfrey Kiprotich. He phoned me a few days before we left Lewa to tell me that he had found a place for us to rent. I'm hoping that he can come and get us and take us to see it, but when I call him he says he doesn't have a car.

"It's in the garage," he says. "But let me see what I can do."

He calls back a little while later to say he has arranged a lift for us. Sure enough, twenty minutes later a low-slung white car with tinted windows rolls into the campsite and a neatly dressed man with a gold watch steps out. His name is Christopher Cheboiboch, he says, looking around warily at the campsite, as though it might make his clothes dirty. "Are you a runner?" I ask, thinking he might be too old.

He smiles. "Yes," he says. "I have the fifth fastest time ever in the New York marathon."

He takes us very slowly in his car up the final stretch of the escarpment to Iten. We glide past a steady stream of people walking along the road. Children with sticks stand watching their cows grazing on the grass verges, or run, barefoot, disappearing into the long grass and undergrowth. At the top of the valley, a rusting sign over the road welcomes us to Iten.

As we drive into town and up along the main street for the first time, we gaze out at the half-collapsed wooden market stalls, the carts pulled by donkeys, ladies sitting on top of piles of clothes for sale. It's market day and the place is full of people. Cows and sheep seem to wander around freely, poking their noses into piles of rubbish left on the dirt verges beside the road. People ride by with their bicycles stacked ten feet high with mattresses, crates of chickens, firewood. Ahead of us, a small bus drives away with two people still hanging out the door.

Christopher calls out to a man in the street, who comes over to the car. They shake hands. Christopher gives the man some money and then drives on. We sail slowly up the road, past a small supermarket with two speakers placed outside blaring crackly music. On the other side of the road sits a pristine, white mosque. Red dirt roads cut through rows of rusted tin roofs rising up the slopes on either side. It looks just like any other roadside town that we passed through on the way from Lewa.

We drive through the town before we realize it, emerging out the other end and pulling off the road, down a rutted track, past a boarded-up wooden bar, to Lornah Kiplagat's training camp. Christopher pulls in regally as the gates are swung open by the security guard. This is the most state-of-the-art training camp in town, with a gym and a swimming pool. There are no Kenyan athletes living here, the camp catering instead to foreign runners. As soon as we get out of the car, I spot the British international runner Helen Clitheroe. She's sitting at a table with her coach and I can hear them going over her training schedule on a laptop. A Greek athlete with a long goatee walks by, lost in the music from his iPod. A man with long, blond hair, looking more like a surfer than an athlete, bounds out of the gym. It's Toby Tanser. I was reading about him in the newspaper in Lewa last week. I've also got his book, *More Fire,* about how to run like a Kenyan, in my bag. I stop him and say hello.

Toby has an encyclopedic knowledge of Kenyan running and is friends with just about every athlete here. He also heads up a charity, Shoe4Africa, which is building a school and a children's hospital near Iten. He is full of optimism about everything. When I tell him we're looking for a house to rent, he says, "Finding accommodation in Iten is not a problem." As he says it, a group of young Kenyan men walk by.

"Erastus," Toby calls to one of the men, who ambles over. Erastus is wearing a neat leather jacket and a big grin. In his hand he has an expensive cellphone. "What's happening with your house?" Toby asks him as they shake hands. "Is it free to rent?"

The man nods.

"There you go," Toby says to me. "This man has the nicest house in Iten. What did I tell you?"

Before he rushes off, Toby offers to take me on a running tour of the town. It's an offer I can't refuse.

While we're talking, Godfrey, my contact with the other house for rent, turns up. He's dressed in jeans and a T-shirt and must be in his midforties. I call Marietta and the children over. While I've been talking, they've been wandering around, trying to keep out of the way of the athletes. Godfrey greets us like long-lost friends, crouching down to shake the children's hands. He's full of apologies for not having a car. It's in the garage, he tells me again. Instead he has hired a taxi and is with another former runner, William Koila. Between Godfrey, Koila, the driver, and the five of us, it's a bit of a squash, but we all bundle in and head out.

Godfrey tells us the house is in a "very nice neighborhood," as we drive along over a bumpy dirt track resembling a dry mogul ski run. It's the sort of road I wouldn't even attempt to drive on in England. The weighed-down taxi scrapes over the bumps as we pass some small houses with smashed windows and overgrown gardens. We stop outside a black, corrugated iron gate. The driver beeps his horn. Out on the street, two men are sitting on the counter of a small, wooden kiosk and staring at us. On the other side of the street, a two-story house is penned in close behind a high wooden fence. Pairs of eyes are peeking out between the gaps. Lila and Uma, leaning out of the car window, peer back.

"See what a nice area this is?" Godfrey says as we wait. He's sitting squashed in the front seat with Koila. I don't know what a bad area looks like, so it's hard to judge. I look over at Marietta and the children. They all look slightly breathless, as though suddenly everything is happening too fast. Marietta holds my hand. Ossian, standing on her lap like the captain of a ship, watches out the front window, an anxious look on his face.

The gate is pulled open by a workman in overalls, revealing a large, sweeping garden with a bungalow about halfway down. It's painted blue and white and has a red tin roof. It looks quite nice. Behind the house is a view out across the valley.

"They've built it the wrong way around," says Marietta, as we walk around it. "Surely the house should face out toward the view." Instead, all the windows overlook the garden and the eight-foot corrugated metal fence that runs around the perimeter, blocking everything else out. To one side is the roof of a neighboring house.

"That house belongs to Ismael Kirui," Koila tells me. That's the athlete who won my favorite race, the 1993 world championships 5,000 meters, by sprinting away from the field with seven laps to go. Before I get too excited, Koila tells me that Kirui doesn't actually live there but rents out the house.

Many of the houses in Iten are owned by former athletes, but, like Kirui's house, they are all surprisingly small and unglamorous. The late Richard Chelimo, a former 10,000 meters world record holder, was the first athlete to invest in Iten. His legacy is a few rows of concrete one-bedroom units now falling into disrepair.

Later we go to look at the house that Toby Tanser found for us to rent. "The nicest house in Iten," he had said. It is actually owned by Erastus's wife, Sylvia Kibet, a world champion 5,000 meters silver medalist. Tucked behind a gas station, it has three small bedrooms looking out onto a brick wall, some old cardboard cabinets in a dark sitting room, and a tiny shared yard.

Godfrey's backward-built house is sumptuous by comparison, with its ample garden and views across the valley. When we see it for the first time, it is being redecorated and is a bit of a mess, but we're assured that it will all be ready within a few days. In the garden there are four sheep and an angry dog tied to a post. The house is split in two and we're told that the man who owns the dog lives in the other half of the house, its windows covered by dirty polyester curtains, but that he will be moved out.

"The landlord is a man who has traveled," Godfrey reassures me. "He understands privacy."

Koila is more succinct: "And *mzungus*." The implication being that we're too finicky and uptight to share our house with a strange man with a wild dog. To be honest, I think we are. But where will he go?

"He will still be your neighbor," says Godfrey, pointing vaguely to where he will live, somewhere over the back fence behind a large plantation of passion fruit trees. It turns out that the man has been squatting in the house and growing passion fruit for some time. We agree to let him back in once a week to spray and harvest his crop.

The day we eventually move into the house, he shows up. He has an unsettling grin and tiptoes around me like an unpredictable pony. He tells me he wants to be a runner, if I sponsor him. I have to admit, I'm a bit worried about letting him in the house even once a week. Godfrey seems to think he's harmless, though, and jokes with the man while helping himself to some passion fruit.

"He says you can eat the fruit whenever you want," Godfrey tells me, as the man grins his approval.

◄ ►

We agree to rent Godfrey's house but are told a few days later that it won't be ready for another week. I get the call while we're in the larger nearby town of Eldoret. We've come here to visit the European-style Nakumatt supermarket. Nakumatt is a big, glossy store that's open twenty-four hours a day and sells everything that a homesick European could dream of, from strollers to bathrobes, and from Barbie dolls to ice cream.

After a few days in our little campsite, cooking rice on the camping stove and sleeping on dirty pillows, it's like stepping back into the comfortable, ordered world we left behind. I realize suddenly how tough life has been for the children over the last few days. Although Alastair, my brother-in-law, has now lent us a car, we've been ferrying the children back and forth in it, from house to house, back to the campsite, then off to visit athletes in training camps, all in the heat, meeting lots of people who talk about running. They get stared at wherever they go. Sometimes they embrace it, waving at everyone, laughing, and shaking hands with all the other children, who shriek with excitement and run along beside us. But sometimes it's too much. Our daughters keep telling us they like England better.

"It will be different when we have our own home," Marietta says. "They're just unsettled."

When the children are unhappy, the whole venture seems like a folly. I feel I've dragged them away from their friends and their home, all for some whimsical goal of running a fast time in a running race. It seems so trivial. I begin to think I should take them home to England.

As we drive back from Nakumatt through the outskirts of Eldoret, the road is lined with collapsing houses and tiny shops built from scraps of metal, cardboard boxes, and anything that people can find. Children play in puddles that are black with grime, or sit among stray dogs on piles of trash, as men whip threadbare and overladen donkeys into a slow, painful walk.

As we reach Iten, we pass a group of European runners. With their fair skin and pristine clothes, they look like creatures from another world. It seems ridiculous that they—and I—have come all this way to preen themselves for some competition. Amid the chaos and poverty, where people struggle to make enough money to buy even the simplest things such as bread and water, here are some of the world's best athletes doing drills, back and forth, along the side of the road.

Yet, ironically, they have come here to be inspired. To live among people who don't think that running is ridiculous, no matter how hard their lives are, but who value running and the opportunity it brings, who revere it, almost. Even if you never become an Olympic champion, or even manage to race abroad, just being an athlete here seems to lift you above the chaos of daily life. It marks you out as one of the special people, who have chosen a path of dedication and commitment. You can see it in the runners' eyes when they talk to you. Even the slowest of the runners talk about their training with an almost religious devotion. They may live in makeshift houses, without running water, and sit by candlelight each night, but their best times for the half marathon are recalled with reverence. Running matters.

Six

Cross-country racing in Iten

Toby Tanser tells me to meet him at the gates to Lornah's training camp, where I first bumped into him, at 6:30 A.M.

I wake up at dawn, feeling a thrill of excitement as I pull on my running clothes, which I left ready and laid out on the floor. Lila and Uma are sleeping soundly, curled up on their beds, their heads fallen off the hard pillows. I slip out of the room. The awakening Rift Valley drops away outside the door, the sound of roosters echoing over its majesty. This is it, the first run in Iten. Let the show begin.

The car starts with a purr, and I drive carefully out through the campsite's elaborate entrance gates and up the bumpy road to Iten. Toby is there waiting for me when I arrive, bouncing around on his toes. We head out on a very gentle thirty-minute jog, down through the town, past the famous St. Patrick's school, and out along a dusty, red track into the countryside. The trail we follow is actually a road, snaking its way through farmland and green fields dotted with cedar trees. The only vehicle we pass, though, is a motorbike with two men and two children on it, beeping at us as it bumps along.

We see fewer runners than I was anticipating. Toby says we're a bit late, that most of them start earlier. The few we do pass are running alone or in small groups of two or three. I don't see any large groups blocking the way of taxi drivers.

Every couple of minutes Toby points to a house and tells me the name of an athlete who lives there and the incredible times they have run or the championship medals they have won. He also has a personal story about some wild escapade he once had with each one.

I ask him why the people here are so good at running. Could it be because they run barefoot?

"They don't," he says. "The children run barefoot, but it's not what makes them fast."

I don't press him, I wasn't expecting the barefoot theory to be widely held, even here. I ask him what he thinks it is, then, that makes them so fast.

"It's not one thing," he says. "You'll meet lots of people. You'll get lots of answers. And they will all be right."

As we run, schoolchildren run along beside us. A few call out: "How are you?" but most seem to be running regardless of us. One of the theories often put forward as to why Kenyans are so good at running, often by the athletes themselves, is the fact that they run to school every day.

"Are they already hoping to become athletes?" I ask Toby, assuming he will know the answer. "Is that why they're running?"

"No," he says. "They're running because if they're late they get caned."

Despite the fact that corporal punishment was officially banned in schools in Kenya in 2001, lots of Kenyans later verify that Toby is right. A few weeks later the national newspaper carries a story about one of the country's brightest junior runners, Faith Kipyegon, who has been so badly beaten by her teacher at school that she is unable to train because of her injuries. With the world cross-country championships coming up, it's bad timing, the newspaper reports. There is a distinct lack of outrage in the article.

But surely school beatings can't be the secret behind Kenya's running success. It's not as romantic a secret as barefoot running. One day Godfrey tells me that when he was young, he ran the four miles to school every day because he felt better when he ran.

"I noticed I felt better in my body during the day," he says. "I was able to concentrate much better. When I didn't run, I felt tired and lethargic all day." Perhaps he felt more awake only because by running to school he could sleep in longer, but it's interesting to hear him talk about how running made him feel good. It's this sense of well-being that gets people out running in the West, rather than necessity, but I wonder how many runners here even think about how it makes them feel.

Godfrey admits to me that I'm the first person he has ever told this to. In fact, he says he has only just realized it now, as he was saying it. We're sitting in the cheap Hill Side Hotel café in Iten, and Godfrey has a look of excitement on his face, as if he has just realized something profound. I don't know if it is coincidence or not, but later that day he tells me he wants to run the Lewa Marathon with me. He hasn't run for years, but suddenly he's full of the joys of running. He wants to be my training partner, and keeps saying thank you to me as though I've done something other than just listen to him and nod.

⊲ ⊳

A few days after we arrive in Iten, the national cross-country league comes to town. It's the last leg of a seven-race series and it's all brilliantly organized, with runners doing laps in and around the playing fields in the center of the town. It's a warm day and a big crowd has turned out, lining the hills on two sides of the playing fields. There is even a sound system booming out from the back of a truck, with two women on the stage grinding to the jumped-up music. A few gazebos have been put up by the corporate sponsor, KCB, a Kenyan bank, at the start and finish areas. We make our way over. Marietta initially sits down with the children in the front row, where someone is handing out free bottles of water. But after a few stern looks and poorly disguised coughs, she realizes she is taking up the prime viewing seats in the VIP tent—seats reserved for dignitaries such as the head of the army and the head of the Kenyan Olympic Committee.

Milling around by the start, I bump into both Toby and Godfrey. They introduce me to a seemingly endless number of runners and coaches. Rather than telling me their names, each person is introduced by a time or an achievement—often a world record or an Olympic title. One man in particular seems to be getting handshakes from everyone. He's a short, white man with a ruddy face shaded by a baseball cap. He has his arms folded tightly across his round body as the leading junior girls come by. Quietly, with a strong Irish accent, he tells the girl in second to "Stay there, stay there." I know who he is without being introduced.

In the late 1970s, an Irish priest with no background in athlet-

ics came on a two-year placement to teach at Iten's Catholic boarding school, St. Patrick's. At that time there were no runners training
in Iten. Even though the school had already produced an Olympic
medalist, Mike Boit, who won the bronze medal in the 800 meters
in 1972, it was the influence of the new recruit from Ireland, Brother
Colm O'Connell, that was to turn St. Patrick's into one of the most
successful athletics schools in the world, and turn Iten into the running center it is today.

Soon after Brother Colm started teaching, the school's track
coach returned to Britain and the Irish priest stepped into the va-
cant role. His teams began to do well in national competitions, and
in 1986 he was asked to select the Kenyan team for the first ever
world junior championships in Athens. He picked nine runners,
seven from St. Patrick's. Having never competed internationally, he
didn't know what to expect from his team, but to his surprise they
won nine medals, including four golds.

"It was then I realized we had something special going on here,"
he tells me later. Three years after that, in 1989, he started the first
running camp in Kenya. It was open during school holidays, and
initially it was just for girls.

"I just wanted to give athletics a bit more focus," he says. But the
idea caught on. St. Patrick's went on to produce numerous world
and Olympic champions, and today there are more than 120 training camps in and around Iten. Brother Colm has since retired from
teaching at the school, but he still lives within the school grounds.
Tucked behind his modest house is his training camp—a small
house where the runners share rooms. Currently he has only four
athletes in the camp, but they're all people he has coached since
they were very young. One of them, 22-year-old David Rudisha, has
just been crowned the IAAF World Athlete of the Year after he twice
broke the thirteen-year-old 800 meters world record. The person

who held the record before him was Wilson Kipketer, another St. Patrick's old boy and former charge of Brother Colm.

At the race in Iten, Godfrey, yet another of Brother Colm's former prodigies, introduces him to me as a legend in Kenyan running. Brother Colm, though, is quick to tamp down the hyperbole. "The legend is bigger than the man," he says, looking away as though he's in a hurry to be somewhere else. Godfrey tells him I'm writing a book on Iten and the runners, and that I'd like to talk to him at some point. "What do you want to talk to me for?" he says. "There are lots of other more interesting people."

Every article I've read about Iten talks about the influence of Brother Colm. The athletes themselves talk about him as the godfather of Kenyan running. As Godfrey says, to them he is a legend. But I guess he doesn't like the limelight, because before I have a chance to say a word, he's gone.

I bump into him again the next evening at a bar in the Kerio View hotel, sitting with a young Kenyan woman. "I'm stalking you," I say, only half jokingly. He warms to me a bit more when I tell him that my parents are Irish and that my dad is from Galway. "I went to university in Galway," he says, and starts telling his companion about the beautiful wildness of Connemara. He talks with the wistful tone of a man who has spent a long time away from his homeland and remembers only the most cherished of moments, like little treasures in a box, taken out occasionally, held delicately, turned over, and then placed carefully back again.

◄ ►

Back at the race in Iten, a long line of men stretches out across the dusty field. A few officials are rushing along the front of the line, trying to keep order. I've gone to stand at the first corner, to take pictures of the start, so it's hard to see what sets everyone off, but suddenly half the runners are charging across the field toward me. A shout goes up from the crowd as marshals rush onto the course to halt the runners. Some of them don't want to stop and have to be virtually pulled to the ground. Eventually they all return to the start line to try again.

With all the incredible runners here, competition is stiff, so getting a good start is vital. The second time they get it right and the line quickly becomes a swarm of athletes fighting to get ahead. I hold my camera up as the field arrows toward me and darts around the corner. It is like they are sprinting for their lives. But they still have over seven miles to run, in 85-degree heat.

This is one of the fiercest races you could hope to witness anywhere in the world. At the world cross-country championships, for instance, there are only six Kenyans in each race, most of whom usually finish in the top ten. Here there are three hundred Kenyans in each race. It is quite a sight.

Unlike open cross-country races in Britain, where you will always see a fair sprinkling of gray hair and bandy legs, and many runners who are clearly doing it purely for fun, in Kenya everyone is under forty and fast. I briefly contemplated running, but after watching, I'm glad I didn't. Next time I'll run, I tell myself, not realizing the next race is only a few weeks away.

There is one foreigner in the race. A fair-haired man wearing a Winchester AC running vest. He trails just a few places from the back, and I'm thinking that he is a brave man even to be out there. Later I find out that his name is Tom Payn and that he is the fourth fastest marathon runner in Britain.

The large crowd watches mostly in silence, except at the end when the spectators occasionally rise to an excited cheer at the prospect of a sprint finish. In the women's race, they scream and yell as the world champion 5,000 meters silver medalist, Sylvia Kibet (who almost became our landlady), produces a barnstorming sprint at the end—to finish third. The race is won by one of Godfrey's friends, Lineth Chepkurui. The junior women's race is won by Faith Kipyegon, just days before the reports of her school beating, and a couple of months before she becomes world champion.

The men's race is won by Geoffrey Mutai, who a few months later will go on to win both the Boston and New York City marathons, setting course records in each, while the winner in the junior men's race is Isaiah Koech, who just weeks later will smash the world champion junior 5,000 meters indoor record by an incredible forty seconds. And this is just a national league race.

The quality of the running is slightly lost on my children, who initially enjoy watching, but soon find the sun too hot and the races too long. "Daddy, is it nearly finished yet?" Uma keeps asking me. Eventually Marietta has to take them back to the car.

Ossian may not have been paying close attention to who was winning the races, but later that day he starts playing a new game. Standing at one end of the long veranda that runs across the front of our three rooms at the Lelin campsite, he says, "Ready, steady, go!" Then he starts running, his arms up in the air and a big grin on his face. The Kenyan magic, it seems, is already starting to have an effect.

◄ ► ►

A week later, our house in Iten is finally ready to move into. When we turn up, the only person there is the builder, still working on a few last jobs. The place smells of paint and dust. The rooms are bare, save for unmade beds and an elaborate, handmade sofa set in the sitting room. The new linoleum floors have been badly taped down and are already curling up at the edges.

In the section of the house where the man with the passion fruit was squatting, a half-made bed without a mattress fills a tiny, bleak room. The main room is completely empty, while a third room is filled with junk—an old television, bits of wood, some frayed electrical wires. Flora, a young woman hired by Marietta's sister to work for us, is supposed to live in this half of the house. It feels a bit desolate. The toilet is black with grime and the flush doesn't work.

About an hour after we arrive, the landlady, an elderly, kindly woman in a big, patterned blouse, turns up carrying lots of sheets and blankets for the beds. She immediately sets to mopping the floors and making the beds. Like almost all women in Kenya, she wants to hug and pick up the children, but they back away shyly. This only makes her persist more, giggling to herself as she chases them around the room.

While the rest of the house is put in order, we leave Lila and Uma with Flora and head back to the supermarkets of Eldoret to get supplies such as spoons, plates, knives, pots, pans, and all the other household items. It's quite a job and we don't get back until after dark. On the way home we start worrying about the girls. They seem too young suddenly to spend the day in an empty house in a small Kenyan town, with a 22-year-old woman that they hardly know looking after them. But as we pull in through the gate, they're standing smiling at the front door, a warm glow of yellow light behind them. They run out into the night to meet us. Inside, we find a big bowl of soup that they have made, waiting on the table. We all sit down, and family life in Iten begins.

Seven

The early-morning run

"The time is five thirty-five. It's time to get up. The time is five—" I switch off my alarm before it wakes up Ossian. I look over. He's sleeping soundly. I creep out of bed and put on my running clothes: tights and a long-sleeved top. The door bangs as I open it, but no one in the house stirs.

I step out into a moonlit night. Dogs and roosters are already doing their best to wake the valley, but there's still no sign of the dawn as I walk through Iten toward the meeting point: a junction between one of the many dirt roads and the main paved one. I've been told that runners meet here just after six every morning.

Despite the thousands of athletes in Iten, when you first arrive, there is no program that you can join or center where you can go to put your name down to start training. The many international runners who come here stay at Lornah's camp and run every day by themselves or with other international athletes they meet at the camp. So far I've run a few times with Godfrey, who is just starting to train again after a few years, trying to get himself into shape for Lewa. But if I want to run with the big groups that I see zipping by everywhere, I'm going to have to do what any Kenyan hopeful turning up in Iten has to do: Stand by the side of the road, wait for a group to come by, and join in.

The town is quiet at this time of the morning, and I slip by unnoticed in the darkness. Even at this hour there are people out running. I don't know how they can see well enough to negotiate all the bumps and potholes without twisting an ankle. There are also children running to school already, racing past with their pencil cases rattling in their schoolbags.

I'm the first to arrive at the junction. I do a bit of stretching and jogging up and down to keep warm, as the occasional *matatu* drives slowly by, beeping for customers. After about ten minutes, runners start appearing from everywhere, materializing out of the darkness. Within minutes there are about sixty Kenyan runners standing around. Some of them are talking quietly and stretching. They are mostly men, their long, skinny legs wrapped in tights, some wearing woolly hats. I suddenly feel out of my depth, panicking as more athletes bound down the slopes or appear out from behind trees. But it's too late to turn back now.

Without any announcement, we start running, heading off down the dirt track. *Here we go,* I tell myself, following them off into the darkness. *Buckle up and hang on.* The initial pace is quick without being terrifying, so I edge myself into the middle of the group and try to stay calm, focusing on my style, feeling the gentle *pat,* *pat, pat* of my feet skipping under me. Up ahead the full moon lights the way, while behind us the dawn is creeping across the sky, making it easier to see. The last few stars go out as we hurtle along out of the town and into the African countryside.

I love running like this, in a group. You often hear commentators on television saying that an athlete is getting an easy ride running in the pack. In one way it doesn't make sense. You're still running under your own power, using the same energy to propel yourself forward. Wind resistance isn't usually a big factor in running. But somehow, in a group it is easier. It can feel as though the group is running, not you; as if the movement around you has picked you up and is carrying you along, the switching back and forth of legs focusing the mind, synchronizing it, setting a rhythm for your body to follow. As soon as you become detached from the group, its power evaporates and it feels harder to run.

When I run on my own, particularly in a town or city, I feel like I'm constantly negotiating obstacles, such as curbs, pedestrians, parked cars, and lampposts. Here it is potholes, cows, and bicycles. In a group, though, they all whiz by almost without registering. In the group, everything is swept up and spat out as you pass.

A few of the runners around me are chatting quietly, but mostly we run in silence, passing small settlements of round mud huts, following the red dusty trail as it winds its way farther and farther away from anywhere I recognize. The children who usually call out and get excited when I go by just stand and watch as we run past. I'm lost in the blur of the charge.

It doesn't last long, however. After just a few miles, the pace begins to pick up. I feel it most up the hills, and soon find myself drifting to the back of the group. I ask someone how far we are running. "One hour ten," he says. We must be moving now at a pace of about six minutes per mile, and getting faster with each stride. I will need to have the run of my life not to get lost.

Luckily for me, two women also begin struggling with the ever-increasing pace and I end up sticking with them for the rest of the run. They kindly encourage me whenever I start to fall behind. Up one particularly steep hill near the end, as my legs finally start to rebel, refusing to match the patter-patter rhythm of the two women, one of them turns to me and says simply: "Try."

I can't help but respond, and I manage to stay with them until the end. We finish at the top of the hill outside Lornah's camp back in Iten. The other runners are all standing around in the bright sunshine, joking and stretching. Some are walking home. I'm exhausted, but still standing. It's as much as I could have hoped for.

◄ ►

After thanking my two companions, I make my way slowly through Iten back to our house. The rest of the town is waking up now. Men walk around selling newspapers by the side of the road, while boys on bicycles deliver bread to the various wooden kiosks dotting the town. Outside the big black gates to our house is a tiny kiosk with a grill-covered window across the front. It sells tea and rice and other things that last a long time, in case nobody buys them. There are always a few men sitting on the counter outside, as though at a bar, passing time, watching us as we come and go. I walk over and shake their hands. I can just about make out the face of a man inside the kiosk. "Fine, fine," he says, coming out through a side door to greet me.

His name is Geoffrey, he tells me, smiling. He thought we were German. One of the men, sitting languidly on the shop counter is his brother, Henry, an athlete. "Half marathon," he says.

A third, shorter man is wearing a ripped yellow tracksuit. He gives me a big, bucktooth grin. His name is Japhet.

"Are you an athlete, too?" I ask him.

"Yes," he says. His torn running shoes and old clothes suggest he isn't the most successful athlete in Iten, but I imagine he's still probably pretty fast.

"Two hours twenty-eight," he says. He's talking about the marathon. It's a surprisingly slow time for a Kenyan. Most marathon runners in Iten have a best time of under 2 hours 15 minutes. Even 2 hours 10 minutes is fairly average. But Japhet says it was his first marathon, and he ran it in Kisumu, here in Kenya. He says it was very hot when he ran. "But I ran all the way," he says, smiling. "Position twenty-seven."

I ask him if he trains full time, or whether he has a job, too. He shakes his head.

"If you have a job, you can't run," he says. "You get tired. Too tired."

I tell him that I'm running a marathon in Kenya, too. Perhaps we could train together.

"The Lewa Marathon," I tell him. "Do you know it?"

"Lewa?" he asks. "Yes. Very hard. Very hot."

"Perhaps we could go for a run together, all three of us?"

"Yes," says Japhet, looking at Henry, who nods his approval. "That would be good."

A small herd of cows ambles past along the rutted road, followed by a young girl in a gold, silk evening dress, torn across one shoulder. Her bare feet are caked in mud, and her hair is cropped short. In her hand she carries a stick for prodding the cows. She stares at us as she passes.

"I see you have a soldier," says Geoffrey.

He means our night watchman. Everyone has told me that Iten

is a safe town. But they also said that we should get a security guard. Just in case. I'd heard enough terrible stories of foreigners being robbed in other parts of Kenya to make the first few nights of sleeping in the house an hourly ordeal, as I'd hear a noise, wait quietly to see if it would happen again, and then, if it did, jump up to look out of the window. At about four o'clock in the morning on the first night, Lila woke up shouting. I went in to see her.

"What's that banging noise?" she asked, almost hysterical.

"Shhh, it's nothing," I said, listening hard to see if there was any banging. There was. "Quiet," I said, in an urgent enough tone to make her quiet. She looked at me. I looked at her. "Wait here," I said. The banging seemed to be coming from the kitchen. I opened the door quickly, but there was no one there. It was coming from above.

Marietta called from the bedroom. I went in to see her. "It's just the birds on the roof," she said. "They've been making noises all night."

The problem with not having a watchman is that you can't reliably call the police if something happens.

"What do we do if someone tries to break in?" I asked Godfrey. "Call the police?"

"Yes," he said. Then, thinking about it, he smiled. "No, first call Koila." Koila lives near our house. "Or call me." Godfrey lives thirty miles away, near Eldoret.

In the end we hired a watchman. He arrived in an armored car with about eight other uniformed men, who jumped down and saluted me like members of the A-Team. Deliberately last out of the van was a smooth-talking manager in a shirt and tie. He was all reassuring smiles as he pointed at the armored car. "If anything happens, we send the car from Eldoret," he said.

"How long will that take?"

He smiled at me. "This is your guard," he said, turning to the smallest of the men, who gave me a worried salute. The others looked strong and sturdy, like soldiers. Our man, Alex, looked more like a runner.

That evening he turned up punctually at seven o'clock and started snooping around the garden like a comic book guard with his uniform and watchman's hat, his big, white truncheon held out in front of him. He checked the fence and noted things down on a big clipboard. Later that evening I looked out of the window and saw his torchlight skirting the ground by the fence.

He may not be particularly effective, with his truncheon and his back-up team all the way in Eldoret, but that night I had the best sleep since we moved in. I left the worrying about noises to our man in the garden.

"Yes," I say to Geoffrey, the kiosk owner. "You saw him?"

"Yes," says Geoffrey. He smiles, friendly. "It's best to be safe."

◄ ►

For the next few weeks I find myself running mostly with Godfrey, or with other foreigners in the town, in an attempt to get in better shape before I'm brave enough to join in with another group run. But everyone here is fast. One guy I meet is a young American student called Anders. Godfrey seems to have taken him under his wing.

"His mum," Godfrey tells me, "ran the first ever marathon. In the Olympics. She just jumped in with the men and beat them all."

He repeats this jumbled story to people countless times and each time the result is a puzzled expression, rather than the look of impressed surprise Godfrey is hoping for. Eventually I work out that Anders's mother is Joan Benoit. The story that Godfrey was trying to retell was her victory in the marathon at the 1984 Olympics. It was the first women's Olympic marathon and she didn't jump in with the men, there was a separate race. As well as being an Olympic champion, Joan is also a former world record holder and a two-time winner of the Boston Marathon. She's basically America's greatest ever woman's marathon runner.

Anders is no slouch himself and has a 10K time of thirty-three minutes—five minutes quicker than my best. One morning I head out with him and Godfrey on a steady run through the forest. After a few minutes, Godfrey, the one training partner that I can keep up with, stops, complaining of sore knees. Godfrey was once a great athlete, but at forty-five he is struggling to get back into shape.

"Sorry, guys," he says, as we leave him to hobble back to town. As we run, Anders tells me that he's not sure Godfrey will really run the Lewa Marathon. Godfrey must be the world's most friendly, helpful man, but sometimes that can be a problem. He says yes to everything.

"There's been a change of plan," is his famous refrain, just when you're expecting to do something with him. He's usually on the other end of a long-distance call from Nairobi or western Kenya, where his wife works as a police officer. So I'm not surprised when Anders says Godfrey might not run Lewa, but it leaves me without a training partner. It suddenly feels lonely to go there on my own. I should form a team, I think. It would give me a ready-made group to run with. It would be a great way to get closer to some of the athletes, and to find out what makes them tick. And even if Godfrey doesn't run, perhaps he could be the coach.

When we get back, I mention the team idea to Godfrey. He thinks it's a great plan. "Chris will run, too," he says. He means

Christopher Cheboiboch, the runner who picked us up from the Lelin campsite on our first day in Iten. The man with the fifth fastest time ever in the New York marathon.

"Really? You think so?"

"Sure," he says. "We want only the best."

Eight

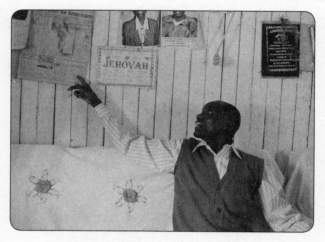

Christopher Cheboiboch at his childhood home

For years I've been saying that one day I would run a marathon, and now, in a few months, I will. I'm slowly getting in shape. Every time Godfrey sees me he mentions that I've lost weight. I must have had a lot to lose. Whenever I mention the Lewa race to any of the other runners, however, they grimace. "That is tough," they say. It's hot, hilly, and run on dirt tracks. Kenyans generally prefer courses where they can run fast times. A fast time can mean an invite to a big city marathon. A slow course is, in many ways, simply a waste of effort.

My neighbor Japhet, though, says he would like to run it with me. He keeps telling me how he is always at the front on the early-morning group runs.

"I'm forming a team," I say. "Would you like to join?"

He grins. "Yes," he says.

Japhet, it turns out, is from the same village as Christopher Cheboiboch, who has also agreed to be part of the team. The village sits on a ridge just below the top of the escarpment, caught between a chiseled rock face rising up behind rolling fields and the vast Rift Valley falling away to the front. It's a beautiful place. Chris says he remembers when Japhet was born. Their family homes are practically next to each other.

◄ ►

Every Kenyan runner has a story. To go from a small *shamba* on the side of a mountain in rural Kenya to winning big city marathons in Europe and America is inevitably a tale filled with drama and adventure. Chris told me that the first time he ever visited Iten he was fourteen years old. It was the first time he had ever seen even a small town. He walked through the streets agog at all the people and buildings. Ten years later he was almost winning the New York City Marathon, racing past huge skyscrapers, being cheered on by hundreds of thousands of people.

Chris took me home to his village one time to meet his family. He looked completely out of place among the raggedy farmers, with his neatly ironed shirt and easy smile. Everywhere we went people waved or stopped to talk to him. The one who had made it. The prodigal son, returning to see his people. But a distance had grown between them. He spoke to most people through the window of his gently purring car, keeping his distance. After we'd spoken to one worker, reaching in to shake my hand, his clothes covered in dust and mud after a hard day's toil, Chris turned to me.

"He was a classmate of mine," he said, aware of the contrast in their fortunes, letting it linger as he drove on.

Chris's family home was a simple mud hut like all the others, but he had bought lots of the surrounding fields. It was hard to keep track of how much he owned. "Those cattle are mine," he said, pointing into the distance. "I bought those two fields for my brother." At his homestead, his sister had prepared a feast for us. Inside, it was like a shrine to Chris, with newspaper clippings about his successes and photographs of him on the walls, all framed and surrounded in tinsel.

After we'd eaten, his mother turned up. She was a tough woman who grunted an unimpressed hello at me. After Chris's father disappeared when he was very young, she started farming the land, bringing up her six children on her own. But Chris was clearly a little embarrassed by her, with her tired scowl and woolen Manchester United hat. They hardly spoke to each other. A few muttered words and then we were gone, heading back to Iten.

Chris is now forty-two, although, like virtually all male Kenyan runners, his official age is much lower, in this case thirty-four. I never get to the bottom of why they all say they are younger than they actually are. Each person has a different story, although it usually involves someone else, such as a manager, getting the date wrong at some point. Bizarrely, around half of Kenya's runners were born on January first, according to their official records. When I fill in Japhet's Lewa entry form with him, I ask him what his date of birth is.

"Nineteen eighty-seven," he says.

"What day and month?" I ask him. He looks at me and starts shuffling around on his seat.

"Let me go and find out," he says.

In 2002, when Chris was thirty-three (officially twenty-five), he came second in both the Boston and the New York City marathons.

He was flying, one of the top athletes at the illustrious stable of the Italian agent Doctor Rosa. Almost immediately, though, he became distracted. He used his money to build a school named after his home village, Salaba.

Like all Kenyan runners, when Chris was young he had to run to school, three miles, back and forth twice a day every day.

"Unknowingly, we were already training," he says. "But it was hard." He says he built Salaba Academy so that his own children didn't have to suffer as he did.

"It's also an investment. It's his retirement," says Godfrey.

A fee-paying boarding school just outside of Iten, Salaba Academy takes up a lot of Chris's time. He seems to do everything himself, from buying the flour for the *ugali* to attending meetings with education officials in Nairobi. One morning we arrange to leave for an early run at 5:00 A.M. and he asks if we can pick him up at the school.

"Why will you be at the school at that time?" I ask.

"I'm always at school early," he says.

"But is anyone even awake?"

"They are in class already," he says, affronted, as though I'm suggesting that his children are lazy.

"At five in the morning?"

"They have exams coming up. They must work hard."

Once his school was up and running, Chris never reached the same level of performance in his running again.

◅ ▻

Chris's story of short-lived glory is common among the athletes here and shows just how vital focus and dedication are to Kenya's running success.

The most famous example of a great athlete becoming distracted by success is Sammy Wanjiru, who blazed away to win the 2008 Olympic marathon at the tender age of twenty-one. A few months after setting up my Lewa team, Wanjiru, one of the most precocious and successful of all of Kenya's runners, is killed in a fall from a balcony at his home in Nyahururu. Wanjiru was known among the other athletes as a heavy drinker. I was told that if I wanted to meet him, I should go to a bar in Eldoret and ask around. According to the stories, he would regularly go into a nightclub and buy everyone a drink. On the night he died, his wife came home to find him in bed with another woman. What happened next no one knows, but Wanjiru ended up dead.

One warm, still afternoon, as a paraglider circles in the sky above, I find the legendary Italian coach Renato Canova sitting in his seat by the vast windows that span one side of the Kerio View hotel, a glass of milk on the table in front of him. He's the only person there, apart from a team of waiters hovering by the kitchen door and talking quietly to one another. I ask him if I can sit down.

"Please do," he says, moving the chair out for me. Renato has a permanent room at the hotel and spends much of his time sitting here, perched above the sky, reading a newspaper or gazing out the window. Since he first came to Iten in 1998 he has been training Kenyan athletes, and virtually all of his runners have gone on to win world titles.

One of the waitresses comes over and asks me what I want to drink. I order a passion fruit juice. She doesn't ask Renato. He has his milk. He'll be back later for supper, at the same time as always.

"So, what did you want to know?" he says.

I ask him why the Kenyans often have short careers. Unlike

the great Ethiopian runners such as Haile Gebrselassie and Kenenisa Bekele, most Kenyans run well for a few years and then disappear.

He looks at me over the top of his fingers, held in a prayer position on the table.

"The runners all come from poor backgrounds, with less education," he says. "When they win, the whole village celebrates their victory, and everyone asks for support. The successful athlete becomes like the chief of the village, so then everyone goes to him with their personal problems." Renato says he once had an athlete who, while at the world championships in 2005, was being phoned every two hours by people back in Kenya asking him where they should put the windows in a building they were constructing. "The athletes need to concentrate on their training," he says. "They need to educate their villagers about their life."

This is why the training camps were started, to remove the athletes from the distraction of their families and relations, and the rest of the outside world. But once athletes become successful, they often decide they don't want to live in the camps anymore, where daily life is stripped down to the bare essentials of run, eat, and sleep, so they move out. "They start dealing with building projects, borrowing money," says Renato. "This is normal behavior for a Kenyan." It is normal behavior in most other countries, too, even for athletes. Those who live in the camps are the unusual ones. But the difference it makes is huge. Without the same intense levels of dedication and focus, when an athlete leaves a camp it often signals the beginning of the end. Wanjiru isn't the only great athlete who ended up propping up the bars of Eldoret.

Chris at least kept running. He tells me that for the month before the Lewa Marathon, he will move away from home, to a hotel, to concentrate on his training. "Of course," he says. "You have to be focused."

I can't imagine this level of intensity, living away from home in basic-training camps for months at a time, being considered normal among athletes in other parts of the world. Yet there are hundreds of these camps in Kenya, all filled with dedicated athletes. Under the heading "Secrets" in my notebook, I jot down the words *focus, dedication, training camps.*

Godfrey calls a Lewa team meeting at a hotel in Iten. Japhet turns up wearing a sleeveless safari jacket that hangs way too big from his shoulders. He sits shyly on the edge of his seat, listening intently as Godfrey talks about what an honor it is to be on the team, that the race will be live on television, that the whole world will be watching. As he's talking, Chris arrives with another runner.

"This is Josphat," he says. "He wants to run, too."

Josphat shakes my hand and gives me an amused smile. Like Chris, it's hard to put an age on him, but it turns out that he's Chris's childhood friend and he's also from the same village.

"Okay," I say. "So together we're five, if Godfrey runs." He has been telling me his knees are too sore. "Otherwise, Godfrey has agreed to be our coach."

Godfrey and Chris take turns to make the most grandiose speech about what the team means, and they keep thanking me profusely for setting it up.

"We are representing Iten," says Godfrey. "When you are interviewed afterward," he says, looking at Japhet, "you must speak well. You mustn't be shy."

"Josphat, what have you got to say for yourself?" says Chris, turning on his friend. "What will you say after the race?"

Josphat, who still hasn't spoken since he arrived, looks unwilling to join in the game. The hotel waitress brings over five cups of tea, buying him some time. She places them down on the table in slow motion, without speaking or looking at anyone.

"So, Josphat," says Chris, sounding like a teacher.

"I don't know," he says.

"Ah, that's no good," says Chris, annoyed.

Later, after the others have gone, Godfrey seems concerned. "I don't know why Chris brought Josphat along. He doesn't add anything to the team. He's way too old. We need a winner."

A week later I get a call from Godfrey. "Finn," he says. "I think I've found our winner." I'm not sure we need a winner. I've agreed to pay the race entry fees and arrange some accommodation for the night before the race. Suddenly everyone wants to be on the team.

"How good is he?" I ask.

"Are you kidding me? He's good. Come and meet him tomorrow. There's a homecoming for some athletes who ran in the African championships. Komen will be there." He means the great Daniel Komen, the 3,000 meters world record holder.

"Okay," I say, not realizing what is in store.

◄ ►

After driving for about two hours along the edge of the escarpment, we swing in through the drive of a school in the village of Kamwosor. "Can we stop?" Godfrey asks. I pull the car to a halt. "I think this is it," he says, "but let me check first." He gets out of the car and disappears through the gate behind us.

"Where's Godfrey going?" Lila asks me, as though I ever know what is going on when Godfrey is around.

"I don't know," I say. We all sit staring out of the front window. A long, corrugated metal building sits at the end of the dirt driveway. I presume it's the school. A few heads appear around the edge of one wall and then disappear. Suddenly the whole school is running up the drive toward us, a huge swarm of red sweaters. We sit trapped in our car as the children clamber around us, laughing and chattering to one another, peering in at us. They reach in through the half-open windows, looking for handshakes, money, candy, anything. Lila and Uma are not sure whether it's funny or terrifying. Uma is standing up on the backseat, while Lila climbs over the seat to the front and curls up on my lap. The car is rocking in the frenzy.

"Finn, Finn." I can hear Godfrey outside, but I can't see him. He manages to push his way through the crowd. Where are the teachers? "Finn, start to come back," he says. I turn the engine on to a big cheer, and start edging the car backward. Godfrey is pulling children out of the way. Finally we make it back out onto the street. The children stand in the open gateway, held back by some invisible force, waving and laughing as we turn the car.

Godfrey gets in. "Sorry about that," he says. "Let's go this way."

We drive up into the village, a single strip of road with painted wooden shops on either side, a few flimsy vegetable stalls, women with big skirts holding long knives, standing staring at us. We park the car and Godfrey takes us into a tiny, blue building with the word HOTEL painted across it. It's actually a café. Inside, a few men sit at wooden tables. They look at us in silence as we sit down. Rickety chairs, benches along the walls, a dusty red floor. There's a wooden counter in one corner, with a pile of rocklike buns on a shelf behind the glass front. In the other corner is a butcher's shop, the skinned and headless body of a cow hanging from a hook.

Godfrey asks us what we want to drink and then disappears out through the front door when we tell him, leaving us sitting there.

"Where's he gone now?" Lila asks me quietly, leaning across the table.

"I don't know," I say, looking at Marietta. She shrugs, amused at his constant comings and goings. Ossian climbs onto her lap and starts banging the table and singing, happy to be out of the car. The other men in the room give up watching us and turn back to their conversations. Eventually Godfrey comes back with a bag full of sodas. He has two men with him. One of them is Shadrack, the runner he has been telling me about.

"Hi," I say, after Godfrey introduces us. "I hear you want to run Lewa?"

"Huh?" he looks at me as though I'm mad.

"Lewa. You know the marathon?"

"Yes," he says.

"You want to run?"

He nods, staring at me now with unblinking eyes. "Yes," he says.

―< >―

About three hours later than planned we make our way back down the road to the village school where the homecoming ceremony is finally about to begin. Four of the children from the village have just come back from the African cross-country championships in Cape Town, where Kenya won every single medal on offer despite sending only a second-string team. The first team was being saved for the world championships two weeks later.

The appearance of the teachers means that we don't get such a raucous reception this time, so we're free to park the car and walk over to where the festivities are taking place. As guests of honor, we are each given tinsel wreaths to wear around our necks and are directed to sit under the shade of a small marquee. The schoolchildren sit on the ground around the tent in the hot sun.

One of the speakers is Daniel Komen. The chairman of the local athletics board, he sits sullenly through the speeches by the other dignitaries, not laughing when everyone else does. Occasionally he calls Godfrey close and whispers something in his ear, his eyes looking around to make sure nobody else is listening.

Tall and smartly dressed, Komen is one of the greatest runners that has ever lived. In 1996, at the age of twenty, he burst onto the international scene like a fireball. The great Ethiopian Haile Gebrselassie was the dominant force in distance running at the time and was breaking world records for fun.* Suddenly he had a challenger. At the end of the 1996 season Komen, upset at not making the Kenyan team for the Olympics, went out and ran one of the most staggering performances ever seen on a track. On a cool September evening in Rieti, Italy, he flew around seven and a half laps like a man possessed, breaking the 3,000 meters world record by over four seconds. Despite all the great names that have tried, nobody has since been able to get even close to the time he ran that night.

However, less than two years later, Komen's career was virtually over. Those who knew him blame the money he won, and people often hold him up as a prime example when they talk about athletes winning money and then becoming distracted. Komen himself, however, blames the shortness of his career not on money but on injuries. I corner him one day at the exclusive Eldoret Golf Club, where he often sits on Sundays, brooding under the shade of an umbrella while his children dive-bomb each other in the pool.

---

*From 1993 until 2000, Gebrselassie won every major 10,000 meters gold medal, including two Olympic games, while during his career he broke an astounding twenty-four world records.

"I had many injuries," he says, looking away. He seems annoyed.

"What injuries did you have?"

"From high school. The teachers wanted the points for the team, so they made me run all the races. Sometimes I had to run two races on the same day. The Ethiopians don't have so much pressure on them in high school, but it's a big problem in Kenya."

Despite Komen's ill feeling, he is heavily involved in junior athletics in Kenya. As chairman of the local athletics board, he seems to show up at every school event, although he says he is stepping down next year to focus on the school that he has set up. He also sponsors talented athletes to go and study in the United States.

"But we have many problems," he says, scowling. "People don't run. They take the money." Just a few months before, one of his sponsored athletes in Alaska hung himself. There's not a lot of light in Komen's world right now.

Back at the homecoming ceremony, he sits glowering as the speeches rumble on, the gold tinsel wreath hanging uncomfortably around his neck. After about three hours, Godfrey is called up to speak. He talks in English, telling the schoolchildren that education is important. That they should work hard at their studies.

Marietta has taken our three children off behind the marquee to play, but a line has formed of people who want to be photographed with them. It's getting late, so we decide to make a break for it. We bundle out as the town's mayor takes up the microphone. Heads follow us as we make our way back to the car. Godfrey, shaking hands with everyone, is dragged on by Lila. A man from a local radio station comes over, wanting to interview me, asking me to talk into his tape recorder as I climb into the car, reversing as someone leans in through the window, alcohol on his breath, telling me he is a great runner.

And then we're off, following the road back along the edge of the escarpment, past round mud huts, flickering wooden fences, bicycles, people walking, the sloping green fields full of the late afternoon, children laughing and chasing each other. And all the while, to one side, the great open space of the Rift Valley falling away below us.

Nine

Kenyan runners at rest

When I can't find anyone to run with, I put on my racing flats and head out on my own. Although I prefer running in a group, here in Kenya sometimes it is a relief to run alone. At my own pace, I can simply enjoy the trails, the countryside, the sense of motion, the earth trundling by under my feet, without having to feel slow and hopeless at the back of the pack, always bursting my lungs to keep up, just waiting to see how long I can survive until I'm cast aside.

On one of these solo runs I strain a toe landing on a stone. I get it massaged by one of Iten's many massage therapists and it's fine a few days later. But the injury makes me question the wisdom of doing all my running in "barefoot" shoes. Lee Saxby, the barefoot expert in London, had told me that Kenyans ran in this kind of shoe, but it clearly isn't the case. Kenyan runners race in low-support shoes, but they mostly train in big, chunky, cushioned sneakers, just like your average, plodding Western jogger. Oddly, though, and contrary to Lee's theories, these big shoes don't force the Kenyans to run heel first. They virtually all run in a lovely, smooth forefoot-first style—what Lee would term "barefoot style." The shoes, it seems, make no difference.

"Your feet are not used to the terrain here," the massage therapist tells me, pressing my toes to a pulp as I lie on the treatment room table in Lornah Kiplagat's training camp (Lornah actually walks in mid-grimace and shakes my hand). "You need more cushioning on your shoes, because of all the stones," the therapist tells me.

So I've come full circle. To run like a Kenyan, it seems, I need to go back to where I started, and get myself a big, padded pair of sneakers. I can't quite bring myself to do it, though.

That afternoon we all walk down to the local *mitumba,* a weekly market selling mostly secondhand clothes shipped over from Europe and America by aid charities. The clothes are piled high on sacks laid out on the floor. Everything from mainstream brands to designer labels. For bargain hunters it's a bonanza of cheap clothes, a jumble sale of epic proportions. Marietta loves it, and she and the children head down most Saturdays to rummage through the bounty. "I could clothe us all for the next two years," she says, not joking.

My family causes quite a stir in the *mitumba.* Marietta disappearing under armfuls of clothes, bartering hard with a woman sitting up high like a queen on a throne of piled-up clothes; Lila drawing giggles as she tries on a pink, faux-fur waistcoat, looking at herself in a shard of broken mirror; Uma, following on, holding tightly to a Barbie tracksuit, folding it up and squashing it under her arm. Even Ossian likes to get in on the act, sitting down on the ground and kicking off his shoes so he can try on endless pairs of high heels and flip-flops.

This being Iten, a couple of the stalls at the *mitumba* are selling running shoes. Lines and lines of scrubbed-up shoes, glistening in the sunshine. I scan them, looking for the pair with the thinnest sole, and stop on a pair of orange Asics. "Yes, my friend," says the seller, sensing I have my eye on a pair. "Which country are you from?" The shoes are slightly worn, but that's all the better, right? I'm confused now. Do I want to be near the ground, or protected from it? They're the only pair in my size that don't have a huge wedge of sponge built in under the heel, so I buy them.

But on my very first run in my new shoes, I land heavily on another stone. I can feel the pain shooting up my leg. After a few minutes it subsides, but the whole barefoot issue is clouded yet further. Clearly my feet are still not tough or strong enough to run forefoot first, even in shoes. But I can't go back now. I've gotten to the point where forefoot first feels completely natural to me. And I'm still convinced it's a more efficient way to run.

I remember the day, back in Exeter, when I went to buy my racing flats, just before we left for Kenya. I'd been practicing my barefoot style for a few weeks and had managed to run two miles without my legs aching too much, but I was nervous about the shop assistant asking me to get up on his treadmill so he could analyze my gait. He might tell me that I shouldn't be buying flats as I needed more support, padding, and everything else. I tried to be as inconspicuous as possible while I picked out the flattest shoes, with the least support, that I could find. But I was the only person in the shop.

"Do you have these in a nine?" I asked.

The man took the shoe from me. "Do you pronate?" he asked.

"Er . . . I don't know," I said, wary of lying outright in case he could tell that I did just by the way I walked.

"Hop up on the treadmill and we'll take a look," he said.

I considered bolting out the door, but decided against it. Instead I obediently put on the sneakers and clambered aboard the treadmill. The machine whirred slowly into action. *Lead with your chest,* I told myself. *Legs like a unicycle.* It started to get faster. *Pad, pad, pad.* The shop assistant was crouching down trying to look under my feet. I tried to look casual, like this was my natural running style, not something I was working hard to maintain. He was checking me out from the side now. After about thirty seconds, I hit the Stop button and the machine came to a halt.

"You're lucky," he said. "You have a lovely forefoot style. It's the most efficient way to run."

Occasionally, during my solitary runs here in Kenya, I try changing back to heel first, just for old times' sake. It's like a car changing down gear suddenly, as I feel my whole body slumping back into a slower motion. No, I'm convinced the barefoot style has to stay. I just need to strengthen my feet. Toby Tanser told me that it was too late, that the Kenyans' ankles and the arches of their feet were so much stronger and more flexible from years of running barefoot that we couldn't hope to compete. But I'm not trying to compete with them. And I'm not actually running barefoot. Just in a forefoot style. Surely that's possible.

◄ ►

Once an aspiring runner arrives in Iten and finds a group to train with, his next aim is to run fast enough to attract the attention of a manager, who will sign him up and send him abroad to race. In return for his services, the manager takes a percentage of the prize winnings. Virtually all the managers are foreigners who have set up training camps in Iten and the surrounding area. When an athlete gets signed up, he usually lives in the manager's training camp, where he receives food and lodging and gets to train with the rest of the athletes in the camp. Most camps also have a massage therapist on hand to revitalize tired limbs and treat any niggling injuries. It's amazing how some heavy-duty thumb pressing can usually fix an injured athlete, as though he's simply made of modeling clay.

Although I'm never going to impress a manager, after a few weeks of running around Iten I've gradually gotten to know some of the other athletes, and one of them invites me to spend a day at his camp. The imaginatively named Run Fast camp is one of Iten's newest training centers. There are ten athletes living at the camp in five small dormitories, each with a shower, a sofa, and a bunk bed. Nine of the athletes are Kenyan and one is the British runner Tom Payn, whom I saw competing in the Iten cross-country race. Tom was a technical sales engineer for a filtration company in Portsmouth when he decided to give it all up to come out to train in Kenya. With a best marathon time of 2 hours 17 minutes, he's hoping to get himself into shape to make the British team for the Olympics.

To start my day in the camp, I'm told to meet Tom and the other athletes at 6:20 A.M. outside a hotel on the main road in Iten. When I arrive, quite a big group has already gathered there. As well as the ten athletes in the camp, Run Fast has a group of second-string runners who live outside the camp but come to the training sessions. A few days before I turn up, two of the runners in the camp were told that they had to leave because they weren't training or racing as well as expected. They got quite upset. Two runners from the outside group were invited to take their place.

The Run Fast manager is an Englishman named Peter

McHugh. He has told the group that by the end of the week he will pick six runners to travel to Europe to compete in a series of races. Once they get there, all they have to do is run like Kenyans and watch the money start rolling in. Last year the camp's star runner won enough prize money to buy himself a plot of land in Iten when he got back.

There's a lot of tension in the camp right now as the runners wait to find out if they will be among the chosen six. Most of them have never raced abroad before. They stand on the threshold of the promised land. This is what they've been training for, dreaming about. But if their name is not on the list, they'll be left standing outside in the cold, watching as their friends head off without them. One of the athletes, Eliud, has been running for twelve years and has made a total of one thousand Kenyan shillings—about twelve dollars—in his entire career. Even a small race abroad could net him two thousand dollars. But only if he gets picked.

The problem is, Peter tells me, that finding races for Kenyans is getting harder and harder. With the global recession, prize money at races is down, and people are getting bored of watching Kenyans win everything. Race organizers are desperate for top runners from other countries. When a manager calls up a race director with the offer of a few unknown Kenyans, the response is usually a bored shrug. "Is that all you've got? More Kenyans?"

Peter set up his Run Fast camp only recently, but the other managers I speak to don't think he has much of a chance of making it a success. It's not that he doesn't know what he's doing, but that the landscape is dominated by a handful of über-managers. "The governing body passed a new rule recently," explains one American manager, who is pulling out of Kenya after twenty years of working with athletes here. "Contracts need to be renewed every year. It's good for the athletes, because it means they can move on if they're not getting a fair deal. But it makes it easy for athletes to get poached by other managers."

He says that once a smaller manager like Peter discovers a promising talent, the bigger names will simply move in, offering short-term incentives to the athlete to switch. "There's no loyalty anymore," he tells me. "The Kenyan runners don't understand the longer-term view. So if you offer them five hundred dollars up front, they'll jump at it, even if the terms of the contract mean they'll lose out in the long term." When I mention this to Peter, he just shrugs. "Hopefully that won't happen," he says. "If they're happy with me, I don't think they'll feel the need to change."

Despite promising murmurs, Eliud doesn't get picked to travel. It's all too much for him. "An athlete can't keep in good shape forever," he tells me. "I'm in good shape, but what for? I don't have a race." He looks close to tears. A few days later he leaves the camp and sends a message to Peter to tear up his contract. But where else can he go? He moves in with some friends and continues training.

"He's an idiot," Tom Payn tells me. He likes Eliud and is sad that he has left the camp. "I think Peter was about to give him a race, but now he has no chance." It may be Murphy's law, that he left just as he was about to get a race, or perhaps the race would have remained forever a mirage, always about to happen. Eliud was too proud to sit and wait any longer. He would rather face the impossible route of going it alone. Unless he wins a big race in Kenya, though, it could now be game over.

Although the Run Fast camp is pretty second rate by local standards—there are no Kenyan internationals in the camp, for example—through my eyes it's still a formidable bunch of athletes standing around outside the tiny hotel in the morning half-light. Each person who arrives shakes hands with everyone else and then stands waiting for the runners from the camp to turn up. I spot my neighbor and Lewa teammate Japhet among the crowd. He shakes my hand nervously, his usually big smile slightly terse this morning.

We all travel together to the university track in Eldoret squashed in the back of a pickup truck. It's still only 7:00 A.M. when we arrive, but already there are a few groups of runners hurtling around in midsession. The Run Fast schedule is for them to run lots of 600 meters and lots of 400 meters. I decide to run 400 meters with them when they're running 600 meters, and 200 meters when they're running 400 meters. Hopefully, with the shorter distances and the longer rest between each one, I'll be able to keep up.

It's evident right from the first one, however, that that won't be the case. I find myself almost sprinting around the dirt track, stumbling all over the place trying to run in the trench that has been worn all around the inside lane. A Russian man back in Iten told me that if you run on the track with Kenyans, you feel disabled. I now know what he means. I manage to stick just behind Tom, but the others are far ahead.

Tom is the slowest runner in the group. But, perversely, he is the only one who is sponsored, by Adidas. And he has the best chance of anyone in the group of making it to the Olympics. It seems unfair, but the Kenyans just grin ruefully when I mention it to them. They're just here to run. They don't seem to dwell on whether it's fair or not. Peter, who has come to watch the training, says that the British runners are usually the ones claiming an injustice. "I've been getting a hard time back in the UK," he says. "The British runners don't like me bringing Kenyans over there to race. They complain that the Kenyans are taking all the prize money. But it's an open race."

He's talking to me as I sit on the grass watching the other runners carry on without me. I struggled around for less than a quarter of the session, falling farther and farther behind. Determined to carry on, I switched over to the women's group; three runners, toiling around at what looked like a much slower pace. They nodded shyly, hardly glancing up, when I approached and asked if I could join them. But they were also too fast. I managed to keep close to the slowest of them for a few intervals, even battling to overtake her once or twice. But she just kept going, lap after lap, until I had to drop out, exhausted. After she finished, I went over to shake her hand.

"You're too fast," I say. She grins. "What's your name?"

"Beatrice," she says, looking away.

The men's group is still charging around the track. A few others drop out, and Tom doesn't get any farther behind. Little Japhet seems to be struggling with the pace, dropping off from the main group. Even Tom is almost catching him. It's amazing that Japhet has chosen to live and train as a full-time athlete when he clearly has little chance of success. Hope, or optimism, or a lack of alternatives drive many of the Kenyans on. But you can't eat hope.

Besides the large groups of Kenyans, I spot the odd Italian athlete and another British runner. The Serbian team is also here; stocky men with big hair grinding their way around the track.

Finally, the Run Fast group stops, and we head back to Iten for breakfast. At the camp we get a mango and a banana each. We sit down and drink sweet, milky tea and eat dry bread. The food is doled out by the camp cook as people find themselves chairs to kick back in. The remainder of the day, until the afternoon run at 5:00 P.M., is dedicated to resting.

For Kenyan runners rest is a serious business. None of the athletes have jobs. Even the athletes who don't live in the camps rarely do anything other than run, eat, and sleep. I met one athlete who had worked in the Hill Side café in Iten, but he told me he had to give it up because it made him too tired to run. Without a job, most of them rely on the kindness of relatives, or other successful runners, to see them through. They don't require much, living frugal lives, with no electricity or running water, and eating a simple diet of rice, beans, and *ugali*.

The athletes in the camps, who don't have to worry about buying and cooking food, can sit for hours on plastic garden chairs talking or just staring into space. And when they get bored with that, they go to sleep. Lornah Kiplagat is famous for sleeping sixteen hours a day when she is in serious training. I spoke to some top British athletes who had come to Kenya to train and I asked them what they thought the biggest difference was between the Kenyans' training and their own. "Rest," they all said unanimously. "In England when we're not running, we go shopping, cook food, meet up with friends. Here they just rest."

It could also be called focus or dedication, and, like barefoot running, the scientific research is playing catch-up with the intuition and simplicity of the Kenyan approach. If you ask a Kenyan athlete why he sleeps so much, he won't quote the recent paper from Stanford University that found that its basketball players ran faster in time trials and had a 9 percent improved shooting accuracy after increasing the amount of time they slept. No, the Kenyan athlete will tell you that he needs to sleep more when he's in training because his body gets tired.

Stanford researcher Cheri Mah says that this wisdom isn't unique to the Kenyans. "Intuitively many players and coaches in the United States know that rest and sleep are important," she says. "But it is often the first thing to be sacrificed." But in Kenya, where the daily schedule is simply run, sleep, and eat, there is nothing to sacrifice it for. I note "rest" on my list of possible secrets. "Barefoot running, training camps, running to school, rest . . ." The list is growing.

At some point in the midafternoon, after we've eaten lunch, I find that I'm the only person still sitting out in the garden. One by one the athletes have gotten up and wandered off, disappearing into the short row of dormitories. I get up to see where they've all gone. Some are sleeping. In Tom's room I find four of the runners watching music videos on a fuzzy television.

After lounging around all day, by 5 P.M. the Run Fast athletes don't seem too keen to do their evening run. A few of them decide that they are too tired, while the rest of us head out for a forty-minute run. It's a lovely time of day out along the lanes around Iten, the air just cooling, the light turning yellow. It's a rare thing for me to train twice in one day, but I feel surprisingly good. For the others, of course, it's only an easy run, but in my head we're racing along, the wind in our hair. People watch as we fly by, tightly bunched. I may be bursting my lungs, but here I am, a month after arriving in Iten, running with the Kenyans, and keeping up.

◄◆►

Gradually, achingly, but just about perceptibly, I begin to get into shape. Shortly after my day with Run Fast, I return to one of the big early-morning group runs.

I meet Japhet again one evening while I'm watching Lila and Uma playing with the other children from the neighborhood in the dirt strip of a street outside our house. (Uma, who loves to unbolt the gate and run outside like a celebrity mingling with her fans, has caused great excitement by bringing out an inflatable beach ball.) Japhet sidles over with one arm outstretched, his other hand resting on his wrist as a sign of respect. We shake hands. "They are having fun," he says. "It is good." He asks me when we'll go on our first training run with our Lewa team. I tell him I'll talk to Godfrey. I'm still not quite sure how the team training is going to work, so for now Japhet offers to join me on one of the early-morning runs. He says he will stay at my pace the whole way. It's a kind offer. It means I won't have to worry about getting lost. We agree to meet at the kiosk at 5:50 A.M. the next morning.

It's pitch black as Alex, our guard, unbolts the gate and lets me out. In the darkness, I can just about make out two figures, waiting. It's Japhet and his friend Henry, the brother of the man who owns the kiosk. They look cold as I walk over and shake their hands. There's no moon, so we walk carefully and slowly along the bumpy path down to the meeting point, feeling the way with our feet. Today we're going to run with a group known as the *mwisho wa lami,* or the End of the Road group, because they meet at the point where the paved road ends. Wilson Kipsang, one of the fastest marathon runners in history, is part of the group, Japhet and Henry tell me. I stop, and pretend to turn back, making them laugh.

"It's okay," says Japhet. "Today is easy."

Henry nods. "Easy," he says.

A few runners jog past us out of the blackness, calling out in Kalenjin to Japhet and Henry. Roosters, somehow spotting the imperceptible paling in the eastern sky, call out among the scattering of tin roofs. About sixty people have gathered for the run, stretching their long arms in the air, shaking hands, or standing huddled in silence. Someone starts speaking to the group, explaining the route. Japhet nudges me. "Kipsang," he says, nodding toward the man talking. A few people ask questions. I'm sticking to Japhet like glue. Despite his small stature and tatty clothes, he's bubbly and friendly with everyone, even making a joke about the route that gets a few chuckles from the other runners. I remind him that I'm slow, and not to forget about me amid the banter, but he says it's okay and that he is happy to run as slow as I want.

It's still dark as we take off. *"Pole, pole,"* (Slowly, slowly) says Kipsang, as we begin running up the main road into town. At St. Patrick's school we turn right, down a side track. The first seepage of light is beginning to pick out the silhouettes of trees. As I run along beside Japhet in the midst of the group, something strange happens. I don't get left behind. Even as the pace begins to increase, my breath remains steady—strong almost.

Occasionally a car coming the other way forces everyone to slow down and bunch together, and I get to catch up any lost yards and gather myself. And then we're off again. For the first forty minutes I'm motoring along amid the scattering of feet and swishing of tracksuits, feeling fine. Eventually, as the charge to the finish begins to gather pace, I start to lose ground. Japhet, good to his word, sticks with me, and we run the rest of the route within sight of the main group. At the end, as we're stretching by the side of the road, Japhet's friend Henry comes dawdling up the track. He's dripping in sweat as he stops next to us.

"You're fast," he says, clearly out of breath. I look around to see who he's talking to, before I realize it's me.

Ten

Barefoot children after a race at Salaba Academy

Foolishly buoyed by my run with Japhet and the End of the Road group, two days later I find myself standing on the start line of a local cross-country race. It's a hot but windy day in Eldoret. We've all woken up early so that Lila and Uma can run in the children's race. Memories of the fun run at the Great West Run back in England have prompted their enthusiasm. That day Uma refused to run, and Granny Bee had to carry her around the two-mile loop. But today's race is less than a mile, and she's now five—she was only three and a half then.

They get dressed in their best racing outfits—shorts, sneakers, and Hello Kitty T-shirts—and we talk tactics in the car on the way to the course. As we enter the gates to the Eldoret Sports Club it's still only 8:30 A.M., but the place is heaving with excitement, people in race numbers and bare feet darting around everywhere. Heads turn to look at us as we enter, children giggling and passing comments behind cupped hands. A man at a desk sees us and ushers us over. Lila, though, has changed her mind. She doesn't want to run. Uma, in a blur of bodies and early-morning chaos, lets me register her. The race is about to start, we're told, so I guide Uma through the crowd—a parting sea of staring eyes—and out onto the course. The sun is getting hotter. Announcements are blaring out over the PA. There are children zipping around everywhere. Skinny, bony children, light on their feet. Uma is one of the youngest. She looks confused.

"It's okay," I say. "Look, that girl is smaller than you." A little girl watches us from the side with unblinking eyes. She has a race number on her chest, but doesn't appear to be heading to the start. "If you don't want to run, you don't have to," I say. Uma looks at me and leaps up into my arms, burying her head in my neck. It's an intimidating atmosphere for two little English girls just turned seven and five. I sympathize completely. In three hours' time, it will be my turn.

Instead of racing, we take the girls and Ossian to sit in the small stand by the clubhouse. Inside, we find Godfrey with some friends. He is in his element, chatting with former runners, reminiscing about old times. He introduces me to a man in a smart, brown jacket and sunglasses who won the silver medal in the marathon at the 2001 world championships, finishing just one second behind the winner.

"I was that close," he says, holding up his thumb and forefinger.

Also sitting in the stands is the Chinese national team. They're here to watch and learn, their coach tells me. This is no ordinary local cross-country race. The whole thing is sponsored by Nike and is used as a way to unearth emerging talent. As the event organizer, the legendary manager Doctor Rosa gets to pick a few of the most promising young athletes to invite to train at his camp.

As stewards hand out water to everyone in the stands, two announcers tag-team on the PA. They say everything twice, in Swahili and English, and take turns talking, so there's no letup in the noise booming from the speakers that have been set up just in front of the stand. Meanwhile, the races are trundling by. Every now and then a crowd of barefoot children flies past. Interestingly, in each race there are a few children wearing running shoes, but they all invariably finish near the back of the field, particularly in the younger age groups.

A week later I find myself watching a race at Chris Cheboiboch's school, Salaba Academy. Again the same pattern is evident: The children wearing shoes are all at the back of the field. I seem to be the only one noticing it. Whenever I point it out to people, they smile and say, "Oh, yes, how funny," as though it's a quirky coincidence. They don't seem to make the connection, that running barefoot could actually be a key part of the Kenyan secret. But the evidence is mounting. At one training camp in Iten, a top marathon runner tells me that when he was at school, his parents had a bit of money so they bought him some running shoes. But the children without shoes kept beating him, so he took his off and started winning races.

Ironically, the prize for the winners at Chris's school race is a pair of running shoes. It's as if the organizers not only don't appreciate the benefits of barefoot running, but see it as some kind of disadvantage. It seems ridiculous to be giving the fastest runner in each race something to help him run which, on the face of the evidence in front of us, will only slow him down. In one race, the farther back in the field the girls finish, the better their shoes, to the absurd extent that the girl with the newest, sleekest running shoes of all comes in last, while the girl whose shoes are only slightly worse finishes second to last. Each time, the runners without shoes seem light and graceful, while those wearing sneakers seem to be plodding, burdened by heavy weights tied to their feet.

At the cross-country race in Iten a few weeks before, the junior girls winner, Faith Kipyegon, tried on a pair of running spikes for the first time.

"They felt uncomfortable," she said. "Even though they were very elegant, they felt very heavy to run in." So she stuck to what she knew best, her bare feet, and she won. A few months later she would go on to win the world cross-country championships, also barefoot. To Faith, used to running barefoot, even running spikes, the lightest shoes imaginable, seemed heavy.

Despite the recent boom in barefoot running in the West, it is not a new idea. In 1962, a young Briton named Bruce Tulloh won the European 5,000 meters title running without shoes. (Tulloh would later train the Kenyan national team in the run-up to the 1972 Olympics.) I met him just before leaving for Kenya and asked him why he chose to run barefoot. "I ran a lot on grass tracks in those days and it was just much easier in bare feet. I could adapt more quickly to changes in the uneven surface. Also, when I ran barefoot, I had a shorter stride and a faster leg turnover." Tulloh agreed to be a guinea pig for Dr. Griffiths Pugh, a leading exercise physiologist of the time. "He managed to plot a straight-line relationship between the weight of the shoe and the energy cost of running," said Tulloh.

Few men have looked as closely at the phenomenon of Kenyan running as sports scientist Dr. Yannis Pitsiladis, from the University of Glasgow in Scotland, who has spent the last ten years trying to work out what it is that makes East African runners so good. Across many trips to Kenya and Ethiopia he has become close friends with many of the athletes, and is now a visiting professor at both Moi University in Eldoret and Addis Ababa University. He was recently asked by the great Ethiopian runner and marathon world record holder Haile Gebrselassie* to give a seminar on how to get a human to run under two hours for the marathon.

Dr. Pitsiladis went through a whole predictive lecture on what would be required, and one thing he thought would help would be if someone such as Haile, who had not run with shoes until he was in his late teens, didn't move to shoes but remained barefoot. But even Haile, the doctor says, couldn't run a marathon barefoot if he wanted to now because his feet had become used to running in shoes. Yet Dr. Pitsiladis is confident that if he put Haile on a treadmill without his shoes on and measured his oxygen uptake, based on his previous studies, Haile would be at least 5 percent more economical than with his shoes on.

But surely someone running a marathon barefoot on concrete roads would be risking injury? "These kids we study in Kenya," Dr. Pitsiladis retorts, "the soles of their feet are as strong as any shoes. They can walk on glass and it doesn't hurt." As well as landing more lightly, Dr. Pitsiladis says that running barefoot gives you stronger feet, which allows you to train harder with less chance of getting injured.

But if running barefoot is such a clear advantage, why do all the adult athletes in Kenya run in sneakers? It's an interesting conundrum. Abebe Bikila, from Ethiopia, broke the world record on his way to winning the 1960 Olympic marathon, running barefoot

---

*Haile Gebrselassie's marathon world record of 2:03:59 was broken by the Kenyan Patrick Makau on September 25, 2011, when he won the Berlin Marathon in 2:03:38.

through the streets of Rome. But in Tokyo four years later, he won the gold medal and broke the world record again, this time wearing shoes. So was he better off with shoes or without them?

The biggest advantage of running barefoot is that it forces you to adopt a better running style. Without shoes on, all the senses in your feet are suddenly activated, and your inbuilt running software, developed over millions of years, is switched on. You instinctively start to control your impact on the ground, landing lightly on your feet. You quickly learn that the energy you put into the ground, as your foot lands, will return and propel you on. I've seen it happen, to me. It really works. The problem for those of us not used to it, is that our feet are soft, our arches are flat, and the muscles we need to run like this, both in our feet and in our calves, are out of shape. If we try it, we're likely to end up with sore feet and calves after even a short run.

So we have to start slowly. Barefoot shoes can help protect the soles of our feet from abrasions, but we still need to start with short, gentle runs. It takes time, and we get out of shape. But if we stick to it, our muscles will strengthen, and our style will start to change. And as our foot muscles strengthen, our arches will rise. Arches are like springs, and the higher they are, the more spring we have in our step.

It's interesting to note, in trying to determine how much of a factor all this can be, that Kenya's dominance is greater in one particular event than any other: the steeplechase. This is a 3,000 meters track race where the runners have to hurdle five 91-centimeter (35.8-inch) barriers on each lap, including one with a pool of water on the other side. To be good at this event you clearly need to have good springs in your feet, probably more so than in any other event. Yet despite the fact that there are virtually no facilities to practice steeplechase in Kenya and very little steeplechase-specific coaching, Kenyans have won every single men's steeplechase Olympic gold medal since 1968 (except for the two that Kenya boycotted, in 1976 and 1980).

Once you have bounce and good running form, you do not lose them the minute you put on conventional running shoes. So the Kenyans may wear shoes, but they're still running in what would be called a "barefoot style." Essentially, the key advantages of barefoot running are retained.

Lee Saxby said that the Kenyans wore shoes so they didn't hurt themselves landing on sharp stones. The roads in Kenya are made of dirt, but every now and then you land on a stone half-buried in the ground and it can really hurt—my two sprained toe injuries testify to that (and I was wearing shoes). But that's not a reason to ditch the shoes completely. You could still do what people like Bruce Tulloh did and run barefoot in races and when the conditions underfoot were conducive to it, such as in track races and on grassy cross-country courses. But it is rare to see a top Kenyan runner racing anywhere without shoes. Tulloh tells me that during his time in Kenya he sometimes ran races in bare feet. "I was the only one," he says. "They all just thought I was a crazy *mzungu*."

One reason the adult runners give for wearing big shoes is to make their training harder. One runner tells me they always look for the biggest, heaviest shoes they can find. "Then, when you put on your racing flats, you feel so light," he says, as though it's a magic trick.

But why even wear racing flats? According to Nicholas Leong, a cycling coach based in Iten, the real reason is cultural. "Kenyans have too much respect for Europeans," he says. "They don't have enough confidence in their culture to say, 'You know, I've grown up running barefoot, I've been winning races, I'll keep running barefoot.'"

Nicholas is from Singapore. As a sports fan, he remembers watching as gradually more and more black athletes began to flourish in sport after sport. "I remember the first black footballers in England," he says. "Then you had the dominance of the African runners. Then the Williams sisters in tennis, and even Tiger Woods in golf." But Nicholas was a cycling nut. "It never happened in cycling," he says. "To this day, there has never been a single black rider in the Tour de France.* I thought to myself, if no one is doing anything about this, then I will." He decided the best place to start would be Kenya. If they were so good at running, he thought, then perhaps they would be good at cycling, too.

Nicholas hatched a mad plan to find the Kenyan runners. He booked himself a flight to Nairobi on the same night as the Singapore Marathon, figuring that some top Kenyan runners would be on the plane. Sure enough, as he waited to board, he saw a group of Africans in running clothes milling around. He went over and asked them if they'd just run the marathon. They had. "Who won?" he asked. One of the men grinned as the others pointed him out.

"Where do you live?" Nicholas asked the man, who said he lived in Eldoret. "Do you mind if I come home with you?"

He eventually ended up in Iten, where he started a cycling team. To recruit his cyclists he tried some unusual tactics. One was to place a sign at the bottom of the Kerio Valley offering a prize of 200,000 Kenyan shillings (about three times the average annual income) to anyone who could cycle more than fifteen miles up the road to Iten, a 4,000-foot ascent, in under 1 hour 8 minutes. Only one man ever achieved it, riding a heavy, fixed gear bicycle, but Nicholas signed up anyone who came close, giving them a good

---

*In 2011, France's Yohann Gène became the first black cyclist to compete in the Tour de France.

monthly salary, board, and lodging while they followed his training program.

"In the past, people have looked at African cycling and said, The big problem is that they don't have the right bikes." Nicholas has the harassed look of a prospector, as though he's in a race to find the golden formula that will produce Kenyan cyclists on a par with Kenyan runners. "There are so few things from Africa that generate such genuine awe, fear, unreserved respect, like a Kenyan runner on the start line of a marathon," he says. "It is such an achievement. We need to tap into that."

But instead of tapping into it, of empowering them, giving them brand-new bikes makes them helpless, he says. "Here we have guys straight from the *shamba* who can hit 5.8 watts per kilo. That's cycling talk, but trust me, that's good. That's the same power as a top cyclist. Yet you give them a new bike, and they don't know what to do with it. They don't know how to use it, so they feel helpless. You're imposing a European system on them. You're saying, right, now you should do what we say. And it simply doesn't work." It's just like giving them shoes to run in, he says.

In the short time I've been in Kenya, I've been frequently taken aback by the levels of respect we've been afforded simply because of the color of our skin. At every event we've been to we've been immediately afforded VIP status and given the best seats. Sitting in the sun in the Run Fast camp that afternoon, one of the athletes told me that Kenyans needed European coaches and managers "because you have more brains than us. We need to learn from you." At one school I visited, the head teacher started telling the children about all the great things the British had done, and about how the British had brought civilization to Kenya. It's a view I hear frequently, when I was expecting the opposite, that the British had stolen their lands and destroyed their cultures.

So when Westerners turn up and see their bare feet and think, *Oh, look at the poor kids running around without shoes on, we must do something to help them,* the Kenyans, too, begin to believe that running barefoot must be wrong, or inferior. Something to frown upon. Ironically, they see the Western runners wearing shoes and want to emulate them.

"Have you spoken to Brother Colm yet?" Nicholas asks me.

"Briefly," I say, nodding.

"Has he done his Yoda thing on you?" I'm not sure what his Yoda thing is, but I don't think so. "When he talks about feeling the earth through your feet?" Nicholas says Brother Colm is the only coach who gets his athletes to train and do drills barefoot. This is a man with no European coaching experience, a man who works principally with youngsters, a man who says he learned all he knows "from watching the athletes." He is also one of Kenya's most successful coaches. I make a note to ask him about it the next time I see him.

Eleven

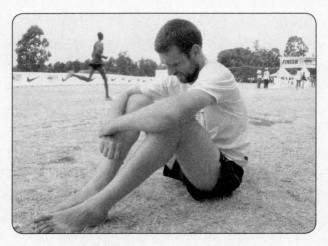

Nike Discovery cross-country in Eldoret

So here at the Nike-sponsored cross-country race in Eldoret, barefoot children streak away at the front of each race. In the girls' under-twelve race, the first two runners across the line are not only barefoot but are wearing frilly, silk dresses. They are quite a sight, sprinting away at the front in their Sunday-best outfits, like two shaven-headed Cinderellas racing home after midnight. It obviously isn't a marketing ploy, they probably didn't have anything else to wear, but the scouts at Nike seem to like it, as the winner is one of the two athletes "discovered" on the day and invited to train at Doctor Rosa's camp in nearby Kaptagat. She collects her award wearing the event's free Nike T-shirt pulled over her dress. She stares ahead throughout the ceremony, looking more annoyed than anything, as photographers snap pictures and dignitaries hand her bits of paper. When it's over, she scuttles away into the crowd.

The races tick slowly by: under-fourteen boys and girls, junior boys and girls . . . my race is the last one. To register to run I have to join a long line of athletes. They all have the bearing of serious runners. I couldn't feel more out of place, with my pasty white skin, shaggy beard, and a few excess pounds of fat. Not for the first time since I arrived in Kenya, I have to ask myself what on earth I am doing. It is like I keep volunteering to fly an airplane, only realizing once I'm at the controls that I don't have a clue what to do.

The longest line of athletes is at the table for the under-twenty junior boys race. Kenyan runners seem to take a flexible approach to age, basing the category they enter more on how they feel their career is progressing than on how old they are. "I'll run the 12K [senior race] when I'm ready. Maybe next year," many of them tell me, despite the fact that they are obviously in their midtwenties. The officials take a slightly different view, however, and it is someone's job to walk along the line and pull out people who look too old.

Once I've registered, I head back to the grandstand. Ossian has dragged Marietta up to the highest seats, which are empty, to play with his toy cars. Uma says she is hungry, but there's nowhere to buy any food. Lila is sitting on Godfrey's lap, pulling him around while he tries to talk with his old running friends. When I sit down, she clambers across onto my lap instead. Then Uma starts hanging from my neck, telling me she wants to go home. It isn't ideal preparation for my race.

Finally the time comes for me to start warming up. I take off my tracksuit and hand it to Marietta. The girls look concerned. "Wish me luck," I say, and trot off to the start to warm up.

Behind the start area, hundreds of athletes are jogging around in a large circle, like a parade ring. I slip in and join them. The hot sun is already making me sweat. I feel like a cart horse that has somehow wandered into the wrong enclosure. Someone is talking about me. I can tell because I hear the word *mzungu*. I look over.

"Where are you from?" the runner asks. He's friendly really. He asks me how I'm hoping to run today. Flush with confidence, I tell him my aim is not to come last. To beat at least one person. He looks at me as he pins his number to his vest. "I'm sure you can beat two," he says.

Soon we're called over to the start. I try to hide at the back, out of the way of the impending stampede, but one of the organizers walking along the line spots me. It's not hard. "Yes, my friend," he says, as a hundred faces turn to look at me. "Where are you from?"

"England," I say. He's writing it down.

"And what is your name?"

"Finn," I say—it's just easier.

"Vin?"

I spell it out for him.

"F for Freddy. I. N. N."

He writes it down. "And?" He wants another name.

Okay, you asked for it. "Adharanand."

My parents were hippies in the early 1970s when I came into the world. They followed a thirteen-year-old guru from India called Maharaji and, getting swept up in the peace and love swirling around them, they named me Adharanand. It means Eternal Bliss in Sanskrit.

The organizer looks at me, mock startled, and then puts the pen away without writing anything down. It gets him a few laughs. A few minutes later I hear the PA announcing that Finn from England is here racing today. If only they knew how good I was. I don't hear the starting pistol, but suddenly we're off. My plan is to stick at the very back of the field, but it's as though I've been shot and I'm falling backward through the air as they all charge off. I'm sprinting, trying to stay upright, but it's no good. It's like a bad dream in which your legs won't move.

At the first corner there's a lot of congestion in front of me, so I manage to catch up with the tail end of the field. As we head past the stand for the first time I'm nicely tucked in. There are almost four hundred runners ahead of me, but I'm sure that some people have started too fast and I'll soon begin picking them off. But it's me who has started too fast, and now I'm struggling to stay with anyone. I battle to keep up with an elderly man in front of me, but he's too strong and I'm soon drifting on my own. I think there's a runner behind me, but everyone else is disappearing into the distance.

The course is six laps of a route that doubles back on itself constantly so that people watching can see nearly the whole race. Once we get to the only part of the course where there are no spectators, I find myself running past about fifteen athletes, standing around looking sheepishly at one another. They've all dropped out already, after less than a mile. If I can just keep going, I'll have beaten *them* at least.

The crowd that lines most of the route watches in virtual silence as I pass. Have I shocked them into dumbness with my ineptitude? I get the odd patter of applause, for trying, I presume, and hear the odd muttering of *"mzungu,"* but otherwise it's just faces watching. I try to focus on my running, but I'm not feeling great. My legs are heavy, sinking into the dirt that seems to get softer with each step. I don't know if I'm running heel or forefoot first. I don't care. Near the end of the first lap I try to swallow and nearly get sick. This is going to be a long race.

I trundle on in a blur. The soft dirt, the watching faces, the fluttering of the tape marking the course. I keep hearing *"mzungu."* People seem to be laughing. Someone somewhere calls out "Finn." I raise my hand to thank whoever it was. Halfway around the third lap the leaders hurtle by to lap me. One after another after another after another they fly by. It makes me feel even slower. I'm sure people are laughing now. There's a fine line between humbling and humiliating, and I think I've just crossed it.

As we pass the stand for the third time, I see Marietta and the children watching. They look concerned. I'm still only halfway around, but I'm finding it hard to will myself on. It's too easy to stop. I've seen enough. I wave both hands as though something is wrong. It's not me, it's the engine. I jog to the side and sit down. I'm dropping out. It feels blissful to just sit on the grass. I pull off my shoes and socks, releasing my feet. They look so white. I watch as a slow runner struggles past, among all the charging athletes. Then another, a man who must be in his seventies. So there were two runners behind me. But they're still going. Suddenly I feel bad. My body feels fine now. I could have kept going. I briefly contemplate joining in again. I could even run barefoot. But it's too late. The two runners are gone, off on their weary way. I hoist myself up and walk back to the stands. People smile at me as I sit down.

"Thank you for trying our race," says one man. I can't answer, so I just shrug and shake my head. "Next time you will do it," he says.

◄ ►

My sense of failure is tempered slightly when I later find out that the three-time London Marathon winner, Martin Lel, finished in thirty-third position, and the reigning 1,500 meters Olympic champion Asbel Kiprop, like me, dropped out. That's some serious competition.

After the race I sit with Marietta and the children in the venue's clubhouse eating French fries. The Kenyan version of MTV plays quietly on the screen in the corner. "Dad," Uma asks me, with one eye on the TV, "did you win?"

Just over a year ago, in England, I did win a race. But here in Kenya's Rift Valley, things are very different. I feel as though I've fallen into a cultural chasm, and it's one that right now I'm not sure I can get across. In England, running is largely a hobby, practiced gamely by enthusiasts who squeeze in training runs whenever they can among all the other things in their lives. A handful of people take it more seriously, training regularly, turning out on freezing winter mornings for races with their local athletics club. But here in Kenya, anyone who can run dedicates his life to it. And that dedication seems to be spreading. There are more training camps than ever before. More runners. All pushing one another, training harder, every single day. Here, athletics is like a religion. On the way to the race, Marietta commented that in such a fervently Christian place, it didn't seem like a good idea to hold the race on a Sunday. But it didn't stop thousands of people from turning out, arriving in busloads from the surrounding villages, both to run and to watch.

In a land where running is so revered, my goals of running a marathon, or beating my personal best times, seem feeble and half-hearted. Here people are running to change their lives. To feed their families. To break world records. "I'm not sure this is going to work," I say to Marietta. "I'm too out of my depth."

She looks at me. We both know I'm just looking for some reassurance. It has been a tough day. "You've only just started," she says. "You just have to give yourself a chance. You never thought you were going to win. You came here to learn from the Kenyans, not beat them."

Of course I can't give up. I've come too far for that. Running is a simple activity. Just lace up your shoes and go, one step at a time, like each breath. But the question is, where do I go from here?

Twelve

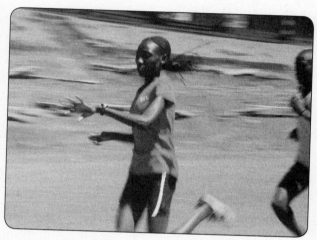

World 10,000 meters champion Linet Masai checks her watch

After the race in Eldoret, I decide I need to ratchet up my training. I'm still in my old mindset, training every other day, treating running as a side activity. I need a dose of Kenyan dedication. That's what I came here for. But the weeks are ticking by. I call Godfrey up. "Godfrey, we need to organize a run with the Lewa team. The marathon is in a few months." But he's already on it.

"I know, Finn," he says. "That's just what I was thinking. We need to do a long run this Saturday. Thirty kilometers. Almost nineteen miles. I've already spoken to Chris, and Shadrack says he will come. You just need to tell Japhet."

To get myself ready for the long team run, I decide to brave Iten's weekly *fartlek* session. The other runners have been telling me about it for weeks. Every Thursday morning in Iten, all the various groups and training camps come together in one huge force of runners. A common form of training around the world, *fartlek* involves alternating fast bursts of running with slow recovery jogs. It comes from a Swedish word meaning "speed play." For most of the athletes it is one of the week's toughest sessions.

"Daddy, where are you going?" Uma asks me as I lace up my shoes. The sun is streaming in through the garden doors. Flora is ladling the oatmeal into bowls on the table. Usually I'm back from my run at this time, but the *fartlek* sessions don't start until a leisurely nine o'clock.

"I'm going running," I say.

"Why?" she asks. It's a good question, but right now, just before a run, is not the best moment to try to answer it. Right before you head out running, it can be hard to remember exactly why you're doing it. You often have to override a nagging sense of futility, lacing up your shoes, telling yourself that no matter how unlikely it seems right now, after you finish you will be glad you went. It's only afterward that it makes sense, although even then it's hard to rationalize why. You just feel right. After a run, you feel at one with the world, as though some unspecified, innate need has been fulfilled.

"Because it's fun," I say. She smiles. It's an answer that makes sense to her. Fun is always a good reason to do something.

It takes me twenty minutes just to jog to the start of the "speed play" at the bottom of a long hill, heading out of Iten along the edge of the escarpment. All along the way, people emerge running from side streets, shops, doorways, joining the flow of runners, everyone going the same way, to the same starting point, as though we're part of some mass celebration. By the time I get there, two hundred or so runners are gathered, milling around, chatting. The men stand to one side of the road while the few women that have turned up stand quietly on the other side. I walk into the crowd as it edges its way across to the start. Long, skinny legs, an array of faded colors, rustling jackets, T-shirts. Then everything goes quiet. A team leader of some sort is standing up on a mound explaining the day's session to the runners like some biblical preacher. Even if I could speak Kalenjin, I can't hear what he is saying from all the way at the back. Someone tells me it's "Twenty-five, one, one." That means we jog for a minute, then run hard for a minute, twenty-five times.

Before I know it, the floodgates have opened and I'm being carried off down the dusty road into the countryside. The pace is easy, for a minute. I'm jogging along in what feels like a sea of runners, people bobbing around in front of me like I'm heading into choppy waters.

By the sides, up on the banked earth, farm workers stand taking a break, watching us pass. It feels like it should be an incongruous sight, this huge mass of Lycra-clad runners streaming by amid the hand-plowed fields and mud huts of this rural African outpost. Things seem even more unlikely when two hundred watches start beeping simultaneously. But here in Iten, it's the most natural thing in the world. The watches set everyone off like wound-up toys being released, zipping and flying away. I attempt to keep up, working my arms, trying to find the smoothest part of the track to run along. But I'm rapidly slipping backward, runners nipping past me on both sides.

A minute later the scattering of beeps catches the galloping herd, pulling it to a halt. As the group slows to a jog, it begins to bunch up again. A few stragglers like me have become detached already. Behind me there are others; mostly, if not all, women, their arms working side to side, trying to catch up. But it's a cruel game. Before we can make contact again with the group, the swarm of watches goes off, and the main group is gone, stringing its way out along the distant track. At the back, we team up in twos and threes for support. I find myself running next to a tall girl with short hair. I hope she doesn't mind me running next to her. "I don't have a watch," I say, by way of explanation.

"Three, two, one, up," she says, and we're off again.

◀ ▶

I must be the only runner here without a watch. Before I came to Kenya, I had naively imagined everyone racing along without a thought for anything as controlling and analytical as a stopwatch. It would be just them and the open road, I thought, their bare feet pounding on effortlessly, the wind in their hair. It turns out that's not the case. However, while in the West we time everything so that we can measure and analyze it afterward, or keep track of our running pace so we can calculate whether we need to slow down or speed up, Kenyans use their watches in a completely different way.

By running their intervals according to the regimented beeps of their watches, Kenyans are actually taking the thinking and analysis out of their running. When the watch beeps, they speed up. When it beeps again, they slow down. Although they say they are doing twenty-five sets of intervals, in reality they just run, speeding up and slowing down, until they get to the end of the route. Afterward, no one could honestly tell you how many intervals he had run. Nobody keeps a training log or adds up their weekly mileage. Each session is forgotten as soon as it is done. The timing is just a way of structuring the training, of telling them when to start and when to stop.

With hill training as well, Kenyans don't run up a set number of hills but run up and down for a set amount of time, usually an hour. This saves them from having to count the number of hills they've run, which may not sound that difficult, but as you get tired your brain becomes easily addled. I've often done hill sessions on my own and even by the third one I'm struggling to remember how many I've done. I have to keep repeating the number over and over to myself, which can get tiring. Having a watch doing the counting means you can just run, unthinking, back and forth, up and down, until the beeps tell you to stop.

"In the West we break it all down and analyze everything," says Brother Colm when I track him down, standing on the playing fields at St. Patrick's high school watching David Rudisha going through his warm-up routine. "But sometimes by doing that you lose the bigger picture. Kenyans might wear watches, but they're not using them to analyze their training. They just take it as they see it. It's a simpler approach."

Most of the athletes in Kenya follow virtually the same training schedule. Toby Tanser told me it was set up by Bruce Tulloh when he was in Kenya in the early 1970s. Other people date it back further to the British system of the colonial days. An integral part of the schedule is the regular 6:00 A.M. run. I often ask the athletes why they always have to start at six when it's still dark. If they waited even thirty minutes, it would be light and they would be able to see. "It is best to run early," is all they can say, laughing when I try to debate the point. Accepting the schedule, rather than questioning it, makes things simpler. They don't have to lie in bed trying to convince themselves to get up in the morning. At 5:45 A.M. when their alarm goes off like a barking sergeant major, they just get up and, like disciplined soldiers, they run.

Of course, you don't break world records, like David Rudisha has done, without some analysis and careful thought going into your training. But this process is usually kept from the athletes. "I might spot something in his training that needs changing," says Brother Colm, "but I won't discuss it with Rudisha. I'll just alter the training a bit without him knowing." For those without a coach, it is the watch that does all the thinking.

◄ ►

"Three, two, one, up," my companion repeats, and we're off again, her watch beeping along.

Eventually we catch up with groups of people walking slowly along the road, like stunned survivors making their way from the scene of some terrible catastrophe. All along the dusty road we pass people in sweaty T-shirts, leggings, and running shoes, hands on hips, not talking. They've all finished the *fartlek,* it seems, and they're walking the rest of the way back to Iten.

My companion doesn't stop, though. "Three, two, one, up," she says as her watch beeps again. We weave through the bodies that turn to watch us, the *mzungu* and the girl, still going. Up the final hill back into Iten I drop back. She is too strong. The altitude still zaps me when I try to run uphill. At the top, she stops and I catch up. She's walking now. That must be the end.

"*Asante sana,*" I say, shaking her hand, catching a glimpse of her face for the first time. She looks young, still a teenager. I wonder if she would like to join our Lewa team. She's about the same speed as me. "Do you run marathons?" I ask.

Her eyes skirt away when I talk, looking down at the ground. I feel like I'm crossing some forbidden barrier. I'm being too friendly. "No, track and field," she says.

Others, intrigued, are walking next to us now. They're looking hard at me, as though trying to fathom whether I'm real. We walk in silence the rest of the way back into town. The sun is hot on the back of my neck. I'm tired, but still standing, my first *fartlek* session done.

Thirteen

The Iten Town Harriers are born. From left to right:
Chris, Shadrack, Josphat (crouching), Godfrey, Japhet,
Adharanand, Uma, Flora, and Lila

"It's like we're going to war," jokes Godfrey as we pile out from the back of the pickup truck and start stripping down to our shorts and T-shirts. Marietta is scooting around taking photographs, while the children watch sleepy eyed from the truck cab, piles of water bottles on their laps, a bunch of bananas up on the dashboard.

We're about to set off on our first Lewa Marathon group training run. We're now officially the Iten Town Harriers. The rest of the team didn't fully join in the debate about choosing the name, but looked at me blankly as I offered up a number of alternatives. They liked them all, they said. Godfrey tried to humor me and get involved, but his suggestions, the Iten Runners or the Iten Warriors, were made tentatively. It was like asking hardened farmers what color they would like the handles of their shovels to be. These were serious runners and I was drifting into the territory of fun running, coming up with team names. Next I'd be asking them what color vests we should wear. (In the end I made that decision by myself: yellow.)

I'm amazed this team run is happening at all. The night before, Godfrey rang to say that the truck he was hoping to borrow was being used by someone else, but that Chris was going to find another one. I get nervous when Chris is organizing things. He is always telling me to relax and to trust him the whole time. But true to his word, the gates to our house swing open at 6:00 A.M. and a big, shiny pickup truck comes rolling through, a grinning Godfrey at the wheel and Chris running behind after having opened the gate. The truck actually belongs to a top runner named Isaac Songok, one of Brother Colm's athletes. He needs it back by nine, so we've got to get moving.

Our newest team member, Shadrack, has come all the way from Kamwosor for the run, traveling to Iten the night before. It's a big effort for a training run. Godfrey tells me that Shadrack has been running with David Barmasai. The two have been best friends since they were children. Barmasai, however, has just won both the Nairobi marathon and the Dubai marathon, one of the richest races in the world, where he collected over $250,000 in prize money. Shadrack, I suspect, is feeling a little left behind.

"But they say Barmasai can't keep up with him in training," Godfrey tells me.

If that's true, then he has huge potential. It's exciting having him on our team, although I can tell that Chris is less thrilled. He nods toward him, looking at me for an explanation. "Godfrey knows him," I say. "He says he's good."

"Ah-kay," Chris says, in that clipped way he does when he's not entirely happy.

The two runners shake hands, not saying anything to each other. All around us, Iten is waking up, stretching and yawning in the yellow glow of morning. Godfrey gives us a little pep talk. "No racing," he says. "Take it nice and easy for the first fifteen kilometers and then push on. I'll be in the truck with water and I'll give you your splits every five kilometers. Everyone okay? Japhet, you okay?" Japhet grins at being singled out. "Finn, ready?" I nod. "Okay, let's go."

The plan is to run thirty kilometers (almost nineteen miles), although I'll be happy if I can keep up with them for ten miles. Marietta, Flora, and the children are to ride with Godfrey in the truck.

We set off at a gentle pace (we go through the first five kilometers in twenty-four minutes), and I run at the head of the group with Chris. We follow the path that runs along beside the main road, down and up and out of town toward Eldoret. My legs are feeling fresh after a massage the day before, and I'm even able to chat with Chris as we run. After about ten minutes, the truck drives past us along the paved road, the children waving, Marietta crouched in the back snapping away like a war photographer.

"It's good how much support you have," says Chris. "Your whole family is here supporting you."

Marietta later tells me how much she enjoyed coming along. I realize that through running I have been able to explore the surrounding countryside, while she and the children have been largely confined to our compound and our tightly packed neighborhood. We occasionally attempt to venture off farther for a walk, but at every corner we are stopped by people who want to chat with us, shake hands with the children, or invite us home for tea. It's nice to feel so welcomed, but it means we rarely get very far.

Soon after the five-kilometer mark, the route turns off the main road and we head out through the lush patchwork of fields that surround Iten. The dirt road wanders gently through small homesteads, clusters of huts dotting the landscape like huge kilns. Occasionally a car or motorbike will come by in a cloud of red dust, beeping at us to get out of the way.

At ten kilometers, Godfrey stops the truck and Lila and Uma hand out water bottles, which we grab on the run as Godfrey shouts out that we've completed the last five kilometers in twenty-two minutes. Things are speeding up. "Keep it up," he says. "Finn, you're looking strong. Just maintain. Maintain." He's a good coach.

"Where's Chris?" Japhet suddenly asks. We look around, but he's not in sight. We carry on running, hitting a long hill that rises up through fields back to the main road. I push on. Although I struggle with the hills out here, I've decided that the best approach is to attack them. If I give in to them and slow down, they grind me into the ground, sucking at my legs until I'm shuffling like a dead weight on sticks. But if I shoot up them, I'm past before they get a chance to grab me. Of course, it's a risky strategy. If the hill is too long, it wakes up while I'm only halfway there, spying me with a wry grin, and then, as though it has tipped up suddenly against me, I'm done for. Today, however, I'm feeling fine and I lead the charge up the hill, passing my water bottle to Shadrack as we go. He keeps coughing and blowing his nose as we run, and sweating hard. Right now he doesn't seem like a Lewa champion.

At the top of the hill, I spot Tom Payn, chugging along behind his pacemaker. We're like busy trains heading this way and that, runners crossing the endless network of roads and tracks.

On we run, over the main road and into the countryside on the other side. Behind us we hear the quick patter of feet. We all glance behind as, without a word, Chris comes past. We follow on, close to him, but the pace has increased. I don't know if Chris is trying to assert his authority, but suddenly the talking and joking stops.

The route seems to be heading slightly downhill, so the pace has no chance to slacken. Josphat, who is running up front with Chris, beckons me to take his place. I oblige, but we're really on the charge now. I'm not sure how long I can keep this up. Chris turns to me with a grin. "You okay?" he asks.

Surprisingly, I am. I'm quite enjoying the new pace, even. But I feel as though I'm pushing my luck. Chris's question sends doubts, excuses pinging around in my head. Before I've fully made the decision, I blurt out: "I'm just going to run fifteen-K."

"Sure," says Chris. I feel like I've given him the answer he was expecting. "We're nearly at fifteen-K," he says. "Just two more corners."

I should go on, but the pronouncement has been made. Once you decide where you're going to stop, it takes a reckless surge of energy to overrule yourself. *You've done enough,* I tell myself, *you've kept up this far. This is just a first run.* Reasons, reasons, reasons. The decision is final. Up ahead I see the truck stopped at the fifteen-kilometer point. "I'm stopping here," I announce, just to be clear, as I move into a sprint. I hear a few chuckles as I leave them behind for a moment, charging to little Lila who is running to meet me with a bottle of water.

It feels good to stop. The others run past, and on, following the dusty road disappearing into some trees.

"That last five kilometers was just under twenty minutes," God-frey tells me. "That's fast." It's not bad, but I can't help feeling I bailed out too early. I clamber into the open back of the truck and sit down on the spare tire next to Uma. Godfrey starts the car and we drive on to catch up with the others.

About two miles farther on we see Chris walking along the track. He hops in the back of the truck. "I twisted my ankle," he says.

"Does it hurt?"

"No, man. It's fine," he says, giving me his million-dollar smile. "I just didn't want to push it."

As we pass the others, Godfrey holds out water bottles while he drives alongside of them. "Time to push," he says. "Just five kilome-ters to go." They're flying now. Little Japhet is hanging on, his ripped shoes almost falling apart on him as his feet pound back and forth. Along the last stretch, Shadrack, the young buck, pushes on, but Japhet matches him stride for stride. Josphat, to Chris's annoyance, starts to drop off the pace.

"Come on, Josphat," he says. He turns to us, giggling. "Josphat is too slow," he says.

A few minutes later they're done. We gather by the truck as they catch their breath. Godfrey hands out bananas while Marietta, get-ting into her role as the official team photographer, gets us to line up beside the truck for a group photograph. Then we jog the last mile back to Iten for a cool down. Inspired by watching the run, or perhaps just fed up with sitting in the truck, Lila joins us, skipping along up and down the banks at the side of the road like the Kenyan children on their way to school. By the end of the run, she's feeling very pleased with herself, her face beaming as Chris lifts her back into the truck. Godfrey drops us all off back in Iten and we head our separate ways, resolving to meet up again for another group run in a few weeks. The Iten Town Harriers, it seems, are up and running.

◄ ►

Later that afternoon, Chris arrives at my house with a friend. A few days before, he called to ask if there was a prize at Lewa for the first masters runner (one who is over forty years old). It turns out there is, for the first three over-forty finishers, though it doesn't say on the forms what the prizes are. Never mind, Chris has found a runner who, unlike him, is officially over forty, and Chris wants him on the team. As I've offered to pay the entry and accommodation for everyone, I'm concerned about the rising costs, so I tell him that I think we've got enough runners already. With Shadrack, we're five. That's a good number. But, as Godfrey would say: "You know Chris." I open the gate and he slinks his car in. He gets out, wearing a neatly pressed shirt. The children, getting to know him by now, run over and give him a hug. Another man gets out the other door.

"This is Philip," says Chris. "The masters runner I told you about."

"Hi," I say. He has a friendly face.

"Hi," he says.

It turns out Philip is actually fifty-one, but due to the usual Kenyan age-stretching techniques, he's officially only forty-two. Still, it's old enough to put him within shot of winning a prize.

"You going to run Lewa with us?" I ask.

"Yes," he says, watching me closely. Philip has run around fifty marathons, many of them in Europe, and has a best time of 2 hours 8 minutes. He's an experienced man. It'll be good to have him around.

"Do you need any more runners?" Chris asks me, as though I'm collecting them. Still, I'm thinking it might be good for balance to have a woman on the team. Someone not too fast, who I can keep up with perhaps.

"Maybe a woman?" I suggest.

"Okay," he says thoughtfully, nodding his head. I realize it's a done deal. He'll find me someone.

Fourteen

Beatrice outside her house

"How are you?" a small voice somewhere calls out. It's a sound we're used to by now, a childish, precise call, with all the stress on the *you*. It's a greeting, not a question. There's no expectation of an answer. Ossian is the only one who still reacts, running out the door to look up the garden toward the gate. The flap in the gate, for reaching in to unbolt it from the outside, is open and a little face peers in. "How are you?" it calls again.

"Somebody here," says Ossian, chugging back into the house.

"Why don't you see who it is?" Marietta suggests to Lila and Uma, but they're not interested. They carry on with their game, ignoring her. All the attention is becoming too much for them, and

they're beginning to withdraw more and more from the world outside our garden fence. That is, until the day Flora takes them to the
local salon to get braids put in their hair.

It has been both my daughters' dream, ever since they were old
enough to entertain such dreams, to have long flowing locks like
the Disney princesses in their books. Unfortunately, their hair
grows very slowly, if at all. Sometimes it seems to be getting shorter.
But once they hear that you can actually "make" long hair, they want
to know how. And, more important, when.

So one bright morning we head out of our gate, along the dusty
dirt road into town. Down a small backstreet, through a broken gap
in a stick fence, we find a sign for Limo's hair salon. Ducking
through the gap, we walk along a narrow track through what feels
like someone's backyard, passing an upturned bucket for laundry
and an empty clothesline. At the end of the track are three small
salons arranged in a square, with small, wooden benches, painted
blue and yellow, in front of them. The doorways are draped with
hanging ribbons. On one of the walls there is a painted picture of a
woman in hair braids.

We pull back the ribbons in the first doorway and enter the
salon. Inside, four women are sitting drinking tea and listening to a
crackly radio playing Kalenjin music. They get very excited when
they see us, asking the children to shake their hands and giggling
when they refuse—Lila and Uma are too agog at the rows and rows
of wigs and hair extensions to be greeting people. The walls are
covered with pictures of women with different hairstyles, as well as
the obligatory portrait of Kenya's president.

Despite the cabinets full of hair accessories, the salon doesn't
have enough light-brown extensions to do both Lila and Uma's hair,
so they have to send someone out to buy more. The two girls sit
down quietly on plastic chairs in front of cracked wall mirrors, look-

ing around as we wait until a woman comes back with a plastic bag full of extensions. "Right," she says, handing them out to the other women, who pull up their chairs, and the plaiting begins. It takes four hours, with two women working on each head. Uma sits happily talking to herself in the mirror most of the time, but for Lila it all goes on too long. By the end she is crying and begging to be set free as four women work frantically on her to get it done. "It's finished," she says, looking at me all teary eyed. "Tell them it's finished."

Despite the tears, they run home, bouncing along the path, eager to show Marietta and Ossian. Flora and I watch them go. "I think they like it," says Flora.

From that day on, something changes. I don't know what it is about the braids, whether somehow this crossover with the local fashion has broken down some barrier, or whether they just feel rejuvenated and invigorated to have long hair, but suddenly they want to play with the other children again. Every evening when the other children come home from school, Lila and Uma rush out to meet them, skipping around in their flowing plaits. I have to wander along the rows of tiny wooden huts, ducking under clotheslines, poking my head into lace-walled rooms, looking for the girls. "Sorry, have you seen my daughters?" I'll find them curled up on a velvet sofa with eight other children watching Catholic sermons on TV, or drinking tea and chatting away on someone's front step. They can be gone for hours.

They become particularly good friends with three girls from the neighborhood, Maureen, Hilda, and Brenda. Maureen is a livewire of a child with a little shock of electrified, fuzzy hair and a permanently mischievous grin. Every time I ask her how old she is, she gives me a different answer. Hilda and Brenda are sisters and, as far as I can work out, nieces of Japhet, who lives in the adjoining house. Brenda, who is twelve, is the oldest. Slow moving and easily confused, she is always the last to arrive and the last to leave. Hilda, who is ten, is as bright as a pin and has taken a particular shine to Uma.

"When will they come to our school?" the three girls ask, as they sit with Lila and Uma making passion fruit juice on the back step of our house. Between them they have virtually stripped the passion fruit plantation of its bounty, leaving the poor man who cultivated the plants with nothing left to sell at the market. He hasn't complained, but he has stopped coming so frequently.

"Would you like to go to school?" I ask my two daughters. They both nod at me, only half sure. Marietta is nervous about them going. We've seen classrooms in other schools, with up to one hundred children crammed in, sitting in long rows, learning by rote, repeating their lessons lifelessly. We've heard stories of children being beaten for getting low marks on a test, or for being two minutes late for class. We're not great advocates of school at the best of times. In England our children go to a Waldorf school, where formal learning doesn't even begin until age seven. "And they'll be the center of attention all the time," Marietta says. She's right, it won't be easy for them. But it is part of community life here, and they seem to want to go. We decide they can try it for a day.

So a few days later, at 6:00 A.M., I wake the girls up for school. They packed their bags the night before and even laid out their clothes in anticipation, but as I pull back the curtains, Lila hoists the covers up over her head and says she doesn't want to go. Uma is already up and bustling around, getting dressed, saying "Come on, Lila, I'm not scared."

I promise Lila that I'll stay with her if she wants me to, and so at

7:30 A.M. we arrive at the gates of Sunrise Academy. Most of the children are already in school. A few latecomers, who can't be more than three or four years old, scuffle in behind us, staring as they go, their heads corkscrewing around as they pass us.

The head teacher comes out of his office to greet us. Hilda and Maureen emerge to take Lila and Uma off to their classroom to prepare for assembly. Another student brings over a couple of white plastic chairs for me and Marietta to sit on. Corrugated metal classrooms surround a small, grassy square. From behind the closed doors comes the busy sound of chattering and laughter. Then the doors open and children parade out into the square from every direction. I spot my children, two little blond heads among the melee.

After the assembly, the children return to their classrooms; windowless sheds, the light streaming in from gaps between the walls and the roof, with pairs of wooden desks arranged in rows. Lila and Uma squeeze into small spaces on the benches between their friends. They seem fine, so we leave them unpacking their pencils and notebooks from their bags.

◄ ►

I return at lunchtime to see how they're doing. As I walk into the school, a group of older children is lined up along one side of the small playing field. They all have their arms in the air and are kneeling down in front of their teacher, who has a big, red stick under one arm. In unison, they chant out a chilling refrain: "We will not fail again. We will not fail again." Over and over again.

I walk past them and into the courtyard, where the head teacher, the deputy, and another teacher are sitting on plastic chairs in the sun. They have the slow, unhurried aspect of people who have been there a long time.

"How are they?" I ask.

"They're doing fine," says the head teacher. "They'll be out in a moment."

Lila is the first one out. She walks over to me looking a little dazed and buries her head in my sweater. Uma, however, is in the swirl of a big gang, trying to ignore me. She's the youngest in the class by about five years and all the other children are swooning around to look after her. "Dad, I want to stay for lunch," she says.

"Okay," I say, but she's already gone, carried in the flow of children toward the lunch barn.

The head teacher smiles happily. "And you, Lila?" he asks.

But Lila is burrowing deeper. "You want to come home for lunch?" I ask her. I can feel the nod in my side.

On the way out, we peek into the barn that houses the dining hall. Among the sea of black hair and gray uniforms bustling around sits a little blond girl in a pale blue dress, her face flushed, a fork in one hand, laughing and joking with the other children. We leave her there and head home.

When we return after lunch, the other children bring Uma out of the classroom. She's crying and she looks lost. She gives me a big hug as Lila slips back into the dark classroom, finds her desk, and takes out her books. Uma wants to come home. On the way out of the school, she holds my hand like a captive being led to freedom. I can feel the relief in her step, her voice, which gets almost giddy as we head out through the gates.

I don't go back to collect Lila until five o'clock. Rather than rush to me, though, she walks straight past with Maureen, Brenda, and Hilda. I end up following her home at a distance, trying not to cramp her style as she walks along holding hands with the others, her bag on her back. The people in Iten stand and watch as she walks by in the midst of the other children, just part of the gang, coming home after a day at school.

When she gets home, though, she collapses on the sofa, exhausted. Uma hovers around her, intrigued to find out what the rest of the day was like. But Lila looks shell-shocked and just stares straight ahead, not speaking. I get the feeling she will remember this day for many years to come.

Later that night as they sit in bed, I ask them if they'd like to go back to school.

"Yes," they both say, but they don't sound sure.

"Tomorrow?"

"Maybe not tomorrow," they say.

A few days later, Chris's car is rolling back through my gates, this time with a woman athlete. She is in her early twenties and has just run a local half marathon in seventy-six minutes, which is pretty fast for a race at altitude. She looks familiar as she gets out of the car. Her name is Beatrice. I ran with her on the track one day with the Run Fast camp. I seem to remember being able to keep up with her, which suggests she's not as fast as she says. Chris has her half-marathon time written down on a scrap of paper, as though that's proof that she did it. But Beatrice has a winning smile, and is soon playing with the children on the grass and chatting to Marietta, already part of the team.

She tells us she has been running for only two years, and has never done a marathon before. She says she knows that the Lewa race is tough, but she's confident she can do well.

"Are you a runner, too?" she asks Marietta as we all sit down at the table.

"No," says Marietta, holding up her hands, making it clear she won't be joining the running craze anytime soon. "I just like to watch."

"You look like a runner. You should try," Beatrice insists. "You are slim. I think you would be good."

Unlike most athletes, Beatrice didn't run at school. She says she didn't like running. After she finished primary school, at fifteen, she lived at home for the next five years, helping her mother. "I was big," she tells me one day, as we sit facing the gas stove in her tiny house. "This big," she says, holding her hands out wide. Bored of sitting at home with her mother, she decided to follow her brothers who had moved to Iten to become an athlete. She found a small room behind a noisy café. To get there you have to walk in through the café and out into the backyard. As well as a few wooden huts, there is also a shed with a screen where the café shows English football matches and big running races.

One evening I sit there in the dark, squashed on one of the long wooden benches between Japhet and Beatrice, watching the Boston Marathon. Less than a month before he is found dead, Sammy Wanjiru is sitting on one of the benches in front of us, going wild along with everyone else as the Kenyan Geoffrey Mutai wins in 2:03:02, the fastest marathon time ever run.

When she moved to Iten, Beatrice started running at 5:00 A.M., when it was still dark, so that people wouldn't see her. Slowly the weight started to drop off. Now, two years later, she's a 76-minute half-marathon runner (at least, that's what she says). She's still quite big compared to the typical Kenyan runner, but extremely slight by the usual parameters.

Despite Beatrice's initial lack of promise, her mother agreed to fund her running, giving her what little money she could to cover the cost of her rent (about six dollars a month), fuel, and food. There aren't many countries in the world where you can tell your poverty-stricken family that you want to leave to become an athlete, spending most of your days resting and sleeping, and they will reply,

Great, let us give you the tiny amount we have to help you. But like their children, the parents in Kenya are aware of the bounty that running can bring.

Many people in Kenya, however, mistakenly assume that all athletes are wealthy. One moderately successful runner told me that when he runs, children shout out to him, "Buy me a car!"

"Who has told them that just because I'm a runner, I'm rich?" he asks. "Where do they get that idea from?" Yet it's an assumption that drives many poor men and women toward running. Training is regarded not as some frivolous way to spend your time but as serious work, even by those struggling to put food on the table. All around the Rift Valley there are role models proving that running can bring you your fortune. Virtually every village has its running star, someone who has packed a bag and gone off to win world titles or big road races abroad, returning rich (at least by Kenyan standards), driving a big 4x4 Land Cruiser, building a brick house, and buying a cow, and some land to plant maize.

As Bruce Tulloh pointed out to me, the great growth in Kenyan running coincided with the rise in financial rewards. While running was still an amateur sport, Kenya produced a few great athletes who had come through the military system, or via track scholarships with American universities. But once professionalism took off in the mid-1980s, with prize money and appearance money being offered to the fastest athletes, Kenyan runners really started to dominate.

Recently, Kenya's success on the world's road-racing circuit, where most of the money now is, has far outstripped its performances on the track. At virtually every big city marathon or half marathon, from Brussels to Bogotá to Boston, the winner is almost always a Kenyan. However, over the last two world athletics championships, Kenyan men have won only one bronze medal in the 5,000 meters and 10,000 meters events.

Of course, a desire to escape poverty is not unique to Kenya or East Africa. And all over the world people are running barefoot to school. The difference is that here in Kenya there is an established running culture ready to take advantage of it. The origins of this culture are hazy, built on the folklore of Kipchoge Keino, who won gold medals in the 1968 and 1972 Olympics, and developed through the running camps set up by Brother Colm and others. As Yannis Pitsiladis puts it: "How many athletes training camps are there in India or Bolivia?"

Now that running is firmly established as the way out, as football is in Brazil or cricket is in India, all over the Rift Valley people like Beatrice and Japhet are taking it up in the thousands, and the result is that Kenya is now dominating long-distance running even more than ever.

Fifteen

Mary Keitany and her husband, Charles

Iten wasn't always the home of Kenya's conveyor belt of running talent. When Kenyans first started to raise eyebrows with their running exploits, it was mainly the runners from the Nandi Hills, farther south, who dominated.

"When I came here in 1976," says Brother Colm, "there were no runners in Iten." I'm sitting in his dimly lit living room, sunk back into an old armchair. In one corner is a small TV with piles of videos stacked up in the sideboard underneath. Godfrey tells me that Brother Colm records every race that gets shown on television. The room is sparsely furnished, with a clock and a picture of a saint on the wall, alongside a free tractor calendar. He doesn't offer me any tea. A packet of ginger nut cookies on the table remains unopened.

It was the influence of Brother Colm and his St. Patrick's boys' school, and to a lesser extent Signore girls' school just outside of Iten, that were to turn the town into the running center it is today. With the repeated success of their teams in national and international competitions, Iten began to build a reputation as the place to train. "St. Patrick's and Signore were the beacons that made Iten the running center," says Brother Colm, as he walks me back out to the school gate. He has his cap pulled down low over his eyes and walks, where he can, in the shade. "We put Kericho [the Iten region] at the center of the map. Now everything emanates from Kericho."

As we stand at the gate, a car pulls up and a man gets out and starts shaking Brother Colm's hand. "Henry, how are you?" says Brother Colm. He looks at me. "Henry was one of my students. He's now a university lecturer."

Henry turns to shake my hand. "We are all his products," he says, pointing at Brother Colm, clearly delighted to have bumped into him again.

Iten's influence is celebrated each year at its annual sports and tourism day. "Iten is the factory of Kenyan running," the day's organizer tells me as we stand in the sports field at the center of town. "So we thought we should have a factory day." The festivities begin, aptly, with a race. Starting down in the hot, cactus-pimpled belly of the valley, the route winds its way thirteen miles up to the cool freshness of Iten. A half marathon, uphill all the way. I'm hurrying the children to get dressed. The race is supposed to start at 8:30 A.M., and I've just received word that not only is it starting on time, but it is starting only half a mile down the road, so the runners will be passing through the town in about five minutes. Uma says she

doesn't want to come; I'm sensing her passion for running is wearing thin. Lila seems happy to tag along, though, so we leave Uma
with Flora and hurry down into town, Marietta strapping Ossian on
her back as we go.

There are very few spectators around, but we spy a couple of the
men from the Run Fast camp standing by the side of the road. Before we've had time to shake everyone's hand, the runners are in
sight and pushing up the hill. Somewhere among the heaving bodies is Japhet, gamely throwing his hat into the ring. The prize money
on offer, organized by the local council, is fairly small, which keeps
most of the top runners from competing. For someone like Japhet,
this is ideal, as it gives him a better chance of winning something.
Even if he comes in sixth he will win 8,000 Kenyan shillings, which
for most people here would be a decent month's salary. We clap as
the runners surge by. And then they're gone.

"They'll be back in an hour," I say, wondering what we should
do until then. We decide to amble up the street to see if anything is
happening by the finish. As we set off, a 1970s school bus, with ST.
PATRICK'S HIGH SCHOOL printed on the side, pulls up beside us. I
get out my camera to take a photo. As I do, a man comes over and
asks if we'd like to ride in the bus. A large group of women in tracksuits is starting to board it.

"Okay," I say. "Where is it going?"

"To the start of the women's race," he says. It turns out the
courses have been altered at the last minute because the council
couldn't find enough buses to take all the athletes down to the bottom of the valley. So this St. Patrick's bus is taking the women six
miles down the flatter road toward Eldoret. From there they'll run
straight back to Iten.

I'm not sure how the athletes are supposed to prepare for these
races when things like start times, courses, and race distances are

decided at the last minute and news is spread purely by word of mouth. Somehow, though, they always seem to know what is happening.

Lila's thrilled to be on a bus. "Is this a school bus?" she asks me as we sit down. "It's like an airplane."

A runner named Rose sits down next to Marietta and Ossian, who is peeking blearily out of his sling. She tells Marietta she has four children but her husband has left her. She can't afford to send her two daughters to school, she says.

"Where are they now?" asks Marietta.

"At home," she says.

"But who's looking after them?"

"They're alone," Rose says, looking out of the window. They're six and four.

Rose has come to Iten in the hope of becoming an athlete, but she has been injured for seven months, so she has been working as a housemaid for Nicholas, the cycling coach from Singapore.

After about ten minutes, the bus pulls off the road. An army officer with a stick under his arm is standing by the roadside, peering out from under the brim of his hat. The women rush to get changed into their running clothes and then hop off the bus and run over to the start line. A skinny man in a tracksuit is yelling instructions and waving his arms around. It's Chris Cheboiboch. He spots me.

"Hey, man. Want a ride?" he asks, walking over to his car and opening the door.

"Okay," I say. I don't know how else we're going to get back to Iten. I look at Marietta, who nods and climbs into the rear seat with Ossian. Lila looks slightly confused as I bundle her straight from the bus into a car, but the race has already started and we're speeding off ahead of the runners. Chris's job, it seems, is to warn oncoming traffic about the race. He does this by driving headlong at top speed toward anything coming in the opposite direction. Once the oncoming vehicle is forced off the road, he stops briefly beside it and fires off a ream of instructions about being careful of the runners. It's a hellfire ride back into town.

The race finishes in the field in the center of Iten. Chris arrives just in time to leap out of the car and get someone to hold up a finishing tape before the leading man comes sprinting across the field. Chris seems to have organized the race single-handedly. He leaps back into his car and skids off, leaving the following runners with no obvious finish line. They have to keep running, charging past the people trying to record their times and hand them bottles of water. Someone eventually realizes what's going on and puts a bit of tape down on the ground as a makeshift finish.

Japhet ends up in around twenty-fifth position. He seems happy enough when I see him afterward, holding his free bottle of water like it was a gold medal. "Did you enjoy that?" I ask him.

"Yes," he says, beaming with happiness. "I enjoyed it, yes."

After the men, come the women. Rose, unfortunately, limps in way down the field, almost at the back. It doesn't bode well for her career prospects. This is easily the slowest race I've seen since I arrived in Kenya.

As the last runners come through, a truck drives onto the field and pulls up beside the finish. Two men get out and begin unloading a marquee and stacks of white plastic chairs. It seems a bit late to be setting up a viewing area, but the men press ahead, working without haste, lining up the chairs in neat rows.

Afterward, I meet lots of familiar faces milling around. Godfrey's friend Koila is there. The marquee and chairs, Koila tells me, are for events later on. The race, the actual running, is just the appetizer. But before anything else happens, we have to wait for the guest of honor to arrive. The rumor going around the field is that it's the deputy prime minister of Kenya, Musalia Mudavadi.

It's now 11:00 A.M. "I'd better go back and see how Uma is getting on," says Marietta, clearly not enthused by the prospect of a political rally. The sun is coming out and people are beginning to congregate. It has all the rumblings of a long, drawn-out occasion, the sort of event that leaves the children hot and flustered. "I'll take Lila and Ossian with me," she says.

By midday, Godfrey has shown up and has taken a pew in the front row of the VIP tent. But the deputy prime minister is still not here. I decide to head back home for some lunch. Two hours later I call Godfrey to see what is happening.

"I advise you to come now," he says, not elaborating.

Crestfallen after missing out on a bus ride this morning, Uma now wants to come with me. Lila, worried that she might miss out on something else, is coming along, too.

When we get to the field, groups of schoolchildren are performing traditional songs and dances. We sit down next to Godfrey and settle in for the show. The children are drilled to perfection, pulling eye-popping faces as they perform. Lila and Uma watch fascinated, particularly when their friends Hilda and Maureen stand up to do a performance. The guest of honor, however, has still not arrived.

As we sit waiting, I spot on the road running along the far end of the field about fifteen shiny 4x4s zipping by one after the other. "The deputy prime minister," Godfrey tells me, as the convoy of cars zooms onto the field. One by one the cars stop, the doors swing open, and large men in suits step out. It's instantly clear which one is Mr. Mudavadi. He has a large, self-satisfied smile across his ample face. He has people crowding around him, and he's waving cordially in all directions.

The announcer is suddenly very excited and starts trying to organize the schoolchildren into lines so they can perform again for the guests. As well as the deputy prime minister, there are about thirty civic officers and local politicians in tow. Once they're all seated and have finished congratulating one another, the children begin their songs again.

Each time, one of the honored guests gets up and starts dancing along with the children. Then another one joins in. Sometimes the deputy PM himself gets up and shimmies around to the music, smiling for the cameras snapping pictures of him. Someone is handing out sheets of paper around the tent. It's a schedule of the day's events. According to the timetable, the whole thing was due to end at 2:00 P.M., but it's now 3:30. The announcer is hurrying the singers along. "We have a lot of speeches," he says. "So, please, just one song each."

By now a few thousand people have gathered to watch the proceedings, among them Marietta and Ossian, who were wondering what was keeping us. It's almost four o'clock. Time, finally, for the speeches to begin. On and on they go, one politician after another, talking in a haphazard combination of Swahili and English about corruption, the coalition, the political parties, and many things I can't understand. At one point, Daniel Komen bravely stands up and starts berating the politicians. "You politicians," he says. "You take the money from Kenya and put it in foreign bank accounts. Then the athletes have to go and win it back." The politicians don't look amused.

After a couple of hours we take the children home. But, curious to see how the day ends, I return alone back to the field. It's past six o'clock and the speeches are still going on. I sit down next to Komen. "They're still talking?" I ask.

"This is Kenya," he says. "It's twenty-five laps. There are two more to go."

Eventually, the deputy PM says *"Asante sana"* and it's over. The crowd claps politely. The faint sound of a tractor can be heard struggling along up a hill somewhere. The prizes for the runners, who finished running over nine hours ago, are finally handed out. The curtain comes down.

◄ ►

As I cross the field back toward my house, I spot Beatrice. She stops, surprised to see me. In the darkness I'm not sure it's actually her. "Hi, Beatrice?"

"Hi," she says, holding out a limp hand for me to shake.

"Did you run today?"

"No."

"Why not?" She doesn't answer, but just grins bashfully as though I've asked her a personal question. "You might have won a prize," I venture, still unsure how fast she really is. "There were prizes for the top ten."

"Top ten?" She looks surprised, shaking her head. "For the women, too?"

I nod. She looks thoughtful, but doesn't say anything else. The headlights of a *matatu* swing around into my eyes for a second and then drive on. "I should get back," I say. She just nods shyly. "Well, good night. I'll let you know when we're doing our next run." She wanders off into the night. There are no streetlights in Iten and once night falls, it can be very hard to see where you're walking if you don't carry a flashlight. I scamper off home while I can still see the ground.

◄ ►

Beatrice may not say much, but she is actually quite outgoing for a Kenyan athlete, particularly a woman. Despite the country's incredible dominance of one of the world's most popular sports, if you stopped a stranger in the street in any Western city and asked him to name even one Kenyan runner, he would probably struggle. One reason for this is the shyness of the athletes. Their awkward looks and monosyllabic answers when placed in front of the media can drive their agents mad. Marketing a Kenyan runner in a saturated field is already hard enough.

Unlike athletes from other parts of the world, such as the Jamaican Usain Bolt, Kenyan runners rarely seek out the limelight. Even when they win gold medals, they always bring their teammates with them on their lap of honor. The teammates, who may have finished in last place, can often seem as happy as the winner. Kenyan runners will also often race as a team, with one of the athletes sacrificing his chances of winning to act as a pacemaker for his countrymen. All this selflessness is simply a reflection of how Kenyans are raised.

"Very few of the Kenyan champions come from a sheltered family unit," Toby Tanser explains to me one day, sitting on the grass in our garden. "Instead, they are brought up as part of the wider community of a village, almost like pieces of a bicycle chain. They soon learn about *harambee*." *Harambee* is a Kenyan tradition, in which a whole community will come together to help itself. It literally means "all pull together" and is the official motto of Kenya. "When a Kenyan wins a medal, or a large amount of money," says Toby, "he reflects on the journey that took him to that moment, and he realizes, perhaps better than we do, that no person achieves without the help and support of those around him."

One of the fastest runners around right now is Mary Keitany, yet she's also one of the most shy. I first meet her at the cross-country race at Salaba Academy, Chris Cheboiboch's school. She is there as a guest, sitting along with everyone else under the flapping gazebo as the winners are presented with their prizes. Dressed in a purple suit, she could easily be one of the many school administrators who are also sitting with us on the rows of plastic chairs.

When I see her again at the Iten race, she is wearing the same purple suit. She has just broken Lornah Kiplagat's half-marathon world record, winning $75,000. I ask her if I can visit her. As one of the fastest female athletes in the world, perhaps she can add another piece to the puzzle of why Kenyan runners are so good.

One of the runners from the Run Fast camp, Raymond, is Mary's brother-in-law (his brother Charles is married to her). When Raymond hears that I'm paying a visit, he says he wants to come, too. It's only about five minutes outside of Iten, but he says he wants us to drive there. He's been coveting my car since he first saw it. To me it looks just like any other car in Kenya, a slightly beaten, old, white Toyota. But to most Kenyan men I've met it's a gleaming dream on wheels. Wherever I go, they stand staring at it, shaking their heads in disbelief. "You don't often see a car like that," they say. "You can tell it's a *mzungu* car. *Mzungus* know how to look after their cars." Raymond asks me to sell it to him, but it's not mine. It was lent to me by my brother-in-law, Alastair. And I've already promised Godfrey that he can buy it if Alastair wants to sell it. But Raymond isn't giving up. He tells me not to tell anyone that he wants it. I'm not sure what his strategy is, but I agree to keep it as our secret.

We drive out of town and then immediately turn off the paved road and down a dirt track, clouds of red dust billowing behind us. The car is as hot as a sauna after being parked in the midday sun with the windows shut. Up ahead a woman in tracksuit bottoms and a bright yellow T-shirt, with a small boy holding her hand, stand by the side of the road. They watch us as we pass.

"That was Mary," says Raymond, after we've gone by.

"Really? Should I stop?"

He doesn't say anything. I look over at him. He's grinning at me. He nods. I pull the car to a stop and wait. In the mirror I can see that she's walking back toward us. I wind the window down.

"Hello," I say as she comes over. But she's looking past me, to Raymond. They talk hurriedly, as though there's a problem. I lean back in my seat so they can see each other.

Raymond looks at me and points ahead to a gate. "In there," he says. I look at Mary. She smiles, stepping back to let me drive.

"She was going to a neighbor's house. She forgot we were coming," Raymond tells me.

We drive through into a small compound. To one side is some farm machinery and two men. One of them, Mary's husband, Charles, watches us suspiciously as I park the car. I get out and wave to him. "Hello," I say. He gives me a small nod, not returning the smile, as Mary and the boy follow us in and then disappear inside the house. Raymond gets out and stands by the car, stretching his hands in the air as though we've just been on a long journey. I'm not sure where to go.

Charles eventually comes over and shakes my hand and gestures toward the front door. *"Karibu,"* he says. "Welcome."

I step through into a small living room so crammed with sofas and coffee tables that there's almost no space to stand. Mary, who still hasn't spoken to me, is fixing up two glasses of a toxic-colored orange drink. I sit down in one of the armchairs. Raymond, following along behind, sits in the far corner of the room. Mary gives us each a drink and sits down somewhere midway between us.

I look around the room. The walls are full of photographs. Most of them are of Mary or Charles running. The biggest pictures are all of Charles. Medals hang from the corners of a few of the pictures. A shiny, gold HAPPY CHRISTMAS sign hangs over the door.

"You must have been happy to break the world record last week," I say. She looks at me confused, perhaps surprised by my accent. "Did you know you could break the record, or was it a surprise?"

"A surprise," she says, looking away. Charles comes into the room with their son and sits down beside her. He picks up the remote control and clicks on the TV. It's just behind my head, so I can't see it. They all stare at it. It feels like they're staring at me. Mary is running the London Marathon in a few weeks. I ask her if she thinks she can win. She laughs. I'm not sure if it's in answer to my question or at something on the TV. Our stilted conversation goes on for about ten minutes, Mary looking away shyly every time I ask her a question, while Charles and Raymond sit watching on silently, their eyes flicking back and forth between me and the TV above my head.

"Well, I'd better leave you to get ready for your afternoon run," I say at last. Mary just nods.

Once we're outside, Mary disappears. Charles takes me around the back of the house to see the cows. I ask him if they'll use the money from Mary's world record to build a bigger house. He looks at me, confused. "Why?" he asks. I feel like I've insulted him. Their place is nice, but it's fairly simple. It's not the house you imagine a world record holder living in.

Money is clearly an awkward subject. Mary has been a fairly late developer. She's twenty-nine and is only just starting to make a mark on the world stage. Up until recently, Charles was the star runner in the household. The house was probably built with his winnings.

A farmhand is milking one of the cows. "Do you sell the milk?" I ask him. Again he looks at me as though I'm mad. "No," he says. "It's for us." The majority of the people in the Rift Valley are brought up as subsistence farmers, so when the athletes win any money, the first thing they do is buy a cow for milk. I can't help thinking it would be easier and cheaper just to go to the shop and buy it every day. Every street has a tiny kiosk selling fresh milk for virtually nothing. But the mindset is to own a cow. A person without a cow is not really a person. You can judge the importance of someone by the number of cows he owns.

Charles tells me that when they were younger, they used to drain some of the blood from the cows to mix with *mursik*, a fermented milk drink. They would make a tiny hole in the cow's neck to get the blood out, and then seal it back up, letting the cow run off unharmed. "It made us strong," he says. The mixture of blood and *mursik* is often cited by runners as the Kalenjin secret, even though it is rarely drunk these days. Mixed with charcoal, it is an unpalatable but potent tonic. When triumphant athletes return home after winning a big competition, they are often met at the airport by a ceremonial gourd of *mursik,* which they drink to loud cheers.

Charles and Mary also have a small field of maize growing nearby. "For *ugali,*" Charles tells me. Yet another Kenyan secret. Mary is certainly running fast on it. A few weeks later she does indeed win the London Marathon, with the fourth fastest marathon time in history.

Raymond is standing by the car, waiting to go. We walk over. Charles wants to know where I got the car. "KXE," he says, referring to the license plate. "It's a very nice car. You don't see KXE like that, in that condition." He asks if he can look under the hood. He stares at the engine, fascinated. "Do you want to sell it?" he asks. I tell him it's my brother-in-law's car. "Well, tell him," he says, "that if he wants to sell it . . ."

I assure him I will. Raymond has climbed into his seat and is waiting like a moody teenager to go, so I wave good-bye. "Say thanks and good-bye to Mary for me," I say, as we pull out through the gates and up the bumpy road back to Iten.

Sixteen

The Kenyan national championships, Nairobi

The next day I hop back into our coveted Toyota Corolla and set out on the long, perilous drive down to Nairobi. Godfrey and I have a pilgrimage to make. In some ways it's just another race. A bunch of people running around a field. But the Kenyan national cross-country championships is probably the toughest, most competitive running race in the world. The top hundred or so Kenyans in each age group come together, the very fastest of the fast, racing one another for a few coveted spots on the national team for the world championships. It's the most densely concentrated gathering of running brilliance anywhere in the world. I simply have to be there to witness the spectacle.

Godfrey had said that he would give me a lift, but a few days before, he rang to tell me that there had been a change of plan. His car was still in the garage, he said. He was now going to take the bus to Nairobi a day early with Anders as he had to help an athlete get a visa. So that afternoon I find myself standing by my car in a hot, dusty town about 50 miles from Iten, waiting for another runner and his wife. Godfrey has arranged for me to give them a lift, so they can keep me company and help me find the way.

A man in a striped shirt carrying a big jacket under his arm approaches me as I stand there, his hand stretched out. "Yes, my friend," he says as I shake his hand. "Where are you going?"

"Nairobi," I say.

"I'll come," he says. It's only half a question. I can't tell if he has just decided to go to Nairobi because I've suggested it, or whether he was going there anyway. Spotting my concerns, he says: "I am a police officer."

I agree to give him a lift. He's heading home to see his family for the weekend. The runner I'm waiting for and his wife turn up soon after, looking harassed and complaining about the *matatu* journey from their home village nearby.

As the midafternoon sun burns in patches of light across the town, we all climb into the car and head out along the potholed road into a landscape scattered with spiky cactus plants and dry, stony riverbeds. It's a straight four-hour drive to Nairobi, past small, ramshackle crossroad settlements, big school gates, and up into the hills, overtaking tractors, trucks, avoiding the *matatu*s and smoking cars coming the other way. At one point we pass a group of baboons sitting right by the roadside grooming their young and watching the passing vehicles with disinterest. Finally the road drops down into Nairobi.

As we drive, my passengers make an effort to speak in English and include me in the conversations, but gradually they slip into Swahili. I let them go, my gaze drifting off into the rainy hills. The grass here is green and soft, with rows and rows of healthy-looking crops rising up the hillsides. People cycle by in rain jackets under gray skies.

Once we get to Nairobi, we meet Godfrey and Anders as arranged at the YMCA. Godfrey has supposedly booked a room for the three of us, but it turns out that it has only one single bed.

"It's okay," he says. "I know another place nearby."

We park my car and hop into a vehicle that Godfrey has managed to procure from somewhere. He drives us farther and farther out of town, past bigger and bigger houses, until we've been going for about forty-five minutes. Finally, with night bringing its curtain down, he turns down a side road that leads us to what looks like a deserted conference center. A sign at the entrance says: KCB BANK LEADERSHIP CENTER. It doesn't look much like a hotel. Anders glances at me, doubtful, but Godfrey is as confident as ever.

"Trust me," he says. "You are going to love this place."

The guard at the gate looks surprised to see us. Godfrey winds down his window with a big smile. But the guard is nonplussed. He seems to be telling Godfrey that the place is only used for conferences; it's not a hotel. Godfrey bids the man good night and reverses the car out into the road. "It's full," he says. "There's a conference on."

Instead, a few minutes away, we pull in at the Shade Hotel. It has some cheap, quirky rooms and a restaurant. We're tired and hungry, so we take it.

◄ ►

Half of Iten seems to be at the race in Uhuru Gardens in the center of Nairobi, sprinting back and forth around the course to get as many glimpses of the runners as possible. Besides enthusiasts like myself, there are the coaches and agents, encouraging their runners along with gruff shouts. When one of their athletes wins, they grin and high-five one another like traders watching their stock rising in value. A few thousand local fans have also turned out to watch. For a cross-country race this is quite a lot, but I can't help thinking that here, in the capital city of the world's most passionate running nation, there would be a few more. Some fans are appreciating it, though. One man turns to me with a big grin as the lead women go by, and says: "I've just seen Linet Masai [the eventual winner] with my own eyes. Not on the Internet."

The athletes parade out to the start at the beginning of each race like warriors, their arms swinging, bouncing up and down on their toes. It's a warm, wind-swept morning and I spend much of the time rushing around trying to take photographs. I want to somehow capture the majesty of it all, the power and speed with which they charge around. But it seems to get lost amid the wide-open space of the park. Occasional planes sink down across the sky, landing at the nearby Wilson Airport, dwarfing the runners still more. Perhaps it's because I want to be overwhelmed by it, because I've come so far to see it, that I'm straining to fully appreciate just how fast the runners are moving.

Then in the last race, as the men's winner, Geoffrey Mutai, hurtles around the last corner right in front of me, he almost goes the wrong way. It's like trying to redirect a speeding train to get him back on course. We have to leap out of the way as he flies straight at us, heading off on yet another lap, as though he could just keep going forever. Somehow the marshals manage to grab him and send him back along the funnel to the finish. He completes the twelve-kilometer course (7.4 miles)—over rough, hilly terrain, on a windy day, at altitude—in a staggering 34 minutes 35 seconds.

To illustrate just how tough these races are, the four current world champions—senior and junior men and women—are all running, but none of them manages to finish even in the top ten. Leonard Komon, who in the previous few months has broken the 15K and 10K world records, can manage only sixth place in the men's race.

Before I leave, Godfrey introduces me to a young girl from a small village somewhere in the Rift Valley. Her head is shaved like most Kenyan schoolgirls', and her teeth are stained. She could have just arrived after a day of planting maize in the fields. She offers me an embarrassed handshake as I'm told she is Mercy Cherono, the world junior champion from the year before. Today, though, she came in thirteenth, herself outrun by a host of other girls from small, dusty villages.

◄ ►

My meeting with Mercy Cherono gets me thinking. Something about her seemed to encapsulate the Kenyan running phenomenon. There was something accidental, unconscious even, about her brilliance.

One evening, weeks earlier, in the Kerio View hotel in Iten, Marietta and I met a couple drinking wine on the terrace. The man, an executive with the country's biggest telecommunications company, Safaricom, in Nairobi, was from the Eldoret area. I asked him what he thought was the secret to the Kenyans' running success. He looked at me over his glass. "Ask any top runner about his background," he said, "and you will find out he comes from a poor family."

At the time I thought it was a slightly crass observation, but the more I think about it, the more significant it seems. Talking to Mercy Cherono, it was clear that her success hadn't come as the result of years of dedication, being driven to training sessions and races by her parents. Her school probably didn't even have a track to train on. Instead, simply from the inherent physical toughness of her daily life had come a talent to outrun the world.

Brother Colm nods when I put this theory to him, that all the Kenyan runners come from a poor background. "I'll add something else," he says. "They all come from a poor, rural family. We've yet to have a good runner from a city."

The life of the rural poor in Kenya is tough. From a young age children have to work hard, herding goats or digging in the fields, and they run or walk everywhere. You see them at dawn shuffling along the trails on their way to school. It's the perfect groundwork for an endurance athlete.

I remember the day I had lunch with Daniel Komen at the Eldoret Golf Club. He wore a dark green suit. It was a hot day, children were playing in the pool. A buffet barbecue was in full swing. Waiters in crisp white shirts carried trays of sunburst drinks across the lawn. "Every day I used to milk the cows, run to school, run home for lunch, back to school, home, tend the cows." He didn't smile as he spoke. It wasn't a happy memory. "This is the Kenyan way."

Chris Cheboiboch once told me a similar story. "We were training already without knowing it," he said. "Every day running, running, running."

Not only are they training from a young age, but they're doing it at high altitude. There is a broad scientific consensus that training at high altitude helps endurance athletes to run faster by increasing their blood's ability to carry oxygen around the body. Virtually every international distance runner will include spells of high-altitude training in their schedules. But the Kenyans are born and raised at altitude, running around everywhere from a young age, which gives them a big advantage.

I head back to the Kerio View in search of Renato Canova and find him sitting in the same seat, his glass of milk on the table. He motions for me to sit down when he sees me, and orders me a glass of passion fruit juice. I ask him about this theory that it is their tough, rural upbringing that makes Kenyans such good runners. He thinks for a moment, measuring his words as though he could answer the question in a hundred different ways. "It's true," he says. "In the West, we have a good quality of life, no? But if you think about what 'quality of life' means, it means less fatigue. Making things easier. Running, on the other hand, is about how much fatigue can you do."

My list is growing, but all the reasons—the secrets—that I'm discovering are beginning to join up. The tough, physical upbringing, the barefoot running, the altitude, the running to school, they all arise naturally from the Kenyans' daily lives. None of it is done with the intention of becoming an athlete. It's just how they live. Simply through growing up on the slopes of the Rift Valley, far from cities and the technologies that the West has invented to make life more comfortable, they have found themselves excelling at the world's most natural sport.

When my children turned up in Eldoret for the cross-country race, it was unlike the fun runs they had enjoyed before in England. There were no pudgy legs or flushed faces, children running at a cute waddle, happy to be doing something active for a change. In Eldoret the children were all charged with energy, rushing, darting back and forth on the start line. Something was already afoot, long before any athletic training had started to take place. Lila and Uma took one look and were terrified.

"To build your aerobic house, to have enough of an endurance base to run long distances, takes about ten years," Canova tells me.

"By the time a Kenyan is sixteen," he says, smiling, as though this, my friend, is everything boiled down to one small, neat point, a little sound bite that you can take away with you, "by the time a Kenyan is sixteen, he has built his house."

◄ ►

Meanwhile, in Nairobi, I'm preparing to set out on another run. I'm training almost every day now, as the Lewa Marathon gets closer. Training is starting to become a daily practice like it is for Japhet, Beatrice, and all the other runners in Iten. Except that here in the city, things are very different.

"Right everyone, stop wanking and gather round."

It's a motley crew that assembles around the big, red 4x4 in the parking lot of the Nest Hotel in Ngong, a satellite town just north of Nairobi. The majority of the forty or so people in the group are overweight. A few are drinking fizzy drinks. One lady, with a face like a snarling dog, is smoking a cigarette. Everyone is wearing running clothes. "Today's long route is ten kilometers," says the man in charge. "The short route is eight kilometers. Enjoy." Most of the people here look like they'd struggle to make it up the stairs to the bar. But with good-natured smiles and jokes, we all file out of the parking lot, on to the road, and start jogging.

Before I return to Iten, I go visit some old friends of Bruce Tulloh's, Ray and Doreen Meynick. Ray told me he was good friends with two of Kenya's greatest running legends, Catherine Ndereba and Paul Tergat. They live just around the corner from his house in the leafy suburb of Karen, he told me. They often come for dinner. I was hoping they would have something to add as to why Kenyans are such good runners, but unfortunately neither of them is answering the phone.

Ray insists that instead I meet up with some of the non-elite Kenyan runners in Nairobi—fun runners, mostly, which in Kenya is an unusual concept. "Running with the Kenyans?" he says, giving me a pointed look. "Well, they're Kenyans, too."

With over 1,700 groups meeting in most major cities around the world, the Hash House Harriers is an international phenomenon. More a social club than a typical running club—they like to describe themselves as "a drinking club with a running problem"— they nevertheless head out on regular runs all across their respective cities. Rather than run along a set route, the Hashers follow a trail marked out in advance with white chalk.

The pace is excruciatingly slow at the back of the group as the runners heave themselves along the Ngong Road, almost being knocked over by buses crammed full of commuters heading home after work. At the head of the group, a few lean runners are getting away. I chase after them, but as soon as I catch them, they step behind a wall and stop. They're all grinning.

"What's going on?"

One of them, an elderly man with one of his front teeth missing, points at two white chalk lines on the ground. "That means it's a false trail," he says. But he doesn't want the others to realize it, at least not until they have come all the way down the dusty side road as we have. This is going to be very different from running in Iten.

Once we get back on track, returning en masse to the main road and taking a different chalk-marked side road, the same few runners hurtle off at the front again, and I stick with them. We soon find ourselves running through the backyards of some collapsing wooden houses, ducking under clotheslines, leaping over small children playing in the mud. But we seem to have lost the trail. As we stand around deliberating, a man in a doorway points down a narrow gap between two of the houses. Without thanking him, we rush down it, and sure enough there are more chalk marks.

"On, on," the others shout at the top of their lungs, as the slower runners begin to catch up. And so it goes. Every time we get stuck at a turning, it gives the other runners a chance to catch up. When we find the right way, we yell "On, on," and the charge resumes.

Despite having initial reservations, I'm finding it all quite exhilarating. We're running like loonies through tumbledown backstreets, looking for white chalk marks. I even find myself yelling out when I find one, "On, on." Two women sit in a doorway watching me run by. Behind comes a long line of plodding Kenyans in tracksuits and florescent bibs.

At about halfway we find a car parked with the trunk open. Inside are cups of water, slices of melon, and chunks of sugarcane to suck on. Sitting in the front of the car is the woman who was smoking at the start. I'm one of the first to arrive, but soon everyone has caught up. As we stand around eating and getting our breath back, someone says, "Let's have a song." Spontaneously, everyone breaks into a hearty version of "Singing in the Rain," with actions like wiggling bums and sticking out tongues. The people living down this particular backstreet, with its dusty hair salons and mango stalls, stand around in groups, agog.

Although there are a few other *mzungus* in the group, the Hash is mainly made up of black Kenyans. They all drive big cars and are perfectly content to hand over 150 Kenyan shillings ($1.50) just to run, which is more than many people in Kenya earn in a day. After the run, the Hashers drink the night away, with beers at specially reduced prices and rooms booked at the hotel for those too drunk to get home. I've heard stories about humiliating initiation ceremonies for "virgins" like me, so rather than investigate further, I cowardly sneak off under the darkening sky.

◄ ►

In terms of the quality of the running, my sojourn with the Hash House Harriers is like taking a little space capsule to a running club back home for the night. All the bandy legs and beer bellies setting off at a ten-minute-mile pace. One contributing factor in East Africa's dominance of long-distance running is the fact that in the West we're getting slower. Despite all the advances in training technology, nutrition, and physiotherapy, in the increase in the quality and quantity of races, and the introduction of prize money, in the West we're stuck on a conveyor belt going the wrong way. In 1975, for example, thirty-four marathons were run in under 2 hours 20 minutes by American runners, twenty-three by British runners, and none by Kenyan runners. By 2005, however, there were 22 sub-2:20 marathon performances by Americans, 12 by Britons, and a staggering 490 by Kenyans.

For every reason for Kenyan success, we see the opposite trend occurring in the West. While Kenyans lead incredibly active child-hoods, we're becoming ever more sedentary. A recent study by the University of Essex found that even in the last ten years, the average English ten-year-old has become weaker, less muscular, and less able to do simple physical tasks. They're not talking about running three miles to school twice a day, but the most basic activities such as hanging from wall bars in a gym. The academics who conducted the study pinned the blame on our modern lifestyles. The study's author, Dr. Gavin Sandercock, said, "It's probably due to changes in activity patterns, such as taking part in fewer activities like rope-climbing in PE and tree-climbing for fun."

Back in the 1970s we weren't exactly running barefoot, but the majority of running shoes were thin soled and lightweight, much like the "barefoot shoes" selling like hotcakes today. And what's more, we were growing up wearing them, which meant we had good form, strong calves, and higher arches.

Our diets, too, are getting worse. While Kenyans have their carbohydrate-rich *ugali,* we're eating more salt and more fatty foods than ever before. Obesity and diabetes rates are rising. According to the World Health Organization, the obesity rates in the United States and United Kingdom have risen at least threefold since 1980.

Kenyans also have an abundance of successful role models, which encourages them to try running and makes them believe they can be good at it. The success stories are everywhere. Nicolas, the cycling coach from Singapore, says he doesn't have this advantage when it comes to his cycling team. "If we pick cyclists at fifteen or sixteen, they don't want to join us," he says. "They don't have the role models like in running. There are no Paul Tergats in cycling." Of course, the more success Kenyans have, the more that runners from other countries are squeezed out, leaving fewer role models for everyone else.

Scientists have found that the ever-growing perception that Kenyans are better runners can also give them a psychological advantage during races. If a European runner automatically expects the Kenyans in the race to be faster than him, this has the potential to affect his performance negatively, especially if the belief is supported by everyone else around him. Conversely, if a Kenyan runner believes the same thing, that he is faster because he is a Kenyan, it can have a positive effect on his performance.

When a runner from another country does break through, the impact can be significant on the subsequent generation. Before Kelly Holmes won the 800 meters and 1,500 meters gold medals at the 2004 Olympics, for example, Britain hardly had an illustrious history in women's middle-distance running. But five years later, it was a major force, winning 1,500 meters silver and 800 meters bronze in the world championships in 2009.

With fewer role models and less potential for success, fewer people are willing to give up everything for a career in athletics. The fewer full-time athletes you have, the fewer stars are likely to emerge. Put altogether, it's a sliding scale of factors that has all the weights pushed over on one side. It's no wonder the Kenyans are better. The fact that someone like Paula Radcliffe can come through a field so skewed against her to shatter the world marathon record is, in some respects, a minor miracle.

Seventeen

Japhet with his father and niece

There's a metal pole in the ground outside the post office in Iten that all the athletes use as the starting point for their long runs. We line up beside it, gazing up the road into the dawn sky. Two figures appear over the horizon, running toward us. Marietta and the children, looking sleepy, are sitting in the cab of the truck as we prepare to set off on our second Lewa team run. Our two newest recruits,

Philip and Beatrice, are also joining us this time. Godfrey tells us that we need to start faster than before. "But no pushing, Chris," he says. "Just maintain." Chris smirks like a naughty schoolboy not taking his lessons seriously. Godfrey and Chris are good friends, although both think they are the senior partner in their relationship, which means that Chris doesn't like taking advice from Godfrey.

Chris starts off at the front, as if to make his point, but he's not pushing too hard. After a steady few miles, we turn off the road, following the same route as before, and drop down into the fields. Beatrice, however, is already dropping off the pace. I look behind. She has a short, heavy stride, her arms held up high across her chest. Japhet drops back to check if she's okay as the rest of us push on.

I'm determined to make it to twelve miles this time, so as the pace starts ratcheting up, around the seven-mile mark, I let them go. Marietta watches me from the back of the truck, concerned. "Are you okay?" she asks as I drift farther back.

"I'm fine," I say. "Tell Godfrey he doesn't have to wait." She takes a few more pictures as the truck speeds away, chasing after the others in the main group. I'm actually feeling strong, keeping my form, lifting my legs, relaxing my shoulders. I pass the nine-mile mark three minutes quicker than the last run, in 1 hour 3 minutes, and then push on. The last stretch up to the twelve-mile mark is all uphill. By the time I get there, my legs have gone. All I can manage are short, pathetic steps that edge me slowly along, past groups of watching children, calling one another across the fields to come, quick, to see the *mzungu* running past. They sprint like excited puppies across the ploughed earth to see the strange sight. "Fine, fine," I manage to gasp in response to the singing chorus of "How are you?" that follows me the whole way up.

At the top, Chris is already sitting beside Uma in the back of the truck. This time he doesn't give an excuse for why he has stopped. I put on my jacket and take a water bottle. About five minutes later, an exhausted-looking Beatrice looms into view, her 76-minute half marathon looking more questionable than ever. "You okay?" we all ask, as she puts on her tracksuit top.

She breaks into her big smile, happy to have stopped. "Yes," she says, seemingly unperturbed by how far behind she was. "That was good. Very good."

We all hop in the truck and tear off after the others. Godfrey is supposed to give them water and time splits at each five-kilometer point, but we've become so spread out that he can't catch up with them until almost the thirty-kilometer mark. Josphat is the first we catch up to. Then Philip. Finally we catch up with Japhet and Shadrack. They're sprinting now, flying along the lane. Godfrey hands drinks to them as he drives, which they collect calmly, without breaking stride, drink, and then hand back. "Only one kilometer to go," says Godfrey, driving along beside them. "Push now, push, the last kilometer." They race each other up the last hill, Shadrack still wearing his running jacket, drenched in sweat, and little Japhet's matchstick legs, amazingly, keeping up stride for stride.

◅ ▻

"Welcome to my home," says Japhet, as I step in from the steady rain that has settled over Iten today, through a wooden door, and into a darkened room. Along the back wall is a bed, with clothes hanging from a string stretched above it. Sheets hung from the ceiling divide the room into sections. "Sometimes my uncle stays here," Japhet says, pointing to a covered area at the back. A small kitchen section with a camping stove, a few pots, pans, and two thermos flasks for tea, lines another wall. The whole place is about half the size of my bedroom back home.

Newspaper has been stuck all over the walls. Japhet has pinned athletics reports over the top here and there, and he points them out to me, recalling them fondly as though they were describing his own exploits. He has the customary agricultural calendar, and a few medals hanging from the cardboard ceiling. Behind the door is a huge container of water, which he uses for cooking and washing. When the tap in the yard outside works, he refills it from that. Otherwise he walks down to the river, or collects rainwater. "Sometimes if I hear the rain at night, I get up and put my can under there," he says, pointing to the roof gutter.

I sit on the only chair and he sits on the bed. From a folder he carefully slides out his application form for college. He never sent it off because he couldn't afford the fees. The form is kept, though, as testament to his ambition. It's even on his résumé, which he pulls out and shows me. Under "Talents And Achievements" it says, handwritten in blue pen, "Form filled in for Moi University."

He pours me a cup of millet porridge from one of the flasks. It's sweet and warm, bringing comfort from the rain outside. Japhet gets the little money he has for food and rent from his uncle, who works at the gas station in Iten. I ask him about his father. Does he help, too?

"My father is very old," Japhet says, smiling, perhaps surprised that I want to know, or perhaps because he hasn't thought about his father for a while. The memory makes him chuckle. "He married six times," he tells me. "He wanted to have children, but his first five wives didn't produce." Japhet's mother, though, wife number six, started to go mad when Japhet was very young. "She killed my brother," he says.

He refills my cup. The afternoon is quiet. People are in their houses waiting for the rain to stop.

"How did she kill him?"

"She lay on him. She used to burn houses, and attack my father. One morning we found my father bloodied on the floor. He was once a powerful man in the community, with many cattle, but he had to sell many things to pay for my mother's treatment."

Once, when Japhet was just a baby, the neighbors caught his mother trying to drown him in the river. So they put her in a psychiatric hospital in Nairobi. She was there for seven years, receiving treatment. Eventually she was allowed to go home. The doctors gave the family handcuffs to restrain her with when she turned violent.

"One day she tied a bull up in the house and killed it with a machete."

Driving or walking through the picturesque valley slope where Japhet was brought up, it's hard to imagine such madness lying underneath the peaceful surface; lush, green hillocks, fluffy white clouds drifting through a blue sky, the air soft and warm. Chris took us there one time to meet Japhet's family. He sat in his car while we ran down the track to a small, peaceful compound with a round thatched hut in the middle.

An old man was laying asleep on the grass. When he heard us, he leaped up as though he had seen a ghost. "Who are these people you've brought?" he asked Japhet in Kalenjin, panicked, looking around as if he was trying to remember where he was. The only other people living there, in another small mud hut along one edge of the compound, were Japhet's sister-in-law and her baby. She came over to greet us, shy, but strikingly beautiful. A radio fuzzed away, hanging from a nail in the outside wall of her hut. Josphat, who was also with us, told us we had to go. Chris was waiting, he said. So we left them there, standing in the green fields, wondering what had just happened.

In 1999, either from her madness or from the drugs she had to take, Japhet's mother died. Japhet was twelve years old. It was then that he started running. "I still have the school record for the five thousand and three thousand meters," he tells me, pouring the last of the millet porridge into my cup. One summer, Chris convinced Brother Colm to take Japhet in one of his training camps. "I still do the exercises I learned," he says.

Even though he couldn't afford to pay the school fees, the head teacher at his school let him stay because he was running well. "Sometimes he sent me home, but then he called me back when the races were on." At race meetings, he tried to find a coach, but he says they didn't help him. He had no phone and lived in a remote area, so communication was a problem.

When he was twenty-one, he decided to move to Iten to become an athlete. "First I ran by myself to get into good shape," he says. "I was seeing the athletes, how they behave. I tried joining a few groups, but the End of the Road group was the best. They were talking, explaining the routes, bringing a vehicle for long runs. Kipsang was there."

The rain has stopped. A small boy in a fleecy snowsuit comes in, sees me, screams, and runs off. Japhet seems keen to tell me something else before we're interrupted. "Cheboiboch said he would help me. But he left me," he says. The boy pokes his head back around the door, a woolly hat under his hood, snot running from his nose. When I turn to look at him, he yelps and runs off again.

"Now I am learning how to run," Japhet says. "Before, I used to go home too much to help my father on the *shamba*, with the cows. But I was wasting time. I keep correcting my mistakes. I saw Kipsang going to Paris and thought I could do that. Now I don't go home so much, I just focus. I see others going home, not serious."

I imagine what it would mean for Japhet to win something at Lewa. It would justify all these years of perseverance. All those thousands of miles run in the belief that one day they will pay off. His dedication in the face of such odds is humbling. Perhaps Lewa will be his crowning moment. He has been outrunning some good athletes on our training runs. Godfrey has given him some new shoes. "Hopefully you will do well at Lewa," I say. "There are prizes for the top five, remember."

"I will do it," he says, that big grin of his lighting up his face. "I will do it."

Eighteen

Emmanuel Mutai cleaning his running shoes

The One 4 One camp is just a single grass courtyard surrounded by rows of small dormitories. A water tower stands high in the middle, offering some shade. In one corner are some sheds with the words TOILET and SHOWER painted over the doors. It is one of the top training camps in the country, housing some of the very best Kenyan athletes.

Godfrey and I arrive around midday, when the runners are all resting. We walk in and sit down on the grass. Godfrey knows the coach, and a few of the athletes come over to sit and chat with us. I ask one of the more talkative runners what his specialty race is.

"Marathon," he says.

"This is Emmanuel Mutai," says Godfrey. "Second in New York last year, and second in London." He also came second in the world championships.

Chewing on a piece of grass and watching me closely, his long legs folded up under him like a praying mantis, is a young man called Nixon Chepseba. Although he is only twenty-one and hasn't raced much outside Kenya, the coach is full of praise for him, telling me that he has recently broken the 1,500 meters record at the local track by three seconds. In most places in the world, breaking a local track record is a relatively minor achievement, but considering the roll call of athletes who have raced in the Kipchoge Keino stadium in Eldoret, it is worth noting. "He was reading a book on the last lap, he was so easy," eulogizes the coach.

The athletes invite me to spend a few days training with them, and so a few weeks later, here I am, driving my car back down the bumpy track to the camp, just off the main road between Eldoret and the town of Kaptagat. I drive past a tiny makeshift house built from sticks and plastic, stopping in front of two innocuous metal gates. Who would guess that behind this badly bricked wall live some of the greatest runners on Earth? I'm a little nervous as I get out and push open the gate.

At first no one moves to help me. They all stop in mid-conversation, sitting and watching. Then a few of them, realizing who I am, or what I'm doing, come over to hold the gate open for me while I drive my little Corolla through and park it up beside a glistening Land Cruiser.

Some of the athletes are laying on old mattresses and chatting on the grass. I spot Emmanuel Mutai sitting on a stool washing his running shoes in a bucket of water. I go over and sit next to him, hoping he'll remember me. He nods a hello and carries on scrubbing away at his racing shoes. He has three pairs of them.

"Do you remember me?" I ask. "I came here a few weeks ago. With Godfrey Kiprotich." He nods, not looking up. One of the other athletes brings me a cup of tea and a full flask, which he places on the ground by my chair.

"Thank you." We shake hands.

"Thomas," he says, and goes off to sit in a chair.

I turn my seat around slightly so I'm facing the courtyard. One athlete is hunched over the newspaper, peering into it like a man who needs glasses. Nixon Chepseba is playing cards at a small table with another athlete. Running clothes are drying from lines around the edge of the courtyard. A dumbbell made from two old paint pots filled with concrete lies on the floor.

"You feeling ready for London?" I ask Mutai. In a few weeks he's running the London Marathon again.

He looks up. "Yes," he says, then goes back to his scrubbing. He's not as gregarious as I remember. "Are you running with us in the morning?" he asks suddenly.

I ask him what they're doing.

"Thirty-eight kilometers. We leave at five in the morning."

"Yeah, sure. Sounds good." Sounds terrifying, is what I mean. That's almost twenty-four miles. I've never run more than thirteen miles before. But hopefully they will start slowly, like on the Lewa team runs, and I can bail out when I run out of steam. "Will there be a truck?"

"Yes," he says, laying his shoes out on the grass to dry. And then he walks off and disappears into his room.

For the next few hours I sit listening to the runners chatting away in Kalenjin, the words drifting and bumping around in the still afternoon air, my face slowly burning in the sun. Only one of the athletes in the camp is not a Kalenjin. Daniel Salel is a Masai

10,000 meters runner. When the other athletes talk to him, they speak in Swahili, Kenya's national language, but once they get chatting among themselves, he's left sitting, like me, unable to understand anything.

The afternoon sun is just beginning to weaken when I spot Chepseba and another athlete striding around in their running clothes. "You going for a run?" I ask. "Can I come?"

"Sure."

◄ ►

We walk out through the gate, two of Kenya's finest athletes and me. We make an odd threesome as we set off slowly toward the forest. They're both long and sinewy, gliding along through the trees. I feel like a clown stuttering along beside them.

They have just come back from racing indoors in Europe for the first time. Chepseba ended the season with the fastest 1,500 meters time in the world. Luckily, however, this is just a recovery run and the pace never rises above a slow jog. The forest is quiet. Unlike on the trails around Iten, there are no children calling after me, or running along beside me. Just endless forest, the late-afternoon sunlight dappling the trees, the trails soft under our feet as we run in single file unison.

At one point we come up behind a man herding his cows. At the sound of our feet, the cows start to run on ahead of us along the narrow pathway, and so we keep going, chasing them as if in a backward version of a Spanish bull run. Eventually we come to a clearing and the cows skip and twirl out of our way, their big horns spinning around dangerously. We've run a long way with them, and I wonder how the owner is going to track them down again.

When we get back to the camp, the day is starting to cool. Chepseba, stripped down to his waist, hands me a bucket. He starts to fill his up from the outside tap. "Is this the shower?" I ask, unsure. He grins at me, nodding, amused at my confusion. We take the buckets into the shower sheds and then use the cold water to splash ourselves, scooping it up with our hands.

Later I ask the runners why the camp has such basic facilities. The toilets are just holes in a concrete floor. This is typical in Kenya, but these are wealthy men, most of them. The collection of brand-new cars parked just inside the gate is proof of that. But the athletes even clean the toilets themselves, a handwritten schedule on the wall in the common room listing when each athlete is expected to carry out his chores.

"It's what we're used to," says Emmanuel Mutai. It is this way of life that has gotten him to where he is now. To change it would be to risk everything. The athletes know that those who choose to leave the camps to live a more comfortable life often lose their edge. And with so much competition in this one tiny corner of the world, edge is something that is hard to get back once it is lost.

Soon after darkness falls, the supper is dished out. We all sit in the common room, the fluorescent light glaring along the ceiling, building rubble piled in one corner. The walls are bare except for an article cut out from a newspaper about why carbonated drinks are bad for children. Some twenty athletes are cramped into the room, sitting on white plastic chairs, talking excitedly. Almost everyone is wearing the same puffy, black Adidas overcoat.

The cook passes a tray with a mound of *ugali* on it through the window from the adjoining kitchen, then a pot of *sukuma wiki*, which is basically stewed kale. Pages of an old calendar are used as place mats for the pots. While Chepseba acts as head distributor, slicing the *ugali* with a bread knife, adding a side helping of stew, and handing out the food, Mutai sets up a laptop computer on a chair beside the television. We're going to watch a film. Someone turns out the light and quiet descends as we all sit eating with our fingers, watching as Mutai tries to get his DVD showing on the television. Finally it appears to a halfhearted cheer and the film starts.

It's about an American teenager and martial arts fan who somehow ends up in China learning Kung Fu from Jackie Chan. At first he is hopeless, way out of his depth and racked with doubts. "Just don't forget to breathe," Jackie Chan tells him. It's good advice. Gradually, with months of dedicated practice out in the woods, waking up at dawn every day to train, he becomes brilliant. Then he returns back to his small town in the Midwest to duff up the bullies who had been giving him a hard time before he left.

It's engrossingly similar to my story. Will I, too, return home transformed, stunning people with my speed as I streak by like a Kenyan? I look around. I'm the last person still watching. One by one the others have gone off to bed. We have a 24-mile run in the morning. I turn off the power and cross the courtyard to my room. Lightning flashes across the night sky. Mutai has left me an extra blanket in case I get cold, but there's no pillow. I make one using a sheet and my towel, and climb into the bed. One of the runners said he would wake me, but just to be sure, I set my alarm for 4:30 A.M. and turn off the light.

◄ ►

There's a quiet knock on my door. I roll over and look at the time on my phone: 4:40. I must have fallen back asleep. "Okay," I say, swinging my legs out of bed. It's still dark outside, so I switch on the light. It squashes my sleepy eyes back shut. I sit on the edge of the bed for a moment, trying to wake up, but it's cold, so I start to get dressed. In ten minutes we have to leave. We head out through the gate just before five and walk under the stars to the main road. Athletes stand around in the shadows while we wait for a bus to come and pick us up. A young man of barely twenty asks me how far I will run.

"It depends on the pace," I say. "How fast will you run each five kilometers?"

"Probably sixteen minutes, maybe seventeen," he says casually, as though that's a normal pace for a 24-mile run. At 6:00 A.M. At eight thousand feet elevation. A few months ago I ran a 5K race on a flat course back in England. It took me over eighteen minutes, running flat out.

A minibus pulls up and the door opens. Sleepy faces peer back at us. The bus is already full and there are about ten of us waiting outside. Somehow we all squeeze in, with people sitting on each other's laps, or standing bent over, heads squashed against the ceiling. I manage to get on the edge of a seat next to the window and peer out at the passing verge as the driver cranks up the skipping Kalenjin music. Nobody speaks.

Just before six the bus stops on a lonely dirt road in the middle of nowhere. A few people walk by in the darkness, looking over at us as we tumble out of the bus, some of the athletes disappearing off into the blackness for a last-minute pit stop. The rest of us stand around like early-morning workers about to start a shift. I'm fretting about the pace. I won't even last the first five kilometers. A thin, sickle moon hangs in the sky as an orange glow starts to seep in from the east. It's a beautiful, still morning.

We seem to be waiting for something. "What's going on?" I ask one of the other runners.

"We're waiting for the ladies," he says, nodding over to the road where three women are standing holding their watches, getting some last-minute instructions from the two coaches. "They get a ten-minute head start."

A head start is what I need. I run over. "Perhaps I should go with them?" I say to the coaches. "Sure," they say, and a few seconds later I'm running. The pace is gentle at first, but we're soon moving steadily along. Kenyans are brilliant at slowly cranking up the speed on long runs so you almost don't notice you're getting faster. By the third mile we're overtaking bicycles, as streams of people make their way to work. At each corner the road stretches off again far into the distance, and we keep going, without speaking, our feet *pat*, *patt*ing, the miles passing as the day rises into the sky.

At about the tenth mile the men come past us. First the sound of rushing feet, then they go by, their strides strong, their shoulders leaning forward, little puffs of dust kicked up by their feet. One by one they go. At the front is Emmanual Mutai and an Ugandan athlete named Stephen Kiprotich, who came in sixth at the recent world cross-country championships. The others are not far behind.

As they race past, I feel suddenly worse, as though the harsh contrast in speed has stripped away the belief that I was feeling strong. The women are also getting away from me now. They, too, are running thirty-eight kilometers, but the pace is still picking up. Behind me I hear the motor of the bus. As it passes me the side door slides open. The coach, a former Olympic silver medalist, grins at me. "You want a ride?" he asks. It's a beautiful offer. I leap in through the door and sit down on a long empty seat. My heart is pumping, my body tingling to have stopped.

"You know," says the coach, "it is very high up here." He's giving me an excuse, which is generous of him. But it's for him, too. The offer of a lift was more of a command than a question. The bus has to keep moving from the back of the group to the front, handing out drinks, giving out times, and offering encouragement. The farther behind I get, the harder that is to do. But it's okay, I've done enough. In fact, I'm exhausted. I've run just over ten miles in 1 hour 14 minutes, at altitude. That's slightly faster than my first runs with the Iten Town Harriers. Just over a three-hour marathon pace. Could I keep it going for another fifteen miles over similar terrain? I doubt it.

I sit in the van doing my mental arithmetic as we skirt back past the leaders to the twenty-kilometer point. They're really flying now, and still looking effortless. Mutai is racing away at the front, leaving behind at least five or six world-class marathon runners. As we drive along beside him and hand him his water, he seems calm, as though he's out for a morning stroll. He drinks some, pops the lid back on, and hands it back. Only eleven miles to go.

I've been reading previews of the upcoming London Marathon and nobody is mentioning Mutai as a possible winner, despite the fact that he came second the year before. Why is that? I ask the coach.

"That's because people who write for newspapers don't know what they're talking about," he says, turning around to me, grinning. He knows I work for a newspaper. "But Emmanuel is ready. For sure."

Mutai gets to the end of the 38-kilometer run before us, and is walking around beside some wooden buildings, hands on hips, when we arrive. The coach hands him his jacket. A gentle mist drifts between two picture-book hills rising up behind the wooden houses. The red road winds on beyond them.

The other runners come through one after another. Bernard Kipyego, who a few weeks later will come in second in the Paris marathon, followed by Kiprotich, the Ugandan. They all come to a stop and grab their drinks without saying anything. A twenty-four-mile run is a tough session even for these guys. One of the last to arrive is Thomas. He is clearly a junior member of the camp, perhaps not in age but in terms of success. He doesn't have a car, but when he's bored at camp, he likes to wash the cars of the other runners.

"Do they pay you some money?" I ask him.

"No, I like doing it," he says.

Thomas is excited to hear that I'm running the Lewa Marathon.

"I ran Lewa in 2008," he tells me. Confident he could do well, he managed to scrape together the entry fee from family and friends. He then traveled to Lewa the night before the race and managed to stay in some community housing at the wildlife conservancy. In the race he came in third, winning more than enough to pay back the money he borrowed. The One 4 One camp's manager, Michel, signed him up as a result.

Rather than stopping by the van, though, he runs straight past us and off between the two pointed hills. We catch up with him waiting by the road a few miles farther on.

"I wanted to run forty kilometers," he says, looking at me with serious eyes. He hasn't had a race since he joined the camp and is desperate to compete again.

Back at the camp, the athletes are in chirpy spirits. The day's work is done. All that is left now is to rest. Tea is served by the cook, but hardly anyone eats anything. After all that running, on nothing but the ugali from the night before, breakfast is a solitary cup of tea. For anyone who is hungry, like me, there are slices of dry, white bread. It's not much, but it tastes delicious.

Mutai, more relaxed now after his run, stands looking at my car with a few of the other athletes. I walk over. "Where did you get it?" he asks.

"It's my brother-in-law's. You like it?"

He nods thoughtfully.

Bernard Kipyego is smiling. "KXE," he says, shaking his head.

To me, it looks like an old banger, next to their collection of brand-new 4x4s. But it seems to hold grown men enthralled wherever it goes. The camp's track coach, Metto, didn't recognize me when I turned up the day before. Then he saw the car, and he spun around with a delighted grin on his face. "Oh, you, with the car."

Mutai is still looking at it.

"Do you want to see the engine?" I ask. It sounds almost suggestive. He nods, so I pop open the hood. They all crowd around, talking to each other in Kalenjin. Then Mutai looks at me.

"Do you want to sell it?"

◄ ►

Just over two weeks later, I'm sitting in the Grand Pri restaurant in Eldoret waiting for the start of the London Marathon. The owner, former half-marathon world record holder and world 10,000 meters champion Moses Tanui, has promised a London marathon party, and the whole place is decorated with red balloons and posters. Moses and his friends are all wearing red Virgin London marathon jackets, smiling and handing out whistles.

Downstairs in the underground bar area, hundreds of people are awaiting the start on the big screen. The only problem is that there is no power, and the race is about to begin. Moses seems unperturbed. He has a generator, he says. Things will be up and running in a minute. But when the power eventually comes on, about forty-five minutes later, for some reason the only thing any of the TVs can tune in to is a program called *Gospel Sunday*.

We sit and wait. Moses has invited me to watch the race in his personal office, which has the biggest TV I've ever seen. Also watching the race here is a host of other former star runners, including Emmanuel Mutai's coach. Nobody else seems upset that we are missing the race. They sit chatting calmly as the minutes tick by. After a while I decide to see what the atmosphere is like downstairs in the packed bar. On the way down, I pass Moses on the stairs.

"Sorry," he says as he goes by, talking urgently on his phone. He looks slightly traumatized. The bar is completely empty, the last man just leaving.

"The Klique hotel," he tells me. "It has screens."

I leave Moses fretting with a team of engineers and head to the Klique hotel around the corner. It is rammed to the rafters with people cheering and blowing whistles.

By the time I arrive, Mary Keitany has a big lead in the women's race. A few weeks ago I was sitting in awkward silence in her cramped living room drinking orange drink. Now here she is on the television, racing away to win the London Marathon.

The men's race is just beginning to heat up, with Emmanuel Mutai still in the lead pack, running with the same fluid form and easy air he had on the dusty tracks of Kaptagat just weeks before. A big cheer goes up as he surges to the front of the field at around mile eighteen and starts leaving the others behind, and I find myself cheering and blowing my whistle like everyone else.

He seems to be floating through the streets of London. I can see the people standing by the road there marveling, wondering where he came from, how he can run so fast, so easy. His burst is quite spectacular. He puts in the fastest 10km ever run in a marathon (28 minutes 44 seconds) to leave the rest of the field flailing far behind, winning the race in the fourth fastest marathon time in history and setting a new course record. He really was ready.

After the race, I feel a warm glow of connectivity as I tumble out of the bar with everyone else. Outside in the street, I bump into a few of the other runners from the camp. They smile and shake my hand. "Emmanuel ran well," they say calmly, almost expectantly. He has just run one of the greatest marathons ever, but to them it's just another day's work.

Nineteen

*Brother Colm watches over the runners
at his Easter training camp*

Brother Colm says he has been in Kenya so long that he feels Kenyan now. And like a Kenyan he can be difficult to pin down. One morning I call him to see if I can come and watch his star athlete, David Rudisha, training. He says he doesn't know what time Rudisha will run, and when I push him to see if I can come by another day, he gets suddenly annoyed.

"I don't do schedules," he says, spelling it out for me in the overly pronounced way he talks to his athletes. "Rudisha told me last night he had a cold so probably won't train today. But maybe he'll run in Eldoret. Maybe he'll turn up here [in Iten]. I can't say, 'At ten o'clock we'll be doing so and so.' My athletes are elite athletes. They don't need to be in peak shape until August [for the world championships]. They're not like all those runners you see in Iten, running around hoping some eejit will see them and send them off to some race somewhere. I mean, it's a good thing they're out there running, it's better than sniffing glue in Eldoret, but half of them don't know what they're doing or when they're racing or what."

He's less curmudgeonly about his Easter camp. He tells me to come along at 10:00 A.M. any time during the holiday. These camps were among the first training camps in Kenya, and certainly the first in Iten, set up by Brother Colm in the 1980s to help develop the region's junior talent. Japhet went to one of these camps when he was seventeen. He has a treasured photograph from it on the wall in his house. I ask him what he learned there.

"Form," he says, without hesitating. "He taught me about form." It's a common answer. Nixon Chepseba, the 1,500 meters runner at the One 4 One camp, also went to St. Patrick's school and trained with Brother Colm. He says the same thing: Brother Colm taught him about form. It's an interesting answer, since most Kenyans have a lovely, fluid running form, which I assumed was because they all grow up running barefoot. So how is it that Brother Colm's secret is teaching form?

When I turn up at his house, he's just leaving, full of purpose. This, you can tell, is what he loves doing: nurturing the champions of the future. Before the training begins, he takes me around to the school kitchen where a man is cooking beans in an industrial-sized vat. Brother Colm wants to check that the cooks received the *ugali* flour he sent them. I follow behind, smiling and shaking hands with everyone we pass as we head on through the dimly lit dining hall. Along one side, beyond the rows of benches and tables, is the school's Wall of Fame. It's full of framed photographs of runners. If you look closely, you can spot an incredible array of Kenya's most celebrated athletes. There's former St. Patrick's student Wilson Kipketer (three-time world champion and former 800 meters world record holder) planting a tree on the school grounds, while Richard Chelimo and Matthew Birir sit with Brother Colm on a sofa showing off their medals after the 1992 Olympics. Another grainy shot shows 1988 Olympic gold medalist Peter Rono hurtling around a dusty track.

Brother Colm passes through the hall and out onto the field at the front of the school. Groups of young athletes are gathering, ambling across the grass from their dormitories. Waiting for everyone to arrive is a young man called Ian. Although he is only twenty-five, Brother Colm has signed him up as his assistant. Quietly spoken and baby-faced, he doesn't have the air of a coach, but once the athletes are ready, he stands before them and explains the session.

Brother Colm lets him talk, standing with me a few yards away. "I chose Ian because he has a gymnastics background," he tells me. "He understands form."

Ian sets the athletes off jogging around the small field. They jog slowly, in single file.

"We're looking to see which of them have rhythm," Brother Colm explains. "They should naturally fall into the rhythm of the athlete in front."

"What if they don't have rhythm?" I ask, watching one girl who seems to be struggling to match the easy, synchronized flow of everyone else.

"Then we work on them," he says.

Among the athletes, I spot Rudisha jogging around in the middle of one of the groups. The world athlete of the year, the fastest 800 meters runner in history, taking part in a school holiday camp. Not as a mentor or teacher, but as one of the athletes. That's the level of professionalism that these schoolchildren are working to. Their faces are focused, serious. Each has been hand-selected for the camp by Brother Colm, after a winter he spent traveling to school races across the region. An invite to the camp is an honor. But, more important, it's an opportunity. So many have come here and then gone on to become professional athletes. Brother Colm says he has about a 60 percent success rate. I look around, wondering which of these youngsters will be stepping onto the track at the next Olympics. No doubt a few of them will.

All the athletes, I notice, are wearing shoes. "What do you think about barefoot running?" I ask. For some reason it feels like a naive, almost stupid, question, as though I'm asking him if he thinks athletes run better with shorter hair.

"We do all our exercises at the school in bare feet," he says, looking at me, making sure I'm listening. "In the West we put children in shoes before they can walk. What are we teaching them? We're teaching them that the ground is dangerous, that they need to be protected from it. But Kenyan children can feel the ground, so they have a better relationship with it. They learn to place their foot carefully when they run, so they don't hurt themselves. They learn to land gently, lightly, gliding over the earth rather than pounding it."

Brother Colm says he works on form not because he thinks the Kenyans have bad form, but because he wants to turn good form into perfect form. Breaking world records and winning gold medals requires fine polishing of talent. Running barefoot is just one part of a formula that produces that talent, he says. A talent completely derived from their upbringing. "It is a hard, physical life, one that makes them strong, disciplined, and motivated to succeed," he says. "When the athletes come to me at fifteen or sixteen, they are sixty percent already there." By working on their form, he is giving them the tools to nurture that talent and strength, born out of hardship, and turn it into gold.

After the training, we head back to the dining hall for a mid-morning snack of jam and Blue Band margarine sandwiches. I sit with Brother Colm and Ian, while the athletes sit at an adjoining table eating dry slices of bread. "They don't like jam," says Brother Colm, reaching for another sandwich and then leaning back against the peeling wall, his feet up on the bench. "So these are just for the coaches."

We sit for a moment in silence, munching on the sandwiches, the sound of pots clanking in the kitchen. I'm still mulling over his comments out on the field. I ask them if they've heard about the born-to-run theory that humans evolved through running.

"We had Daniel Liebermann here," says Ian. "He was a nice man." Liebermann was one of the Harvard scientists who developed the theory. He came up with it in part by studying Kenyan athletes. I feel like I'm at the very source of the story. This retired Irish priest and his twenty-five-year-old Kenyan assistant are an unlikely pair of sages.

"After Mike Boit won his Commonwealth gold medal," Brother Colm says, sitting up and putting his feet back on the floor, "they held a big celebration in his home village." Mike Boit, a former student at St. Patrick's, won an Olympic bronze medal in the 800 meters in the 1972 Olympics. In 1978 he won gold in the Commonwealth Games. "At the celebration, his childhood friend came up to him. The two of them used to run around together as children. He shook Boit's hand. 'That's all very well,' he said, pointing to his gold medal. 'But can you still catch an antelope?'"

Brother Colm is leaning forward, watching me, a half smile across his face. Chairs screech across the floor behind us as the athletes all get up and head back outside. They had been so quiet, I had forgotten they were there. Brother Colm sits back against the wall, as though snapping shut a book. That's it, my lesson is over. He has seen many people over the years coming to discover the secrets of the Kenyan runners. Even that morning, a camera crew from Ireland has been setting up, preparing to spend the week following him, no doubt wanting to discover the Kenyan secrets.

"We even had one man from Sweden who wanted to analyze the *ugali*," he says, pulling plastic wrap over the tray of sandwiches. "I told him to bring some of the flour home to test it, but he said he needed to cook it at altitude, in Kenyan water, in a Kenyan pot." Brother Colm is incredulous at the stupidity of it.

"Did he discover anything?" I ask.

"Absolutely nothing," he says, almost spitting in delight.

"You people come to find the secret, but you know what the secret is? That you think there's a secret. There is no secret." I haven't mentioned a secret, but he's fuming now, his arms folded across his chest.

Ian, sitting opposite him, as serene as a poet, suggests that we head outside to see the athletes again before they disappear for their midday naps.

◄ ►

Brother Colm may be convinced that there is no secret to Kenya's running success, but it hasn't stopped an endless number of scientists from coming to Kenya to conduct studies to try and unearth the magic formula. What intrigues many scientists is the fact that most of Kenya's top runners come from one particular ethnic group, the Kalenjin. In 2011, sixty-six of the world's top one hundred marathon runners were from Kenya, almost every one a Kalenjin. Long distance running is one of the most popular participation sports in the world, and Kalenjins account for just 0.06 percent of the global population. It's such a staggering dominance, one of the most remarkable in all the annals of sport, that most people, particularly casual observers, will just throw up their hands and say, *It must be in the genes.*

It is a scientific fact that genes have a significant affect on athletic performance. One person can train for months, getting up at dawn every morning, turning on the *Rocky* music, eating the right food, and will still struggle to break two hours for a half marathon. While another person, with the same upbringing, can show up with minimal training and breeze around in 1 hour 20 minutes. That's down to genetics, or, as we usually refer to it when we're not talking about East African runners, talent.

Genes determine how tall we are, how well we respond to training, the color of our skin, and our gender. The effect of gender on athletic performance is so marked that we split the competitors up. So genetics plays a role in how fast people run, that much is clear. That top athletes are all people with a genetic advantage toward their discipline is also fairly certain. What is less clear, however, is whether Kenyans, and more specifically Kalenjins, have better running genes than people in other parts of the world.

So far there is no scientific evidence that they do. Yannis Pitsiladis has been working tirelessly on this for at least a decade now, spending months on end conducting tests in a laboratory in Eldoret's Moi University, and he says he can't find a single gene or group of genes unique to East Africans to explain their phenomenal running success.

Without the hard evidence, but in light of the huge discrepancy between the size of the Kalenjin population and its dominance in running, many people have looked elsewhere for indicators of genetic advantage. One theory is based on an outdated Kalenjin custom: cattle rustling. Before the British settled in the region at the beginning of the twentieth century, bringing with them new crops and agricultural techniques, the Kalenjin people were largely cattle herders and, often, cattle raiders. The Nandi and Kipsigi ethnic subgroups were particularly aggressive cattle rustlers. Their raids would often take them hundreds of miles from home, after which they would run back with their stolen animals as fast as they could before the owners could catch them. It was a dangerous game that only the fittest, strongest, and fastest runners survived. The better a young man was at raiding, the more cattle he accumulated. The Kalenjin were, and to a lesser extent still are, a largely polygamous society, and so the more cows a man had, the more wives he could buy, and the more children he was likely to father. The theory is that this reproductive advantage may have caused a significant shift in the Kalenjins' genetic makeup over the course of a few centuries, leading to them becoming better runners.

American journalist John Manners, who was partly raised in the Rift Valley, believes that this is the case. "If you weren't good at running," he says, "you were more likely to get killed. If you were [good at running], you were more likely to have children."

A few years ago John set up a program called The Kenya Scholar-Athlete Project (KenSAP), which sends top students to elite colleges in the United States, such as Harvard and Yale. The idea was based on John's belief that virtually all Kalenjins can run. He thought that if he picked the top students from the Rift Valley region, the ones with the best grades on their high school exams, perhaps half of them would be good enough at running to interest the track and cross-country coaches at U.S. colleges, who might then help process their applications. The first year he managed to get scholarships for six students, two of whom he thought were good enough to pitch directly to the track coach at Harvard.

"But it didn't pan out," he tells me. "Once they got there, the students weren't committed enough to the training. They were scared of missing their studies. Essentially, they were duds."

So the experiment failed? If anything, it showed that not all Kalenjins can run after all, right? "Not quite," John says. The next year he put his potential scholars through six weeks of training and got them to run a 1,500 meters time trial, so he had a better idea of which ones to pitch as runners to the American colleges. "In seven years, we've sent seventy-six kids to top U.S. schools," he says. "Of those, twenty-eight were pitched as potential athletes. Fourteen didn't pan out, mainly through lack of commitment. To be on a team at a U.S. college means around three hours of training a day."

Fourteen of his seventy-six A-grade students turned out to be decent enough runners to make the varsity track or cross-country teams. Of those, four were the best athletes in their college, three became All-Americans, and one became a nine-time division three champion. "From what was essentially a random selection of Kalenjins, these achievements are pretty impressive," John rightly points out. "It leads to the conclusion that there is something special about the Kalenjin."

He's right, of course. There *is* something special about the Kalenjin, but I'm not as convinced as he is that it necessarily suggests a genetic advantage. Although none of the students he sent to the United States were athletes before they left—they were too busy studying—they all benefited from active childhoods, no doubt running to and from school, probably barefoot or in flimsy, thin-soled sneakers. They were raised at altitude. They benefited from a carbohydrate-rich, low-fat diet. So they all came to John with a strong, built-in endurance base—their house, as Renato Canova would put it, was already built. So much so that when pushed into running, they were physically ready to go. Of course, some people just aren't great runners, but if we really were all born to run, as some scientists argue, then to get fourteen good runners from a selection of seventy-six fit, healthy teenagers is perhaps not such a surprise.

If you took a comparable group of English or American students, chances are that they would have spent their lives doing very little physical exercise and eating bad food. Stuck on a track and asked to run 1,500 meters, most of them would probably look at you as if you were mad. They would probably never have run that far in their lives, except perhaps on some forced cross-country race in first grade. Would it be such a surprise to find that only one or two of them, if that, could run?

Yannis Pitsiladis says that he has heard the cow-herding theory, but that it doesn't add up. "There just isn't enough time," he says. "Genetic adaptations take thousands of years, and besides, the Kalenjin are not an isolated gene pool, they have been mixing with other ethnic groups. It's a nice story, but that's all."

Of course, just because the hard evidence hasn't been found yet doesn't mean that Kenyans, and more specifically Kalenjins, don't have a genetic advantage. But I don't think we should hypothesize that they do simply on the basis of their performances in races. Not only is that unscientific, but it seems that there are enough other contributory factors that, when taken together, explain Kenya's running dominance. Presuming a genetic advantage also diminishes the incredible achievements of the Kenyan athletes. If they do have a built-in genetic advantage, it changes the way we perceive their victories. It lessens our admiration for all their hard work, determination, and fortitude. It also changes the way other athletes feel about their own chances of competing, of even trying to compete. It's dangerous to conclude that because so many people from one ethnic group win so many races that they must therefore have a genetic advantage. If that's the case, the rest of the world might as well give up.

Twenty

*"If we push on, we begin to feel a vague, tingling
sense of who, or what, we really are."*

"Finn," says Godfrey cheerily when I call him up. "Great to have
you back."

I've been to Ethiopia, Kenya's northern neighbor and the world's
other great running nation. I ran a half marathon there in the town
of Hawassa, about 170 miles south of Addis Ababa. The race was
organized by Haile Gebrselassie, who has a luxury hotel on the
shores of Lake Hawassa.

The night before the half marathon, I bumped into the former
British marathon runner Hugh Jones in the hotel lobby. He told me
he was now an IAAF official and was there to measure the course.

"It's not a PB course," he told me when I said I was hoping to run a personal best time. "It goes off-road along by the lake and the path is quite bumpy."

Still, after all my training, even with the bumpy trail and the altitude (around 5,500 feet), I was hopeful. I'd been training harder than I'd ever done. I felt leaner than I had felt in years. I had visible calf muscles for the first time in my life.

At the start, I was relieved to find the competition less intimidating than the cross-country in Eldoret. The field had been split into two races, an elite race and a mass race. I was in the mass race, along with lots of other foreigners, mainly aid workers based in Addis Ababa. The Ethiopians in the race were mainly aid workers, too, as far as I could gather.

Almost immediately after the horn sounded for the start, I found myself running on my own, with a lead group of about six runners pulling ahead, and everyone else disappearing somewhere behind me. The course headed along a road into town and then detoured down along a dirt track by the lake. Fishermen stopped their work as we ran by, frozen like photographs, their nets half drawn in. A herd of glistening horses hauled themselves up out of the water, crossing the path. The runners in front of me managed to skirt around one side, making the horses skip back. I spotted my chance and nipped through the same gap. I was feeling strong, and starting to reel in the leaders.

Halfway around the second of three large laps, I caught a glimpse of my shadow on the paved road and was surprised to see that I actually looked like an athlete, striding along the wide avenue. Seven miles done and I was feeling great, running at a good pace. "Good, good," people said as I cruised past.

By the time I passed the same point on the third lap, however, it wasn't such a glorious sight. My stride length had shortened, my arms had stopped moving. I was struggling with cramping, which forced me to stop for a moment by the lake and do some stretching. It kept coming and going. The slower I ran, the better it was. Or was that just my mind playing tricks on me? I was caught in a battle of wills between my desire to run as fast as I could, and my body's desire to slow down.

But the desire to run fast was being drowned out by the internal chatter that told me it didn't really matter what time I ran, or where I finished, that nobody really cared, not even me, that I should just enjoy the experience. I ended up virtually jogging the last mile, up the long road to Haile's resort, past a troupe of threadbare white horses grazing among half-built apartment blocks.

Here at the end, the road was lined with spectators, three-people deep, who clapped quietly or just stared out from under their shawls. The runner ahead of me was too far away to chase, and I couldn't see anyone else behind. As I reached sight of the finish, I saw the excited faces of Marietta and the children. They were all smiling and clapping and I mustered a little surge to the line in their honor.

Despite talking myself down from pushing too hard, I managed to finish in seventh place, in a personal best time of 1:26:47. The seconds were important because it was a best time by just seven seconds. The great man, Gebrselassie, was standing there waiting to greet me like a long-lost friend. I gave him a sweaty hug then walked on to collect my medal and free T-shirt.

"That's great to run a PB," Godfrey says when I tell him my time. But it's hard to know how I feel afterward. After four months of training with the greatest runners in the world, I'd knocked seven seconds off my best half-marathon time. With only six weeks left until the Lewa Marathon, I was really hoping for a bigger improvement than that.

"You did brilliantly," says Marietta when I suggest I'm not happy. "You were right near the front." It was certainly better than my performance in Eldoret, so at least I was moving in the right direction.

◄ ►

Sitting by the hotel's infinity pool the next morning, overlooking the dark waters of Lake Hawassa, I was still brooding on the race. I thought hard about how I had lost the psychological battle, running along that long, straight road, my resolve blown away like a silk scarf in the wind. I just wasn't ready, mentally, when the crunch came.

"You've said this before," said Marietta, trying to help. "Is there anything you can do about it? Anything you can learn?"

She was right, it had happened to me before in other races, my mind whispering in my ear, *What's the hurry? Who cares?* until I went, *Okay, you're right,* and I eased down. Kenyans are not so flaky in races. Partly, it's simply because they're usually nearer to the front. During my win in Powderham Castle, such thoughts didn't bother me. Driven on by the growing belief that I could actually win, I managed to stay focused until the end.

But it's not just that. For a Kenyan runner, driven on by a will to change his life, the stakes are much higher. Even for top Western runners, winning a race is unlikely to have the same impact on their lives as it will for a Kenyan runner. For someone who has spent years living at a subsistence level, even one thousand dollars can change everything.

Kenyans are also more used to hardship in their daily lives, so that when it appears rising up at them near the end of a race, they are less cowed by it. One theory about why Kalenjins, specifically the men, are so psychologically tough, comes from the circumcision ceremony that all Kalenjin boys have to go through as adolescents. They are expected to stand in front of the village elders and endure the pain unblinking, without betraying a single flicker of emotion on their faces. One wince and their passage to manhood is forever incomplete and they are cast aside from the community as a coward. Many athletes have told me that after passing through such an ordeal, all other challenges they face in life, such as a sprint finish at the end of a race, seem easy.

Another reason why Kenyans may be mentally tough is that they seem to spend less time analyzing while they're running. If you ask a Kenyan runner what was happening in his head during a race, he will usually say something as simple as, "I felt good, so I ran faster" or "I felt tired, so I stopped." A Western runner, in contrast, will be able to tell you exactly what his thoughts were at each mile, what his time splits were, how his tactics changed during the race. Many of the Kenyan runners I meet tell me that they don't wear a watch when they're racing, that they prefer to run on feeling. For most Western runners, this would be a dangerous approach. It would be like going on a long car journey and switching off the speedometer and fuel gauge.

But as Renato Canova said after one of his Kenyan charges won a big city marathon in the United States recently: "If you want to be a top athlete you have to be a little bit wild, not be an accountant." Wild like Ismael Kirui in Stuttgart in 1993, who went with his feeling, spurred on to a crazy pace with seven laps still to go. He wasn't calculating his average lap times that night, he just felt good and went, and he ended up as world champion.

So what I can learn from the race in Hawassa is that next time I need to be mentally prepared, to find a way to keep my focus and willpower locked in on the target, and to keep my distracting and debilitating thoughts at bay. I don't want to end the Lewa Marathon dawdling home like a tourist on safari, telling myself that I'm too tired to run, that I should just watch the wildlife and not worry about the minutes rushing away, the people streaming past me. I didn't come all this way, and do all this training, to flake out right at the end.

But without the same driving forces pushing me on as the Kenyans, what should I do? I've heard people say that they have their own special chant that they use. I remember Paula Radcliffe once saying that she managed to outrun the great Ethiopian Gete Wami to win the New York marathon by chanting "I love you Isla"—Isla being her baby daughter—over and over in her head. Maybe I should try that next time, although I can already hear my mind reasoning that my kids don't really care about my race position or what time I run. But then, I'm sure Isla didn't care either. What really pushed Paula on was her love for her daughter, not her daughter's approval. But why should love make her run harder?

The actor Sean Connery was once asked in an interview what, if anything, made him cry. After thinking for a few moments, he replied, "Athletics." I often feel the same way. Watching runners racing for the finish line, relying on nothing but themselves, their own willpower, fighting their own limitations, their eyes fixed ahead in complete focus, the dedication of years of hard work etched across their faces, it can bring tears to your eyes. Running is a brutal and emotional sport. It's also a simple, primal sport. As humans, on a most basic level, we get hungry, we sleep, we yearn for love, we run. Just watch small children left to play unsupervised. They can't stop running. It is part of what makes us human.

Perhaps it is to fulfill this primal urge that runners and joggers get up every morning and pound the streets in cities all over the world. To feel the stirring of something primeval deep down in the pits of our bellies. To feel "a little bit wild." Running is not exactly fun. Running hurts. It takes effort. Ask any runner why he runs, and he will probably look at you with a wry smile and say, "I don't know." But something keeps us going. We may obsess about our PBs and mileage count, but these things alone are not enough to get us out running. We could find easier ways to chart and measure things. We could become accountants. No, the times and charts are merely carrots we dangle in front of our rational mind, our overanalytical brain, to give it a reason to come along for the ride. What really drives us is something else, this need to feel human, to reach below the multitude of layers of roles and responsibilities that society has placed on us, down below the company name tags, and even the *father, husband, son* labels, to the pure, raw human being underneath. At such moments, our rational mind becomes redundant. We move from thought to feeling.

Except our mind doesn't just stop. Many runners say that they become aware of their thoughts when they run. All day our thoughts churn away, turning us this way and that, but this doesn't bother us in the slightest. Yet the minute we start moving away from its carefully constructed world of reason, into the wild heart of existence, our mind panics. Our thoughts try to pull us back, to slow us down. But like the marathon monks of Mount Hiei in Japan, who complete one thousand ultra marathons in one thousand days in search of enlightenment, if we push on, we begin to feel a vague, tingling sense of who, or what, we really are. It's a powerful feeling, strong enough to have us coming back for more, again and again.

Love, too, connects us with a primal feeling deep within us, far from the realm of reason, which is why Paula's chant worked. The love she felt for her daughter and the raw emotion of running come from the same source. Evoking love helped push her on, even though rationally it shouldn't have made any difference. Her daughter couldn't hear her internal chant, and even if she could, at nine months old she was oblivious to the whole concept of marathon running. But by calling on such a strong emotion, Paula was able to bypass such reasoning. Her rational brain, which was telling her, no doubt, to slow down, was overcome.

I decide to try it the next time I'm struggling on a run.

Twenty-one

Preparing the ugali

It's Easter Monday, and a beautiful, lazy afternoon in Iten. All morning the streets were deserted as the entire town crammed into the tin churches that sit on virtually every corner. The preachers did their best to outdo one another, their sermons blaring through speakers placed out in the street in an effort to spread the gospel as far as possible.

It's the last day in town for Marietta and the children. For the next few weeks they are going to stay with Jophie and Alastair in Lewa, leaving me to immerse myself in my running. Marietta asks me to take a walk with her through the neighborhood one last time, down to the viewpoint that looks out across the valley. Lila and Uma are off playing with their friends, running along the rows of houses, laughing, and disappearing through doorways. So we take Ossian and wander off down the lane that runs along our high metal fence, past the little kiosk. A lady is digging a small square of earth with her daughter. She stands up as we go by, dropping her hand plow and mopping her brow.

"Marietta," she says. "Where are you going?"

"Just for a walk," says Marietta. "It's my last day in Iten today."

The woman looks shocked. "Why?" she asks. "You should stay and buy a plot here." The woman is a single mother with two children who works at the hospital, runs a little shop, grows maize, and owns two cows for milk. She asks us if we have a cow back home in England, and gives us a look of disbelief and pity when Marietta tells her that we don't. "Then you must buy one when you get home," she says.

As she's talking, one of her cows lumbers across the mud toward the fence, which gets Ossian excited. He has a stick in his hand and is poking it through the stakes and making a noise like a cow herder. "Rarr, rarr," he says, hitting the fence with his twig. The woman laughs as we start to walk on.

"Leave me to my struggle," she says, waving us on our way.

All along the path, we pass small homesteads with families sitting outside preparing food or just drinking tea and talking. Each time, the children run over, giggling and reaching out their hands, while the mothers wave at us.

"*Iyamune?*" we say. It means "how are you" in Kalenjin.

"*Chamage,*" comes the reply. Everyone is fine.

"It seems a shame to be leaving now," says Marietta. "I feel that we're just settling in. It's starting to feel like home." We turn the corner and the sky opens out before us. Small houses continue to dot the landscape farther down the slope, dropping away into the hazy distance. "It's beautiful," she says, stopping to admire it as Ossian ambles along behind us. "I love the way that when you wake up in the morning here, the first thing you do is step outside. In England we're always cooped up in our houses and cars, like in little bubbles, removed from everyone else."

"You think you could live here?" I ask her. Even though she is right, and there is something enviable about the simplicity of life here, I'm not sure I could make the leap to living here. I don't really know why, but somehow I feel tied to my life back in England.

"I don't know," she says.

◅ ▻

Despite feeling settled in Iten, we stick to our plan and I return from Lewa alone, racing Alastair's little car up the Uganda highway, dodging the trucks and *matatus*, winding my way up the patchwork slopes, past the scenes of numerous accidents, and back to the little town of runners.

As usual, the first sight that greets me on arriving in Iten is scores of people running alongside the road. On and on they go, day after day, tearing up mile after mile, in the hope, as Brother Colm puts it, that some eejit will send them to a race. Well, for a few of them, that eejit is me.

I call up all the other Iten Town Harriers to see how they are and to arrange another long run that weekend. We're running out of days now, so it's time for me to make it to eighteen miles.

I'm going to spend my last few weeks in Iten at the Kimbia training camp. This is where Godfrey works, and he has invited me to stay. I've gradually realized, however, that he doesn't really work there. It's a complicated story and different every time, depending on who tells it. The camp was originally set up by a U.S. agent who employed a German coach to train the athletes. But the coach started to become an agent himself, so they split the camp in two. Godfrey was a multipurpose operator—part coach, part scout, part facilitator. But the German coach took a dislike to his laid-back style, and banned him from the house. Neither of the agents live in Kenya, however, and all the athletes like Godfrey, so he comes back surreptitiously now and then when he needs somewhere to stay in Iten. He also invites his friends to stay.

When I first arrive, the only person staying in the house is Anders. He seems happy to have some company, and shows me to my room. "You've got the best room," he says. "It has a great painting on the wall." The painting is a map of the world, painted by some Peace Corps volunteers who stayed here once. Otherwise the room is fairly sparse: a blood-red, chipped concrete floor; two single beds with mosquito nets tied up above them; and a piece of string running from one end of the room to the other for hanging clothes.

A few days later, three of the camp's athletes return from a spell of racing in Germany. They come bustling in one evening, shaking my hand and settling down quickly in front of the television. They've been missing their Mexican soap opera. The TV room is more like a storeroom than a place to relax. There's a fold-up table right in front of the television, a massage table shoved into one corner, three stacks of plastic chairs, and piles of running shoes by the door, next to an empty glass cabinet. The athletes pull out enough chairs for everyone and place them in a circle around the television as Mama Kibet, the camp's cook, brings in a small charcoal stove, which she places on the floor in the middle of the room. The three of them are in heaven when she brings the *ugali*. As they eat hungrily, I ask them if they missed the *ugali* while they were in Germany. They all nod vigorously, their mouths too full to speak.

While we had our own house in Iten, we ate a mixture of Kenyan food and food that the children were more familiar with, such as pasta and soup. We had *ugali* occasionally, but now it is part of my daily diet. I tuck in, trying to will it on, telling myself to enjoy the frugal blandness of it. Mixed with the stewed kale that Mama Kibet has given us it's nice, but on its own, especially after it has gone cold, it feels fairly pointless. The other athletes, in their excitement, try to get me to eat more, but really, I've had enough.

◄ ►

The Kenyans are always joking that it is the *ugali* that makes them so fast. It's not as far-fetched as it might seem. While this staple by itself may not be the secret of Kenyan running, it is a small part of the puzzle that I'm gradually putting together. As Yannis Pitsiladis says, after years of research: "It's not any one thing. But all of them." As well as the physical, active nature of a typical, rural Kenyan childhood, the altitude, the barefoot running, and the intense dedication, the diet of the athletes plays a role, too.

In the Rift Valley, everyone grows up eating a diet full of carbohydrates, with very little fat. Beans, rice, *ugali*, and green vegetables are the staple foods. Occasionally the runners will eat meat or drink milk. It is very hard, in Iten at least, to find cakes, ice cream, cheese, burgers, pizzas—all those fatty foods that we love so much in the West. They just don't exist. When our neighbor Hilda had a party for her tenth birthday, her mother had to get a cake driven in from Eldoret.

Dr. Pitsiladis tells the story of a group of German scientists who wanted to study the Kenyan physiology, but rather than conduct the research in Kenya, they brought some runners back to Germany. "The interesting part for me is that after just two weeks in Germany, the athletes all put on eighteen pounds," Dr. Pitsiladis says.

When I visited the house in Teddington before leaving for

Kenya, one of the athletes asked me, as he stood stirring the *ugali*, how much I weighed. The others were sitting in the kitchen listening to our conversation. The last time I had weighed myself, I was 175 pounds, but I'd been training quite hard, so I knocked off a few pounds. "Seventy-seven kilos," I said. (That's 170 pounds.)

The runner looked at me surprised, and even stopped stirring for a second. One of the other athletes said something in Kalenjin, but I could tell by the tone of his voice that he was asking for confirmation from his friend that what he had just heard was really true. "Seventy-seven kilos?" the athlete asked me, to be sure.

"Yes," I said. "Is that a lot?"

He nodded, still unsure he was hearing me right. He said he was 130 pounds, while one of the other athletes was only 112 pounds.

Two weeks before we leave Iten for Lewa, I manage to find a scale in the gas station where Japhet's uncle works. I'm 152 pounds. I've lost eighteen pounds since leaving England. Of course, all the running is a significant factor, but so, too, is the diet. With hardly any fat in the food I consume, I'm now fighting weight.

Godfrey rings me that night to see how I'm settling in at the Kimbia house, and to tell me there has been a change of plan regarding our Lewa team's long run the next day. The truck has been double booked, and he doesn't sound as though he has the energy to find another one. I suggest that we drive to Eldoret in my car and run back along the paved road. He sounds distracted as he agrees, telling me it's a good idea.

We decide to leave at 7:00 A.M. to mimic the start time of the marathon in Lewa, but when I call Chris, he's not happy. "It's too late," he says. He's also unhappy about the route. "Only *mzungu*s run along the paved road," he says. I tell him we don't have a truck to go off road. Reluctantly he agrees to be picked up just after seven, outside his school.

At 6:30 the next morning my phone rings. It's Chris.

"Hello, sir," he says. "I'm at the school. I'm ready. We need to get started."

Anders has decided to come along, too, so after we get dressed and fill up our water bottles, we roll the car out of the gate and head off to find Japhet and Beatrice. Beatrice has turned up with a friend. I guess she's feeling a little outnumbered by the men on our team. Having a friend will also give her someone to run with, but it means we're now five in the car. Luckily, the team is depleted today, with Shadrack and Philip not running. Josphat also hasn't turned up.

"He's gone to the U.S.," Japhet tells us.

"What for?" I ask, surprised. "Is he coming back?"

"He's gone to race. I don't know when he'll be back."

Even though Chris is good friends with Josphat, he, too, is surprised when he hears the news. "That is not good, man," he says. "He should have at least informed somebody."

Godfrey as well is full of consternation. "He must respect the team," he says, shaking his head. "It's not good."

Personally, I don't mind. He was a troubled character, Josphat. One time we went to visit his home down in the valley. He hadn't seen his wife or children for at least a week, but he just barged into the house, picked up a bag, and left again without a word of greeting to them. His children stood around in bare feet and ripped clothes, watching with their big, silent eyes as we climbed back into the car. I waved a solitary good-bye as Chris started the engine, and we left.

Josphat is certainly no big loss for the team. In fact, everyone is already suggesting we replace him with a good mutual friend named Paul Tanui. Known as The Preacher because of his religious fervor, Paul is one of the nicest men in Iten. When you talk to him, everything is always "fantastic." Like Josphat, Paul is a veteran journeyman athlete who has won numerous smaller races around the world. He is excited when I ask him if he'd like to run with us in Lewa.

"Yes," he says, his voice swooshing the word like a balloon lifting off into the sky. "Of course."

Once we get to Eldoret, Chris starts remonstrating with Godfrey about the route. Why are we running along the paved road back to Iten? he wants to know. Godfrey isn't sure.

"Finn, do you really want to run on the road?" he asks. Kenyans very rarely run on concrete, and having driven along the road from Iten just now, I can see that it's not the nicest run. But I'm worried about the car going off road.

"I know another route nearby," says Godfrey. "Just a few miles away. It's very flat. The car will be fine."

So we pile back in and start out along another paved road. Unfortunately, this road is so potholed it's like trying to drive across stepping stones. I have to keep to a painful crawl, the morning sun rising higher into the sky with each passing minute. Chris grins at me. "I told you," he says, "seven o'clock is too late."

I slalom around the road, left and right, for around twelve miles, with Godfrey telling me at every corner that we're almost there. His promises begin to become meaningless after an hour or so. Eventually we get there. It's a relief to get out of the car. We're in a tiny settlement that's built up around an intersection between two roads, with just a few houses, a gas station, and a school.

We all get ready as Godfrey talks us through the route. This time I'm doing eighteen miles—my longest run ever. As we line up at the start, Godfrey gives us his now customary pep talk, with Chris doing his customary best to look like he's ignoring it. "Right,

as we all know, this town is called . . . ," Godfrey begins, glancing
around. He looks at Chris. "What's this town called?" he asks.

◄ ►

Anders, Beatrice, her friend, and I get a ten-minute head start, running along a straight, flat road that stretches out before us like a
thin pencil line, cutting the landscape in two. I'm wearing a cap
given to me by Anders's mother, Joan Benoit. She has just been in
Iten visiting him. Not really knowing much about her career, I
looked her up on the Internet and managed to find a video of her
Olympic victory in 1984. Amazingly she broke away from the field
with twenty-two miles still left to run and just kept plowing on, a
look of steel on her face as she kept on pushing, unrelenting, until
the end. All the while she had her cap pulled low over her eyes.

I pull my cap down, like blinkers, focusing, ignoring everything
else but the rhythm of our feet. We run mostly four abreast, not
talking. The miles tick by. Beatrice is doing a much better job of
keeping up with us this time. Once in a while Anders pushes the
pace a little, but we claw him back each time with our steady, steady
patter. We pass the occasional house, but mostly it's a deserted landscape, drier here than in Iten. The sun is high now, soaking us with
its heat.

Godfrey, in my little car, pops up from time to time, hopping
out with his arms full of water bottles, telling us to "Maintain,
maintain." Six miles. Ten miles. Shortly after we pass ten miles, we
hear a rushing of feet behind us as Chris and Japhet stride past.
Nobody speaks.

Soon after, Beatrice starts to fall off the pace, and then at twelve
miles Anders stops. Chris has stopped, too. I run by, along the dusty
road. My head is too hot for the cap now, so I throw it to Godfrey. I
feel released, as though everything up until now was only a warm-

up. I push on, leaving Beatrice's friend behind, racking up the miles, feeling like a long-distance runner. The road is more hilly now, but my legs are strong. The car, with the others in it, passes me.

"Good job, Finn," says Anders from the window, as they pass and drive after Japhet, who is off ahead somewhere on his own. I see Beatrice looking out of the back window of the car. She must have stopped at twelve miles, too.

The dust from the car lingers in the air for a while. It's just me now, in the middle of nowhere, running. I find myself smiling. It's like I'm on one of my childhood runs, imagining I'm running across the plains of Africa. I feel fine. The road slopes down and I feel myself striding strongly, faster than ever. I can see the car stopped ahead. They're all waiting. I sprint up to them, grabbing my water bottle as I stop. Eighteen miles. And still standing.

"Well done, Finn. Good running," says Godfrey.

I stand by the car, smiling. "Thanks."

I ran the 18.6-mile route in 2 hours 7 minutes. Considering the altitude and dirt road, that isn't too bad. Another 7.4 miles in under fifty-three minutes and I'd run a sub-three-hour marathon. It suddenly feels within my grasp. Even in Lewa. We've run late today. It won't be that much hotter in Lewa. And the altitude will be lower. I'm suddenly progressing quicker than I had expected.

Japhet walks over, still looking fresh after finishing in 1 hour 48 minutes. We shake hands, the only two to make it to the end today. Once I've recovered, we pile back into the car and begin our slow, bumpy way back to Iten. When we get on the paved road, it's better, although we still have to watch out for police checks. All around Kenya, police stand at the side of the road waving people to stop. Then they walk around the car looking for something wrong. Anything will do, a broken mirror, a bare tire, too many people in the car. At first I never seemed to get stopped, or when they did wave me down, they'd usher me on when they saw that I was a *mzungu*. I don't know if perhaps it was because I began to look more like I belonged here, but after a few months I started getting stopped. One time I was driving with Anders and his mother when a policeman waved us down. He had a serious look on his face as he patrolled around the outside of the car. I sat still, not wanting to annoy him. He circled around, then stopped by my window and told me to get out. He said I'd been driving dangerously, overtaking a truck on a black spot. The road was straight in both directions.

"How is that a black spot?" I asked, looking around at the road.

He gave me a tiny smile, as though that was hardly the point.

As we were driving, Joan had been wanting to stop to use the bathroom, so when I saw her hop out of the car and scuttle away toward the bushes, I knew where she was going. The policeman watched her, a small, elderly white woman with short gray hair. Anders got out of the car and came over to help.

"We were trying to catch our friend who was driving too fast," Anders said by way of explanation, which was true. We were following Godfrey in another car. But it wasn't exactly a good excuse. The officer looked at Anders's running shoes.

"Are you athletes?" he asked.

"Yes," I said, noticing a tiny thaw in his demeanor. "You see that woman who just walked off?" He nodded, hearing me out. "She's an Olympic champion," I said.

He smiled, as though I was trying it on. "That lady? In what?"

"Marathon." He could tell I was serious. He was shaking his head, but in wonderment rather than disbelief. She was shuffling back now from the bushes.

"Joan Benoit. She won the gold medal in Los Angeles in 1984," I told him. Joan walked up to us.

"Madam, can I shake your hand?" he said, bowing his head.

Joan, unsure what was happening, shook his hand, looking at us for an explanation. "It's an honor to meet you," he said. Then, turning to me, smiling like a teddy bear now, "I'll let you off with a warning."

"Thank you," I said, and we all hopped back in the car and drove off in search of Godfrey.

Twenty-two

Track racing in Iten

Time passes slowly at the Kimbia camp. After their morning training, the athletes sit on plastic chairs as Mama Kibet stands in the kitchen cooking up the rice and beans for lunch. A rooster struts around the garden letting out the occasional belated crow, while Mama Kibet's sheep forage nervously at the edges, pulling at the short grass with their teeth.

Mama Kibet is a kindhearted woman, always laughing. You only have to tell her you enjoyed your lunch and she's off, giggling away. One day I ask her why Godfrey was banned from the camp. It seems unfeasible that anyone could take a dislike to Godfrey. He

seems the most benign person on earth, always making sure everyone else is happy. In fact, without a real job, he seems to have made
it his life's work to help people.

"You know, in Kenya, people are not straightforward," she tells
me. She doesn't want to elaborate further, but it adds another layer
of mystery to Godfrey's character. Anders and I often sit in the garden and wonder if everything is as it seems with him. He tells us he
has a wife in western Kenya who is a police officer. He has a son at
the expensive Kip Keino school. He has a house and land just outside Eldoret, and another house down in the valley. However, considering that Godfrey is the world's friendliest man, neither of us
has ever seen anything of his life. Three times he has invited me to
have dinner at his house with his wife, and three times he has can-
celed at the last minute.

The athletes in the camp are of no help when I ask them about
him. They just smile and shake their heads, saying, "Oh, Godfrey,
he's so funny." So it is with a sense of intrigue that I set out with
him one morning on a trip to visit his mother at the family home
down in the valley.

As ever with Godfrey, the plan is a complicated one. We need to
drive about two hours out of Iten along the edge of the escarpment,
where we plan to meet with Shadrack's training partner, David Barmasai. The road down into the valley is too steep and bumpy for my
car, so Barmasai is going to lend us the truck he has just bought
with his winnings from the Dubai marathon. Later we're going to
meet him back at Shadrack's parents' house, where it sounds like
I'm going to be the guest of honor at a big feast.

"They were going to slaughter a goat for you," Godfrey tells me
as we sit waiting for Barmasai. We've parked up beside a small row
of wooden shops pegged onto the edge of the cliff. The sky stretches

out above the valley, as people stand outside the shops watching us. "I told him," Godfrey says, laughing, "'Before you kill that goat, you should know, Finn is a vegetarian.' He was so happy he didn't have to kill the goat. He's going to kill a chicken instead."

Godfrey tries ringing Barmasai, but there is no answer. He should have been here forty minutes ago. A man pulls up beside us on a bicycle. In his basket he has an upside-down sheep. He unties the legs and then hauls it out and ties the rope that's around its neck to a tuft of grass. Then he rides off.

"That must be strong grass," I say, watching as the sheep, without hesitating, simply carries on with its interminable mission in life, to eat. Godfrey tries ringing Barmasai again. This time he gets through.

"He's on his way," he tells me after he has finished talking. "He said they ran later than usual today. I told him it's fine, we're athletes, we understand that training comes first." The man on the bicycle returns with another sheep, which he unties and places down next to the first one. Then he rides off again.

As we wait, Godfrey tells me the story of the time, years ago, when he took an American friend back to his house in the valley. He'd been away racing for quite a few months and arrived back at the house in the middle of the night. "I tried to open the door, but it wouldn't budge," he says. "That's strange, I thought. Then I heard this noise, a hissing noise, and I thought, oh my god."

"What was it?"

"I knew what it was. It was the hissing sound of termites. There was a termite mound behind my door. Inside my house. My friend looked nervous. I told him there could be a snake, because snakes like to sit on termite mounds. As soon as I mentioned snakes, he started running away." Godfrey chuckles as he tells the story. "He got into the car and locked the door. When I went to talk to him he only rolled the window down a tiny bit, enough to hear, he was so nervous. Then he wound it back up again."

Godfrey found a machete and managed to slide it around the door and knock the termite mound over. It crashed down across his bed. "There was mud everywhere. When I went in, I was scared because there could be a snake. I had to sleep on the floor in another room." His friend was still in the car when he woke up in the morning. "He wouldn't come out until he saw me," says Godfrey, shaking his head at the memory.

Finally, about two hours later than arranged, Barmasai arrives, and after swapping cars, we set off.

The road down into the valley has to be one of the most spectacular drives I've ever experienced. A 4,000-foot descent down the side of a sudden, jagged cliff, giving way to steep, sloping fields that slide out into the dry valley below. The road passes through different climates, from thick jungle air down into the dry, baked sunshine of the Fluorspar mine at the bottom. Toby Tanser once told me that I couldn't leave Kenya without running Fluorspar. It's a rite of passage for any aspiring athlete. Moses Tanui claims he ran it every second week before he won the Boston Marathon in 1996. From the bottom, to the shops at the top where we met Baramsai, is exactly 13.1 miles. A half marathon. Uphill all the way.

"Shall we do it with the team before Lewa?" I ask Godfrey.

"Sure. We have to." It takes us almost an hour to drive down, the road is so bumpy. I can't imagine how long it will take to run up it.

◄ ►

By the time we arrive at the gates to Godfrey's family home, it's almost three in the afternoon. The place has a still, lazy feel to it. People sit under the trees and watch as we drive past, too hot to be surprised. The gates open into a little oasis of green grass and tall pine trees, with two neat little houses that look like Swiss chalets nestled at the bottom. "Welcome to my home," says Godfrey as we drive in.

As we step out of the truck, Godfrey's mother walks over to greet us. She has a proud, weathered face with sharp eyes. She's wearing a gray two-piece suit, a colorful headscarf, and a pair of running shoes.

"She always likes to look smart," Godfrey says. She gives me a firm handshake. *"Karibu,"* she says, looking straight at me.

Mama Godfrey worked her whole life in the Fluorspar mine, initially smashing rocks with the men, but eventually as a messenger in the office. She lived with her family in a small company-owned house, and even though her husband left her, she worked hard to send her firstborn, and only, son to St. Patrick's high school in Iten. He wasn't a runner, but once there he met Brother Colm and started doing well in races. One day his cousin, the athlete Joseph Chesire, turned up at the school and asked Godfrey for his identity card. Godfrey, not sure what was going on, handed it over.

"Right," said his cousin. "I've got you a place in the army." Godfrey didn't really want to join the army, but it was a chance to live as an athlete and get paid. "He thought it was the best thing for me," Godfrey explains. Unfortunately, unknown to any of them, Godfrey's scholarship to study in America had just come through, but it was too late. He was a soldier now.

"Brother Colm was so mad," Godfrey tells me. "He's still mad with me today." It seems a shame, he would have made a good student. But as an athlete, Godfrey ended up spending a lot of his time in the United States winning races. He also ran for Kenya numerous times and once finished fourth, ahead of both Paul Tergat and Moses Tanui, in the world half-marathon championships. The boy from the Fluorspar mine did good.

Inside Godfrey's house, which was the first thing he built with his race winnings, the table is laid out with an array of food. Mung bean stew, rice, chapattis, beans, bananas, ground nuts, and freshly made mango juice. I'm starving.

Piled up in one corner of the room are six old suitcases.

"This is my old stuff," says Godfrey, opening up the top case. It is full of magazines, running vests and shorts still wrapped in plastic, medals, and trophies. Among the early 1990s Puma vests and tights, he finds an old copy of *Athletics Weekly* magazine. I skim through it, thinking he must be in it somewhere. I find a page listing the year's world rankings. There he is, Godfrey Kiprotich, ranked ten in the world for the half marathon.

"So funny," he says, pulling out an old Kenya tracksuit. "This is from when I was a junior."

His mother comes in and speaks to him. He looks around.

"Come on, we must eat," he says, realizing where he is. "My mum is worried that we're not eating."

◄ ►

By the time Godfrey has taken me to visit the local school and the mayor of the town, it's getting late. To get to Shadrack's home we need to wind our way up another dirt road that seems to skirt endlessly along the edge of the valley, going up and then down, passing through settlements lost in time, with colorful wooden houses basking in the late afternoon sun. Finally the road careens across a clacking bridge and then up an incline so steep that we have to attempt it three times, the truck's wheels spinning and sliding on the loose gravel.

Shadrack's house is back at the top of the escarpment, perched on a narrow ridge sticking out into the vast horizon. It clings to the edge of the world like the home of a wizard in some fantastical painting. All around it the land falls away so it feels as though it's almost floating in the air. The curves of the distant hills, faded now in the last light of the day, push up from below.

It looks like we've arrived too late to eat. I don't know if the chicken was saved, or has already been eaten. Children and neighbors crowd around to meet Shadrack's exotic visitors. His mother, pretty despite a few missing teeth, wears a dirty overcoat, shaking hands shyly, looking down. His father, older, grinning, proud of his son for bringing such visitors, walks over. He looks as though he has come straight from the fields, dust and sweat dried onto his tough skin. He has a wispy beard and is also missing some teeth.

We stand there awkwardly as the night closes in, chasing away the day's warmth. The children run around giggling, touching my clothes. Shadrack, not used to being a host, stands to one side watching. Smoke is rising through the grass roof of one of the small, round huts. Suddenly, two car lights come swinging around at us from the nearby field. It's Barmasai with my car. We walk over, followed like Pied Pipers by hundreds of children. I'm ready to get back to Iten. We still have about three hours of driving to do, and I've got a morning run to think about.

I shake hands with everyone and then clamber into my car. Shadrack gets in the front beside me. For some reason Godfrey is with Barmasai in the truck. I follow them out of the field, leaving Shadrack's parents and the children peering after us at the disappearing taillights, their faces glowing red for a second before the darkness closes in, reclaiming them.

◄ ►

A week later I'm back in Fluorspar, standing with the Iten Town Harriers posing for a photograph. The road stretches off innocently ahead of us, beginning up a gentle slope. From there, though, it winds and switches back again and again, snaking its way up the side of the valley for thirteen miles. My aim is to keep running the whole way.

On the way down, the other runners discussed the Fluorspar record. It's only a training run, so there are no official records, but they seem to think the fastest time ever is in the region of 1 hour 26 minutes. That's for a half marathon on a route that ascends more than four thousand feet.

Godfrey, as ever, starts us off with his pep talk. He will be right behind us in the truck, he says, handing out water every five kilometers. "It's hot, so it's very important to drink water all the time."

Chris seems more impatient than ever to get going this morning. He called me at 4:30 A.M. to tell me he was ready to go. I still had another thirty minutes' sleep planned before my alarm was due to go off. A few minutes after I spoke to him, I heard Godfrey's phone ringing in the other room.

Besides the Lewa team, David Barmasai has joined us for the run, which should be a good test for young Japhet. Barmasai has just been selected to run the marathon for Kenya at the upcoming world championships.*

"Okay," says Godfrey, "Let's go."

We start off easy in a big group. Beatrice, looking feisty, seems to be pushing the pace at the front. She has a tenacity that's hard not to admire. She rarely speaks when we meet, but when she does, it is always with certainty that she will run well in Lewa. In every training run she starts off at the front, full of confidence. And no matter how far back she drops off the pace, she remains undeterred.

Hill running has never been my strong point, so I'm not expect-

---

*A few months later, Barmasai ended up finishing fifth in the world championships in Daegu.

ing to stay with the others long, but to my surprise I make it around the first two switchbacks in the middle of the pack. Then suddenly they change gear, and they're gone.

Sure and steady, I tell myself as I pitter-patter along, avoiding the biggest stones, trying to take the shortest line around the innumerable corners. I manage to edge my way past Beatrice and her friend, who has joined us again, but the others are farther and farther ahead every time I look up, until they disappear completely.

People stand by the side of the road to watch me as I pass. At first they're friendly and I greet them happily. I'm feeling fine, just taking my time. But as I go on, I start to feel faint. Godfrey hasn't appeared yet, and we must have passed the five-kilometer point. The more tired I get, the more piqued I become. Where is he? I imagine Barmasai thinking we are very unprofessional. *Come on, Godfrey.* I'm not even that thirsty, but it's becoming a distraction. I keep expecting to see him before the next switchback, but he never appears. I don't know if I'm imagining it, but everyone I pass now seems to be laughing at me. It's like a bad dream: the manic laughter, the endless dirt road, the aching in my legs, the pounding sun. And still no sign of Godfrey.

At one point a slow-moving truck comes up behind me. It's barely moving faster than I am, and so for about five minutes it feels like it's following me, its straining engine grunting at me to move aside. I keep running, glancing up at the driver as the truck finally grinds past. He looks at me from his cab, expressionless. At least he's not laughing. Up and up I go, until the mountains that towered above me when I began look like small hills down below. Up and up, back and forth, into the cooler air. Ahead, the clouds cling to the rock face that holds back the highlands.

As I run, my mind keeps speculating how far I have left to go, suggesting that I slow down. I decide to try Paula Radcliffe's chant.

I tell myself that I love my daughter. *I love you, Lila,* I say to myself. *I love you, Lila.* Amazingly, I feel suddenly lighter, as though I've thrown off a heavy cloak. My feet start picking up their pace, switching back and forth under me with an easy flow. *I love you, Lila.* But then I feel bad for singling out Lila. *I love you, Uma,* I say. *I love you, Uma.* But now something has changed. I'm slowing down again. I've been tricked. My mind, like a double agent, has undermined the power of the sentiment by distracting it, mimicking it. I look at the hill rising up, endlessly up. I try again. *I love you, Lila.* But it feels too calculated now.

For a second, though, the chant worked. Maintaining it against such a slippery adversary, however, was not easy. Perhaps I just need to save it up for the crucial moments, when all hope seems lost and I'm about to give in.

The road goes on, turning around and back, around and back, up and up. Just before the end, Godfrey finally appears in the car. A woman, who turns out to be his sister, hands me my drink from the passenger window. I've no idea where she has come from.

"Godfrey, what happened?" I manage to gasp, handing back the water.

"I couldn't start the car," he says, looking distraught. "Sorry."

I push on, refreshed now, until finally I reach the top. My legs are wobbly as I stand there feeling like Edmund Hillary on the peak of Everest. The other runners are all sitting on the grass, drinking lemonade and eating peanuts and boiled eggs as though they've just been out for a gentle stroll.

Japhet, it turns out, was the first one to the top, ahead of Barmasai. Little Japhet. We're going to have to start taking him seriously, I think. He smiles his toothy smile as I tell him how hard I found it. "It is hard," he says.

In the end it took me 1 hour 58 minutes. The other runners

kindly tell me that anyone who can run it in under two hours is "very strong." They, of course, all ran it much quicker, in just over 1 hour 30 minutes. After all this time in Kenya, I still really have no idea how they do it.

As we stand around talking, Godfrey pulls up. He has Beatrice in the truck with him. She ran out of steam at about eleven miles, he tells me later. "I'm worried about her," he says. "How can she run a marathon if she can't do that?"

◄ ►

Back in Iten, there's a buzz around town. The circus and pageantry of the Athletics Kenya track series has come to town. For weeks we've been reading about the results of the other races in the newspaper, stories of Olympic champions being beaten by barefoot upstarts. The biggest race, the last one on the calendar, is a two-day extravaganza in the Kamariny Stadium in Iten.

I make my way up into the stands, ready to watch the action. Godfrey is milling around talking to all his old athlete friends. I'm sure they all come to races just to chat and socialize, as they rarely seem that interested in watching the running.

The meeting itself is a mixture of haplessness, improvisation, and brilliance. In some of the field events it feels like the organizers have simply plucked a few random passersby to compete. Men in Wellington boots fling the discus, while at the pole vault mat the marshals sit chatting and waiting to see if anyone turns up. Nobody does.

The high jump features a host of tall, skinny athletes who rush at the bar and karate kick themselves over. Despite all lack of conventional technique, they manage to reach the impressive height of over six feet, contorting and twisting their bodies somehow up and over the bar.

It all feels a bit like a school sports day, a commendable effort, a bit of fun. That is until the distance athletes file onto the track. Then, suddenly, this sodden track that sits on the edge of the clouds, the vast Rift Valley spread out far below, becomes the stage for some of the most fiercely competitive racing you could find anywhere in the world.

In the men's 1,500 meters, there are nine heats with around twenty athletes in each one. When the starting gun fires, they charge off like sprinters. In the 5,000 meters they seem to start just as fast. And there are just as many runners.

But despite this race being the highlight of the series, none of the most famous Kenyan athletes have turned up.

"They know you can't run fast times on this track," one former runner tells me. The dirt track sits at an altitude of over eight thousand feet, and, by all accounts, is about ten meters too long. So the stage is left to those looking to make a breakthrough. The hundreds of Iten hopefuls filing in through the gates, string shoe bags on their backs carrying borrowed spikes, weave through the crowds to sign up at a small table.

The 800 meters heats, eight of them in all, are run at a break-neck speed, each won in around 1 minute 49 seconds. The 5,000 meters is won in just over fourteen minutes. These are times that would put these athletes near the front in the British national championships—although, of course, those are run at sea level and on an all-weather track that measures precisely 400 meters in circumference.

Japhet runs in one of the 5,000 meters heats, after arriving too late to enter the 10,000 meters. He looks like a child beside the other runners, his short legs moving twice as fast just to keep up. He seems to be holding his shorts the whole way around, and I hope he's not injured. He finishes around the middle of the field in 15 minutes 33 seconds. I go over to talk to him. "Are you injured?" I ask him. He seems dazed, surprised to see me.

"My shorts are too big," he says. "I had to hold them up." Not owning a pair of shorts, he had borrowed some from a friend. Chris spots us and comes over.

"Hello, my friends," he says. "What time did you run, Japhet?" Japhet looks at his watch. "Fifteen thirty," he says.

Chris looks at me in surprise. "Oh, man," he says, laughing. "That's a girl's time." Japhet smiles, but I can tell he's hurt by the comment.

"Don't mind him," I say. "That's a good time on this track." But Chris is already gone, off to talk to another of the former athletes hanging around in the infield. I spot Daniel Komen striding around, looking worried, trying to keep the show on schedule. Japhet, keen to get some clothes on, hurries off, too, leaving me to watch the next race from the inside of the track.

Interestingly, some of the athletes at the back of the races trail home in fairly slow times. I'm amazed to see 1,500 meters runners finishing in times slower than I used to run at school. I know the track is slow, but surely not that slow. The reason is that every athlete sets off as though he is going to win. Even after just two hundred meters, some athletes have started so fast that they are dropping out, sheepish grins on their faces, disappearing off the track and into the crowd. If they don't drop out, those who went off too fast at the beginning end up jogging around to the finish.

Most Kenyan runners that I meet have a strong belief that they can win almost any race regardless of the opposition. They will make outlandish predictions about the times they hope to run, and afterward, when they don't run them, they will just laugh and say: "Next time I will do it."

Among the crowd, I bump into Brother Colm's assistant, Ian. I ask him why everyone starts off so fast. "It's okay," he says calmly. "They already know how to train, but here they are learning to race. After this, they can run in Rome or Oslo."

This is the breeding ground for the great Kenyan runners of tomorrow. They may have natural talent—I see that every day on the roads in Iten—but now, here on the track, the final piece of their apprenticeship is taking place: racing. And it's interesting to see that this is one area where they still have a lot to learn.

◄ ►

On my way home I bump into Paul Tanui, the runner who has replaced Josphat in the Iten Town Harriers. He has been at the track to watch the racing.

"Hello," he says, shaking my hand.

"Are you ready for Lewa?" I ask. It's only a few weeks away now.

"Yes," he says. "But, listen, what are we doing about visas?"

"Visas?"

"Yes, when are we getting them?"

"Lewa is in Kenya," I say. "We don't need visas."

"In Kenya?"

I feel like apologizing. He obviously thought I was taking him abroad to race. One last payday. The problem with racing in Kenya is that the competition is so much tougher, it's harder to win. The outrageous depth of talent just milling around in this tiny corner of the world is illustrated by a telephone conversation I have that same afternoon. I've been trying to pin down Wilson Kipsang, who leads the End of the Road early-morning runs. He's a fairly decent runner even in these parts, ranked in the world all-time top ten in the marathon with a time of 2:04.* Godfrey, who knows everyone, gives me his number, except that by mistake he gives me the number of a completely different person, someone called William Kipsang. Not knowing that, I dial the number.

"Hello."

"Hello, Kipsang?"

"Yes."

"It's Finn here, the *mzungu* writer."

"Eh?"

"We've met a few times. I was talking to you at the track yesterday."

"Eh?"

"Is that Wilson Kipsang?"

"No, William."

"Oh, I thought your name was Wilson. The two-oh-four marathoner, right?"

"No. Two-oh-five."

Even if you dial a wrong number here, you can end up speaking to a person who has run a time three minutes quicker than the British record, set over twenty-five years ago. No wonder Paul was hoping to race abroad.

---

*On October 30, 2011, Wilson Kipsang ran the second fastest time in history, 2:03:42, narrowly missing the world record by four seconds, in the Frankfurt marathon in Germany.

Twenty-three

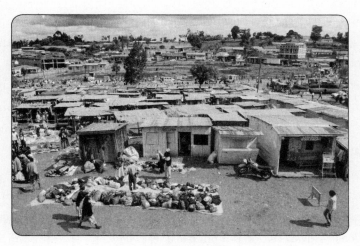

Market day in Iten

"I guarantee that it's nothing," Anders tells me. "It's just because you're getting nervous about the race." I've got a sore foot. I've tried to ignore it for a few days now, but every time I run it feels worse. I can hardly even walk on it. And this time it's not a bent toe from standing on a stone, it's the whole side of my foot. "Then again, it could be plantar fasciitis," he says.

Plantar fasciitis is every runner's worst nightmare. It strikes out of nowhere and the only remedy is to stop running. But I've got only a week now until the race. I can't stop. If worse comes to worst, I'll just run through the pain. I have to make it to that start line in Lewa, no matter what.

The athletes at the Kimbia camp are in no doubt about what I need: a massage. One of the great things about Iten is the ready supply of massage therapists. Some of the former runners retrain in massage after their careers end, or after they fail to take off, and every camp has a man on hand to give the athletes a regular rub down. With very few physiotherapists around to treat injuries, the Kenyans are keenly aware of the value of massages in preventing problems in the first place. Massages release built-up tension in overworked muscles and stimulate the circulation of blood and lymph fluids. Afterward, all the little aches and pains from training are gone, leaving you with a clean pair of legs to punish all over again.

If an injury does set in, a good massage therapist can work on certain trigger points, pressing on them like crazy until you want to scream, to break down knots in the muscles and release tightness. It doesn't always work, but often it does.

The athletes outside the camps, such as Japhet, who can't afford to pay for a massage, have to improvise. Often when I see Japhet, he tells me how he's feeling good after his weekly treatment. "Who gave you the massage?" I ask him one day.

He looks a little downcast, as though I've broken the illusion that he is just like one of the top athletes with a massage therapist on hand. "Henry," he says. His friend from the kiosk. They massage each other, he tells me. And if Henry is not around, Japhet massages himself. Still, as long as you don't press too hard, even a back-street massage, or a self-massage, can help drive fresh blood into tired muscles and rejuvenate them. For runners like Japhet, it's better than nothing.

At the One 4 One camp, the athletes would go in gingerly one at a time to see the massage therapist and spend an hour or so yelping in pain. At one point when I was there, I went in to see what was happening. The massage therapist was up on the table trying to exert as much pressure as he could on Emmanuel Mutai's calf.

Since I've been in Iten I've been mostly avoiding massages, mainly because they're so painful, but now that I'm hobbling I'm worried that that was a big mistake. I call up the massage therapist who was torturing Emmanuel Mutai. He says he will come over straight away.

Over the next three days I get two intensive treatments. During the first treatment, in the Kimbia camp, my feet feel as though they've been in a medieval torture chamber. He presses and presses, chuckling to himself when he hits a pressure point. As I grit my teeth and try to hang in there, he asks about England or my family as if he's simply giving me a haircut. Just when I think I can't take any more, he finally stops. I feel mentally exhausted, and my foot still hurts. He tells me not to worry, that it will be fine for the race. I hope he's right, because a few days before we're due to leave, I'm still limping.

For the second massage, he asks me to come to a house in Eldoret near to where he lives. I've arranged a good-bye lunch with the athletes in the Kimbia camp on the same day, but I'm sure I can fit it all in. Mama Kibet is cooking up pots of beans when I leave. "I'll get back as soon as I can," I tell her as I reverse the car out of the gate and onto the muddy road.

The house where I'm to meet the therapist belongs to a runner. It's a small concrete box down a waterlogged side road. The runner ushers me into a tiny sitting room, chasing his sister and a young child out the back door at the same time. We all sit down around a table.

"First we must eat," says the runner. "As you are the guest in my house." One by one, his sister, mother, and wife carry in large pots of beans, rice, and meat and place them on the table. I'm hosting my own lunch in an hour and I haven't had the massage yet. Next come the plates, a flask of tea, cups, forks, and napkins.

By the time we eat and I get my massage, laying facedown on the sofa, while the runner sits talking to me between my grimaces, it's past one. I make my excuses and head out, refusing, reprehensibly, another round of tea.

As I leave, the massage therapist gives me a small jar of Menthol Plus balm to rub on my feet. On the box it has a picture of a man rubbing it on his head. "This will help?" I ask skeptically.

"Yes, yes," he says, smiling. "You will be fine. For sure."

And so, with my hobble and my jar of headache balm, I get back in the car and return to Iten.

◄ ►

The Kimbia garden has been laid out with a long table surrounded by plastic chairs. Japhet and Henry are there, wearing puffy overcoats and sitting awkwardly among the other athletes. They both get up as soon as I enter and shake my hand. They seem a little startruck to be in the camp, even though none of the athletes here are particularly well known. Beatrice is also there, sitting in the corner sheepishly, trying to blend into the background. She gets up and shakes my hand and then sits back down.

There's a knock on the gate. I open it and Tom Payn walks in with Raymond, Mary Keitany's brother-in-law. Anders is helping Mama Kibet bring out the food. I'm still full from my first lunch, but I can hardly refuse to eat at my own farewell meal. Mama Kibet piles the food up on one of the biggest bowls and hands it to me. "Thank you," I say, raising my eyebrows at the size of it, which sets her off giggling as she starts ladling the food out for the others.

Tom asks me what time I'm hoping to run in Lewa. After my last few training runs, I'm secretly hoping to get somewhere near three hours, but after my half marathon in Ethiopia, and with the heat, the hills, the altitude, and the off-road terrain in Lewa, perhaps I'm being too optimistic. Tom thinks 3 hours 30 minutes would be a more realistic goal.

The other Iten Town Harriers are less circumspect about their chances, of course. When they hear that the race is usually won in around 2 hours 21 minutes, they look happy. "Two hours twenty-five minutes will probably win you some money," I tell them, having studied the previous years' results in detail.

"I will try," says Japhet, struggling to contain his excitement. They all think they can run at least 2 hours 15 minutes, even in Lewa.

Beatrice, too, is hopeful when I tell her that anything under three hours could win her a prize. It seems a very slow time for a Kenyan athlete, but I'm doubtful she can do it. One evening just a few days before, she joined me, Japhet, and Henry on a slow jog. It was the sort of easy run that is not meant to be testing, but just to keep the body ticking over, and ease out any stiffness. Sometimes on these runs the pace gets quite fast for me, but that evening it was very gentle. We chatted as we jogged along past endless small fields, Japhet asking me about England and how slow people run there. After a while, though, Beatrice started to drop behind. We slowed down but she told us to go on. She had a cramp, she said, holding her side. She was still smiling, but it was the first time I'd ever seen a Kenyan athlete struggling with a cramp, or at least admitting to it. As we ran on, I told Japhet that I was worried about Beatrice, that she might struggle even to finish Lewa, but he was as optimistic as ever. "She is strong," he said. "She will be fine."

◄ ►

Mama Kibet is bringing out a huge bowl of fruit salad for dessert. She has made us quite a feast.

"Where's Godfrey?" Japhet asks, putting down his half-finished bowl of beans.

It's a good question. I call him up on his cellphone. "Finn," he says. "I'm just coming."

"Where are you?"

"I'm in western Kenya," he says. "My wife has got malaria."

"Is it bad?"

"Yes," he says gravely.

"Shouldn't you stay with her?" I've been worrying for weeks that he won't make it to Lewa, that something else will happen at the last minute to prevent him from coming. With Godfrey, something else always happens.

"Yes, I might not make your lunch," he says.

"That's fine," I say. The food would be cold, anyway, as he's about a three-hour drive away. "But what about Lewa?"

"No, no, I can't miss Lewa," he says. "No way."

"But what about your wife?"

"She will be fine." It's only two days until we leave. I hope he's right.

I go back to the lunch. It's a happy scene, even without Godfrey. Beatrice is chatting with Raymond, who is dressed neatly in a white shirt, holding his bowl carefully so as not to spill anything. Japhet is chatting with runners from the camp. I'm glad he's getting a decent meal a few days before the race.

Someone outside is beeping for us to open the gates. Two of the athletes from the camp unbolt the lock and hold the gates open as Chris's car slides into the yard, almost bashing into the table. He climbs out of the car, a big, mischievous grin on his face. "Sorry, man," he says. "I had to sort some things out at school."

Twenty-four

"Strength does not come from physical capacity. It comes from an indomitable will."—Mahatma Gandhi

My alarm goes off at 5:45 A.M., as it has many times over the last few months. I reach out from under the mosquito net and switch it off. I get changed into my running clothes and head out into the darkness. Although I felt I should rest my foot until the race, everyone has recommended that I go for one last run before we leave for Lewa. It's a fitting way to say good-bye to Iten.

My foot feels fine as I walk between silent houses, past stinking piles of rubbish, and down to the main road. It has rained during the night, but not too much. A shadow passes by me in the darkness. Down in the town the *matatus* are already circling, lights on, looking for passengers. "Yes, *mzungu*," one conductor says as I walk by. "Eldoret?" I shake my head. I walk up past St. Patrick's school and start off on a slow jog. Ahead of me, the half moon glows in a lightening sky, flicking between the trees as I run. Some children in school uniforms, walking the other way, watch me pass.

I head out past the edge of town and into the countryside. Mist hangs blue in the dips, thick and magical. Pointy-roofed huts and neatly sown fields rise up here and there, the red track stretching out before me. I run on, like Dorothy, through a strange, Technicolor world. And who is that I see now, running toward me, his bright yellow jacket glowing in the first rays of sunlight? The scarecrow? It's Japhet, grinning to see me. He turns and runs beside me, back the way he came.

We run together, easy, passing bigger groups, people running hard, the sweat beading on their anxious foreheads, pushing themselves on in search of the elusive Oz, sure that someday, if they just keep running, they will get there.

Japhet tells me he has a calf injury, but he doesn't seem too worried about it. "I've had it for a long time," he says. "But it will be okay." I guess you have to be prepared for a few niggles if you're going to train for a marathon, even if you're a Kenyan.

It's interesting to note that the runners here still get injured despite their barefoot upbringing, but the types of injuries they get are different. "I don't see many impact injuries," the physiotherapist at Lornah's camp tells me one day. These are common injuries in the West, and are usually the most serious and debilitating; things like runner's knee, shin splints, plantar fasciitis, and stress fractures. In my time in Kenya, I haven't met a single athlete suffering from any of these problems. If someone is injured, it is always something less serious, such as a tight hamstring or a pulled calf muscle. Or a cut leg.

Chris turned up at my good-bye lunch at the Kimbia camp with a huge gash in his leg. He said he fell while out running. It looked nasty and was heavily bandaged. After showing me his leg, he started telling me he had been getting up at 4:00 A.M. to train. It's a strange thing to do. At that hour it's too dark to run. No wonder he fell over. And why did he need to run so early? "To get extra training. I might surprise you and finish in the top ten," he said, as though it was some wild boast. When we first started training, he was talking about winning the race. This is a man who has run the New York marathon in 2 hours 8 minutes. He doesn't need to prove anything to me.

A few nights earlier he invited me to his house for dinner. He lives in a small compound near St. Patrick's school in Iten with his wife and five children. Inside, it's like any other Kenyan runner's house. The walls are covered in Christmas decorations, bright posters of Alpine landscapes and inspirational quotes, and free calendars. On the shelves are bulbous, supersized trophies from Boston, San Diego, and other places.

He takes me out into the yard to show me his room for relaxing. It's a former garage with a few battered old sofas in it, a massage table, and a beautiful mahogany chaise longue. Next door are the staff rooms, although they all seem empty. All the buildings are on top of one another, crammed into his small bit of land, with little space around them. He shows me one of the rooms. A shabby bed is hidden behind a huge cabinet in the middle of the room, its back to the door. "You see how nice it is kept?" he says.

As we sit waiting for supper, he hands me his photo albums. Pictures of him and his wife in Nairobi. He looks young and innocent, his tracksuit waistband pulled up high as he poses proudly beside some tall buildings. For all his slipperiness, Chris is a good man. His talent for running has lurched him from a simple life of farming into an infinitely more complex world where he is expected to be a role model, a picture of success. It's a tough act to hold together.

He sits under the flickering fluorescent light like a king in his big armchair, the pink velvet curtains folded up behind his head. His kids bustle around the cramped room, dark, handsome faces, polite and quiet, wearing thick overcoats. His wife serves up a feast of rice, lentils, baked bananas, meat, and freshly made mango and pineapple juice.

"I might surprise you, man," he says, grinning. "You never know."

◄ ►

After the last morning run, I pack up my things, say good-bye to Anders and the other athletes at the Kimbia camp, and roll the car out of the drive to collect Chris. "You're late, man," he says when he sees me.

Then we head back into town to find Japhet and Beatrice. Japhet is nowhere to be seen. We try calling him on his phone but there's no answer. Chris spots him in the garage. He's getting some last words of encouragement from his uncle.

"Come on, you're late," says Chris, pretending to be annoyed.

Japhet looks at us both, his eyes shot with worry. "It's okay," I say, sensing that he's too nervous for jokes. Chris laughs, sniggering to himself.

As we arrive to pick up Beatrice, she seems to be walking off in the opposite direction. "Beatrice," I call out, "where are you going?" When she sees me, she runs back inside her house then comes out with her bag. She gets in the back next to Japhet. The plan is to meet the others in Eldoret.

"Okay, let's go," I say, driving uphill past Lornah's camp for the last time. "Good-bye, Iten. Thanks for the memories."

◅ ▻

Chris has managed to hire us a *matatu* for the journey, but he decides that he and Philip will travel with me in my car, while everyone else can go with Godfrey in the *matatu*. I had planned to travel with Japhet, but I decide there's no point arguing.

Philip is dressed in a white suit with a Panama hat, while everyone else is in running clothes. We sit waiting in the car while Godfrey arranges the luggage in the bus. His wife seems to have fully recovered from her bout of malaria.

"Let's go," says Chris, impatient as ever.

"We might as well wait for them and all go in convoy," I say.

"No, let's go," says Philip. "They can catch us up."

I don't have the conviction to argue, so I pull the car out of the garage and start on the road to Lewa. I drive slowly, waiting for Godfrey to catch up, but after half an hour he still hasn't appeared in my mirror. I decide to call him.

"Finn," he says. I can hear that he's driving.

"Where are you?" I ask.

"Sorry. Paul said we had to pray before we left. But we're right behind you."

The journey takes most of the day. Chris sits in the front, excited, reading all the signs as we pass. Philip, like a wise old owl, sits in the back twirling his mustache. He used to live near Lewa when he was in the military in the late 1980s, he tells us. As we drive, he explains things to Chris, who sits there like a child taking it all in.

In the van, Godfrey tells me later, they were also staring out the window in wonderment. "It's like a holiday for them," he says. "Especially Japhet. You should have seen him. Shadrack and Beatrice, too. They've never seen this side of Kenya before. They keep saying, 'Wow, look!'" He chuckles to himself, enjoying their excitement.

We finally arrive in Isiolo, the nearest town to Lewa, at about 5:00 P.M. As soon as we arrive at the hotel, they all get changed and head off for a run. I'm too tired from the journey to join them, and besides, I feel like I need to rest my foot. Instead I take a stroll into town.

Isiolo is a dusty, bustling settlement, with people in ripped T-shirts and flip-flops, hustling and looking for money, motorbikes skirting past. It has an aggressive edge that's far removed from the relaxed air of Iten. It feels like a frontier town, and in many ways it is. Even though it's over three hundred miles from the Somali border, it's the last major town on the road and there are many Somalis living here.

It's almost dark when, through the chaos, like six arrows, come the Iten Town Harriers. They seem like creatures from another world, mythical beasts, their muscles rippling as they glide effortlessly over the bumpy surface. Chris leads the charge, unsmiling as he shoots past. Beatrice, her arms swinging high across her chest, chases after him, closely followed by Paul and Philip. Japhet and Shadrack, relaxed, follow at the rear, Japhet waving when he sees me.

◄ ►

We've arrived in Isiolo a day early to give everyone plenty of time to recover from the journey. It means we've got the whole next day just to rest, though it's not as easy as it sounds. I'm lying on the bed in the hotel room staring at the bright peach walls, the sound of the street rattling by outside the open window. Rather than feeling rested, though, my legs are inexplicably starting to feel tired. Aching, almost. It could be nerves, or the fact that I'm thinking about how tired they feel. I should go to sleep, but I'm too awake. Instead, I lie there thinking.

For six months I've been piecing together the puzzle of why Kenyans are such good runners. In the end there was no elixir, no running gene, no training secret that you could neatly package up and present with flashing lights and fireworks. Nothing that Nike could replicate and market as the latest running fad. No, it was too complex, yet too simple, for that. It was everything, and nothing. I list the secrets in my head: the tough, active childhood, the barefoot running, the altitude, the diet, the role models, the simple approach to training, the running camps, the focus and dedication, the desire to succeed, to change their lives, the expectation that they can win, the mental toughness, the lack of alternatives, the abundance of trails to train on, the time spent resting, the running to school, the all-pervasive running culture, the reverence for running.

When I spoke to Yannis Pitsiladis, I pushed him to put one factor above all the others. "Oh, that's tough," he said, thinking hard for a moment. Then he said pointedly: "The hunger to succeed." After a pause, he continued. "Look, my daughter is a great gymnast, but she probably won't become a gymnast. She'll probably go to university and become a doctor. But for a Kenyan child, walking down to the river to collect water, running to school, if he doesn't become an athlete, then there are not many other options. Of course, you need the other factors, too, but this hunger is the driving force."

The will to succeed not only motivates Kenyans to become athletes, but it helps them when they are racing. When the crunch comes in a race and your body is shouting at you to slow down, it is the drive to win that pushes you on. I once complained jokingly to Brother Colm's assistant, Ian, that when I ran with a group of Kenyans, whenever we'd get to a hill, they would all speed up, while my natural inclination was to slow down.

Ian smiled at me. "That's because they want it more than you," he said. "When they see a hill, they see it as an opportunity. An opportunity to train harder, to work harder."

When people in the Rift Valley decide to become athletes, they don't fit their training in around a job or college course, as we might in the West; they dedicate themselves to it completely. A daily diet of run, eat, sleep, run. In Iten alone there are around one thousand full-time athletes living like this—in a town with a population of just four thousand people. Every morning the lanes are full of people on the move, like commuters in any other city, but all of them in running clothes, flying uphill, training, training, training.

Brother Colm once remarked to me, as we stood watching a team of his athletes charging repeatedly up the long hill leading to St. Patrick's school, that, "This is the bit people miss when they look for the Kenyan secret."

Humans evolved as runners over millions of years in order to survive, not because it was a fun thing to do. Catching the antelope meant the difference between life and death. So it makes sense that even in the twenty-first century, if you're running to survive, then you'll become better at it.

I've immersed myself in the world of Kenyan runners, living and training with them, sharing their commitment, and following their almost monastic lifestyles, in the hope that some of their magic would rub off on me. Hopefully it has, but in truth, at thirty-seven, after years of living an easy, Western lifestyle, and without anything driving me other than the joy of running and the desire to use my talent, I never stood a chance.

There's a knock at the door. Godfrey comes in. "Finn, it's getting dark. Shall we go and find some supper?"

This is it, the last supper before Lewa. "Yes," I say, sitting up. "Where are the others?"

"They're all downstairs waiting. Chris says he has found the best place. He says it's cheap, clean, and has lots of vegetarian things."

"Great. Let's go."

◄ ►

They all stand in the lobby, disheveled and bleary-eyed, like they've just woken from a deep sleep. I follow Chris and Philip out the door. Godfrey, smiling at everyone, is clearly the only person not running tomorrow. He is relaxed, chatty, while the rest of us walk along in silence.

Chris's restaurant has two small plastic tables in one corner. The rest of the room is bare concrete. A man with a pencil behind his ear comes over as we crowd around the two tables. He hands us a colorful, laminated menu listing about a thousand different dishes.

"Do they have rice and beans?" I ask Godfrey, feeling too drowsy to ask the waiter myself.

Godfrey speaks to the man. They seem to have a long conversation. "They only have rice," Godfrey says to me, looking concerned. "Anything to go with it? Any vegetables?" Godfrey asks the man in English, but he shakes his head.

"Do you have anything vegetarian? Anything that is not meat?"

The man looks at me, thinking hard. It's a painful pause as he rifles through the list of dishes in his head. Then he shakes his head. "Just rice," he says.

Shadrack is looking more startled than usual. He mutters something to the waiter in Swahili, but the man shakes his head. Another waiter brings two plates of meat over to Chris and Philip, sitting at the other table.

"Godfrey, I can't eat just rice the night before the race," I say.

More plates of meat are arriving. They place one down in front of Shadrack, to his horror. He pulls Godfrey's hand. There's a commotion as they discuss Shadrack's meal. Godfrey tells me that Shadrack wants *ugali,* but they don't have any. He suggests I take Shadrack to another restaurant beside the hotel where they might have something vegetarian.

"What's going on, man?" says Chris from the other table, his mustache glistening with the juice from the meat.

"It's okay," I say. "We'll meet you back at the hotel. Come on, Shadrack, let's go and find some *ugali.*"

Shadrack keeps two paces behind me as we dodge our way through the busy street, avoiding the motorbikes and buses blazing their headlights at us, and watching out for holes in the rutted road. I ask him why he wants *ugali* so badly.

"I always eat ugali before a race," he says, his eyes fixed ahead.

The other restaurant is quiet, with rows of sculpted concrete tables, and artwork on the walls. The woman behind the counter thinks hard when I ask if they have *ugali,* before finally nodding. And vegetables? She nods again. I order two plates and we sit in front of the window. Outside, people in Somali robes stroll by, one man with a goat tied across his back. We eat in silence. This is it. It feels more like the end of the world than just the end of my journey. A bedraggled landscape of broken vans and trucks, a small wind picking up the dust and swirling it in the light from the window. Opposite me sits a lone warrior. Our champion, preparing for the battle ahead. The time has finally come.

He looks up at me midmouthful. "It's good," he says.

"Good." *Eat well, my man, for the moment is nigh.*

Twenty-five

Japhet collects water from a Samburu tribesman

Uma and Lila are waving to me from the sidelines, held aloft by Marietta and Godfrey. A small rope held by security men in bright jackets presses against my legs. Ahead of us lie the empty grasslands, the course narrowing up ahead through a small cluster of trees. Beyond that, twenty-six miles of wilderness. A man with a microphone is talking, telling us about the great work the race does for local charities. He's buying time. Occasionally, the helicopters skirt across the sky.

"I think we're getting the all-clear signal," he says. There are lions on the course. The helicopters are trying to scare them away, so they don't start picking us off like a herd of migrating wildebeest.

But I guess it's not a simple job, getting lions to move by swooping at them in a helicopter.

"We have a few famous athletes in the field today," the man says.

I've been telling Chris that he's the star runner at the race, trying to make him feel special. The whole project has never quite had his seal of approval. At one point, after I returned from Ethiopia, Godfrey told me that Chris was talking about quitting. I wasn't surprised. In every long run he seemed short of training. His enthusiasm for the race was always fragile. He kept asking me questions about it, looking, I always thought, for reasons to drop out. So I kept building it up, to keep him on board.

Godfrey told us that the race would be shown live on national television. "Of course," he said. "It's a big race. They always show it live. Everyone watches it." I told Chris the organizers were excited that he was running. He was a big name, I told him. They had given him a complimentary place in the race. They were even mentioning him in their promotional materials. That last bit was not quite true, but I was getting carried away, wanting to satisfy his need for approval. Godfrey was as bad as me, trying to make Chris happy. He went even further. He told us he had met two filmmakers from the U.S. TV channel ESPN who were filming the race for a newsreel. They were so excited to hear that Chris was running, he told us, that they wanted to film him before the race and interview him afterward. Chris grinned happily. *Really? Me?* I said I was sure the announcer would call out his name at the start. I emailed through the details of our team, with Chris's name at the top, his achievements in bold type.

The day before the race, we found out that it wasn't being televised live on Kenyan TV after all. Then, when I went to collect the race numbers, they told me they didn't have a complimentary place for Chris. I had to call up the race director on her cellphone. She was obviously busy with other things. "Hi," I said. "You agreed to give Christopher Cheboiboch a free race entry."

"Who?"

"Christopher Cheboiboch."

"Who is he?"

"He's a big-name runner. He came second in the New York and Boston marathons." I felt like the agent of a D-list celebrity trying to get him an invitation to the opening of a local supermarket.

"Sorry, we can't do that."

"But you've already agreed. I can send you the emails to prove it."

"Did I? Okay, he can have a place."

With so many amazing runners in Kenya, finishing second in New York ten years ago ranks about as highly as being a man who was once interviewed on the street about the price of gas. Unless an athlete wins the Olympics, he is soon pretty much forgotten in Kenya, even among race organizers.

On the start line, the ESPN TV crew is indeed there, panning along the runners, shuffling through the dry grass, a big camera catching these last moments before we head out on our odyssey. They don't linger as they pass Chris.

"We have a team of elite runners here called the Iten Town Harriers," says the announcer. "They are, Chris"—he hesitates as he reads the name—"Cheboych, who came second in the New York marathon." He's said it wrong. I don't look across at Chris. The announcer is reading the rest of our names out, but nobody is listening. People are talking, preparing to run a marathon. The announcer is a background noise, an outside interference. It's time to focus. Only when he tells us, finally, that we're ready to go, and starts the countdown from five, do we actually hear him. It's as if all the world, all the other sounds, everything that ever existed or happened, is being sucked down into those tumbling numbers—"Three, two, one"—as the rope is dropped and we're off.

◄ ►

The race starts off at a charge. People are sprinting. For some reason I wasn't expecting this surge of runners. I feel myself being swarmed, left behind like a boat still tied to the dock. I catch Chris out of the corner of my vision, streaking away at the front, but the others, like me, seem to have been caught off guard by the fast start. They're running just in front of me as a sea of bodies converges through the trees, the path narrowing, strides chopping, arms out so as not to crash into other people. Philip squeezes past me, but the leaders are already far, far ahead. We've got some catching up to do.

The race is both a marathon and a half marathon run together, with the marathon runners lapping the course twice. We'd talked the night before about how some of the people running the half marathon might go off fast, but that we shouldn't panic because they wouldn't be in our race. But we're already a long way behind. Surely they can't all be half-marathon runners.

After about a mile I start passing people. Some of them seem already spent; slow, thudding strides; big, thick legs; heavy, sweating T-shirts. I'm skipping past them, hopping up on the grass verges when the dirt track is too congested. I'm in a hurry, I seem too far behind. But I need to calm down, I tell myself. This is a marathon. I pull my cap down over my eyes, recalling the steely gaze of Joan Benoit in those YouTube clips, settling into a steadier pace. Beatrice is a few yards ahead of me now. The others have gone off on the chase, somewhere among the long line of runners zigzagging toward the horizon.

After about ten minutes the race seems to settle down. The people around me are now running about the same speed as me. The soft, gray dirt underfoot puffs gently as we run. Everything else is silent. Up ahead I spot another *mzungu*. I start reeling him in, without pushing too hard, just keeping my pace steady, passing him calmly, pressing on along the track. I'm feeling light on my feet, my barefoot style gentle on my racing flats.

At the two-mile marker, we turn sharply and head up the first hill. My legs feel strong as I keep up the pace, not slowing, passing other runners who are hitting their first difficult patch. At the top of the hill is the first water station. It's manned by a team of white women in khaki safari clothes, leaping around and cheering everyone on. "First *mzungu*, first *mzungu*," they shout, going wild as I run by. "Well done, well done." They hand me some water. I take a few sips and discard it like a man in a hurry. The first *mzungu*. Where are all the half-marathon runners?

As I run on, I spy a herd of zebra in the distance. I want to point them out to someone, but I'm running on my own now. I pull my cap down and press on.

At three miles I begin to wonder how fast I'm running. I made a late decision not to wear a watch. Anders thought I was mad, but I've done every training run without one, and the Kenyan runners at the Kimbia camp didn't think it was a problem. Just run how you feel, they said.

The course dips down suddenly into a narrow valley. It feels like the sort of sheltered, shady place you might find wild animals resting. I try not to think about it. The field is more spread out now, but I'm still passing people, people who started off too quickly. I cruise by, discarding them, one by one, in my wake.

At one point, a man battles back past me. His persistence disrupts my rhythm, making me feel as though I'm working hard for the first time in the race. We're at five miles, heading up a steep slope back out of the crevasse. I surge hard to drop him as we rise up, twisting through the rocky grassland, up and up. It's not steep, but every time I think we're at the top, it rises up more. To make matters worse, the ground here is even softer, sandlike, sapping energy from my legs with each stride. I keep crossing over from one side of the track to the other, because it keeps looking firmer on the other side. But it never is. My mind is playing tricks on me, I think, half-joking with myself. I'm becoming delusional. Up ahead, the heat is beginning to make the plains shimmer. It's getting hotter, 80 degrees and still rising.

For the next few miles the course goes up and down, up and down like a roller coaster, except one you have to push along yourself. I try to stride down the slopes, but I'm getting cramps now. I press my stomach with my fingers, which helps, but mainly it just comes and goes with the slopes, returning whenever I go downhill.

At each water stop, the stewards tell me I'm the first *mzungu*. They've been waiting to see how long it would take, I can tell. Well, finally, here I am.

At about nine miles, I see Marietta and the children for the first time. They're cheering, *Come on, Daddy,* Ossian peering out at me with his indifferent what-are-you-doing? look. Jophie, Marietta's sister, is also there. She looks as though she might cry.

"Come on, Dhar, you're the first *mzungu*," she says, disbelieving.

Godfrey is there, too. "Come on, Finn, you're doing great."

I stride through the water station like I'm leading the London Marathon, swiping a bottle of water, grinning at my kids, and heading back out into the silent, open plains. *I've got a job to do, kids, I'll see you soon.*

They all pop up again at the eleven-mile point. Godfrey looks at his watch as I pass. "Eighteen kilometers. One hour sixteen minutes. Looking good, Finn."

It sets my mind off, trying to calculate how fast I'm going. But the heat is pounding on my brain now. I figure I'll hit halfway in under 1 hour 30 minutes, which is pretty fast. I may get that sub-three hours, yet. As we come up to the halfway point, however, ready to set out on the second lap, I imagine for a moment that I'm doing only the half marathon and that I'm gathering myself to sprint to the end. I'm not sure that if I wanted to I could go any faster. I feel totally spent.

Beatrice is still ahead of me, but I'm starting to catch her. If I'm feeling this tired, she must really be struggling. I fear she has gone off too hard. I feel sorry for her. She was so confident, her big smile, telling me she would do it. Two women have passed me in the last few minutes, running strongly. Now they're chasing Beatrice, moving in like two lions for the kill. It's hard to watch.

At the halfway point, I pass Ray, the man I stayed with in Nairobi, who sent me along to run with the Hash House Harriers. His job is to make sure the half-marathon runners go one way, to the finish, and the full marathon runners head out on another lap, to do it all again. I can tell he's excited to see me because he stands up from his plastic chair. "Come on," he screeches. "Get a bloody move on."

A few corners later, I pass a glum-faced Chris negotiating with a motorbike for a lift. He has dropped out. The gash on his leg is the official reason.

"Bad luck, Chris," I say, holding out my hand as I pass.

"Okay," is all he can muster, barely looking at me. We go to slap hands, but miss. It feels symbolic, somehow.

Meanwhile, Shadrack and Japhet have both started off way too slow, but are making steady progress through the field. At halfway they are up into the top fifteen, running together stride for stride. Paul and Philip are strung out some way behind them.

As I run through the start line again to head out on the second lap, everything is eerily quiet. Just ninety minutes ago this place was buzzing with runners, spectators, the announcer on his microphone, the air humming with anticipation, the sense that something epic was about to begin. Now it is just me. It's as though the show has gone home, but for some reason I'm still running.

I head on, leaving the start line behind. Every step now feels nearer to the end. The balance between what I've done and what I still have to do has tipped. I'm on the downward slope. All I have to do is cruise in to the finish. Or so I think. The reality, of course, is that I've only just passed base camp, and instead of going down, the slope keeps rising, getting steeper. The real climbing is only just about to begin.

Up ahead, Beatrice isn't getting any closer. In fact, she seems to be pulling away from me, her shoulders swinging from side to side, pushing on. Good for her, I'm thinking. I can see the two women still chasing her. Can she hold out? There is still a long way to go. At the same time, the fact that I'm not catching her is slightly concerning. I usually pass her at some point, but my legs are tiring. The ground feels softer now than it did on the first lap. The long, straight lines cutting across the parched landscape seem to stretch on farther than before. The gentle wind and the soft *pat, pat, pat* of my feet are the only sounds. I swing a few glances behind me, but there is no one as far as I can see. Just the long path already traveled, empty, as though I'm the last runner on earth.

I have an energy gel in my back pocket. I had planned to take it at eighteen miles, but now, at fifteen miles, it's all I can think about.

It's like magic, someone told me. I pull it out, the yellow tube glistening in the sunlight. I rip it open and squeeze it into my mouth. It tastes of lemon-flavored candy. Sickly sweet. I suck on the packet. I'm in a hurry to finish it, squeezing out the last globs. Even holding it seems like a waste of my precious, fast-depleting energy. I shove the packet back into my pocket as I turn and start to head up what was once the first hill. This time, however, I can't seem to move myself beyond a slow grind, churning my body up the hill with my arms, my feet taking short little steps.

At the top, the excitable women at the water station have also run out of energy. "Well done," says one, quietly, as she hands me a bottle of water.

I guzzle down the whole bottle. I'm suddenly insatiably thirsty. But the water station is gone. I'll have to wait until the next one.

Spurred on by the gel, and the downward slope, I begin to pick my speed back up. But it's so quiet out here. For the first time, as I dip down into the narrow valley again, I start looking around. I'm out in the bush. Alone. There are lions, cheetahs, and leopards out here. I remember the roar of the lions outside the tent in our first week in Kenya. That was only a few miles from here. Out of the corner of my eye, I spot a man sitting beside the track. I almost don't see him. He's dressed in a green uniform, with a gun across his lap. He gives me a friendly wave, as though I just happen to be passing.

Soon I'm running through another water station, at around eighteen miles. A man with a trash bag is collecting the discarded bottles from the first lap. I grab a full water bottle from a young boy and drink it up.

On I go, beginning the series of steep climbs. They continue, up and down, but mostly up, for about six miles. I can barely jog up the slopes now, instead keeping my head down and shuffling as sure and steady as I can. At one point a woman overtakes me. "Come on," she says, urging me to run with her. "Don't give up."

I haven't given up, but I really can't go any faster. My legs feel as though they've been drained of life and refilled with lead. I can barely move. I almost need to use my hands to pull my legs along. *Come on,* I tell myself. I try chanting. *I love you, Lila. I love you, Lila.* But it's no use. The heavy, debilitating exhaustion swamping me swallows the chant whole, sucking it away until I can't even remember what it is. This time it's not a question of willpower. This time I haven't lost the psychological battle. No, my focus is intense. I'm pushing myself as hard as I can. This time it's purely physical. I'm struggling just to keep moving. At each water station I drink more. Two bottles of water. A fizzy energy drink. But my thirst is unforgiving. I squeeze sponges of ice cold water over my head and for a blissful second I feel refreshed. But the burning trail stretches on.

The distance markers become my only sanity, the only evidence that I'm actually still moving forward, and not just drifting aimlessly across a dry ocean. I begin to call them my little magic markers, talking to myself, to the little signs hammered into the ground. "Ah, there you are, my little magic marker. What took you so long?"

Suddenly Godfrey is standing alone on the horizon, calling my name. At least, I think he is. I squint to see if I'm dreaming. When I reach him, he runs along beside me. "Marietta was worried. How do you feel?" He barely has to jog to keep up with me.

"How are the others doing?" I ask him, my voice sounding surprisingly composed, as though we were just walking along the road in Iten. My breathing is steady. It's just my legs that are holding me back, and my overpowering thirst.

"Shadrack is pushing on in about eighth. He can still catch the leaders, but I told him he has to push hard now."

"And Japhet?"

"He's just behind him." He looks at me, worried. "How do you feel?"

"I feel exhausted. My legs just won't move."

As we crawl over the brow of the hill, I see Lila standing at the water stop, holding out a bottle of water. When I reach her, I grab it. "Thank you," I say, smiling at her.

"First *mzungu* coming through," Jophie announces to everyone else gathered there.

I don't know how much longer I can hold out. I'm getting slower and slower, surely someone must be catching me. But I push on, refreshed, feeling back in control of my senses, for the moment at least. I try to focus on my form, keeping my legs in order, leaning forward. It's as though my body is desperately trying to shut down and I have to do everything I can to keep it in operation.

Between each magic marker, I lose track of how far we've gone, and I'm not sure which number to expect next. They seem to count erratically: 34KM, 36KM, 35KM, 36KM. But even if I'm losing count, each one represents progress, proof that I'm still moving.

And still no other *mzungu* passes me. Beatrice has long since disappeared into the distance, but amazingly nobody else comes by. I'm passing the slowest half-marathon runners now, still on their first lap, most of them walking. I try to weave past them, but I'm barely moving faster than they are.

At thirty-nine kilometers we reach the last water stop. I don't know what happens. I reach for a drink, and then stop, completely stock-still. My legs, charged with sweet relief, feel as though they're singing hymns. I pick up an energy drink and suck it down. Half-marathon runners, their big bellies hoisted up over their shorts, are standing around drinking and joking. This is the greatest party ever. I feel like a gatecrasher, my eyes wide. This is where it's happening. At the back of the field. This is where the real action takes place. Just when I think life couldn't get any sweeter, a man comes over and squeezes about eight wet sponges over my head. Ice cold water. I'm in heaven.

But I have to get on. I tell myself to stop having fun, to pull myself together. I start off again, into the dry wastelands, the dust sticking now to my wet shoes. The taste of dirty water running into my mouth. I wonder whether I could walk the rest of the way and still be the first *mzungu*. No, it's too risky. I have to keep going. Just one foot in front of the other, no matter how slow, just keep running. I look down, watching them, my feet moving back and forth.

Finally, miraculously, I make it to where Ray is sitting on his plastic chair. He leaps up. "Come on," he bellows. "What's wrong with you?"

I can't help grinning at him. It's half a mile to go from here. "Thanks, Ray."

Then Godfrey, the omnipresent, appears. "Come on, Finn, you're going to win."

He means the *mzungu* race. It's a victory of sorts, I suppose, although it's hard to fathom how right now. I feel more pathetic than heroic as I lumber along. Godfrey, the real hero of the piece, runs beside me, encouraging me. Somehow, with his help, I begin to get moving again, to move my legs once more like a runner. As I round the last corner, the beautiful, arched finish rises up to meet me. The clock ticks on to 3 hours 20 minutes. And then I'm there. I've done it. I've won. I've finished. I've survived. I've finally stopped.

Marietta is there, smiling, proud, holding my hand. The children are there. It's beautiful. I want to cry. I can hardly stand. A man is moving me on, directing me to a chair. I hold on to it, to stop myself from collapsing. The girls are buzzing around me, offering me a cupcake they've baked for me, a beautiful mess of melting chocolate. But I need water, an energy drink, anything liquid. I collapse into the chair.

Hands are reaching down, wanting to shake mine. Paul is there, his big grin. "Fantastic," he says. Chris walks over. Lila runs up and gives him a big hug. Godfrey is smiling under his hat. I have to look away, to stop myself from crying. I'm overcome with emotion. I get up, to try walking around.

Alastair comes over. "Man, that was some run," he says, offering me a big handshake. I can't look. I totter off, unstable, toward a sign that says RECOVERY TENT. Inside it's like a war zone, with exhausted people collapsed everywhere. Those on bales of hay are getting massages, while those on the floor have simply been left to die, it seems. I slide down next to a hay bale, out of the sun, among the pungent smells of sweat and Deep Heat, hidden from the emotions running wild outside. I need a moment to breathe.

I hear a voice I recognize. It's Ray. I need to stand up, at least. He wants me to meet someone from the charity that runs the event, but when he introduces me, I can't speak. I can barely blubber my name. I'll come back, I tell the man. I just need to get my breath back. He smiles knowingly. He's seen it before, of course.

When I finally remerge, composed, the others are all still there. Beatrice is talking and laughing with Flora. She ended up finishing fourth, in her first marathon ever, and she won forty thousand Kenyan shillings. Enough to pay her rent for more than three years. Where did she get the strength from?

"It was very hot," is all she can say when I congratulate her. From just after the halfway point, which was around the last time I saw her, she managed to stick with a Masai runner from Isiolo. His encouragement kept the other women runners chasing her at bay, until, at around sixteen miles, amazingly she began to pick up the pace. "I left the Masai runner," she says. She can't stop smiling.

"But it was very tough. At forty kilometers my legs felt so weak." She had no idea that she was in the top five, but she kept on pushing. "I thought I was number ten," she says, which makes Flora laugh. They say something to each other in Swahili and start giggling.

Japhet and Shadrack are not there. Godfrey says they've gone off to get showered and changed. I ask him how they did.

He shakes his head. "Not good," he says, disappointed. "It's my fault. I should have told Shadrack to drink more."

Shadrack and Japhet spent most of the race moving up through the field, but they had left themselves too much to do. Shadrack had not taken enough water, and despite getting up to eighth, he almost fainted from dehydration with less than a mile to go.

"Japhet passed him, and told him, 'Let's run together,'" Godfrey tells me. "But he was doubled over. 'Go on without me,' he said."

In the end, Japhet finished in tenth place in 2 hours 28 minutes, with Shadrack struggling home in eleventh, a minute later. Paul, who had malaria only a few weeks before the race, ran 2 hours 45 minutes, while Philip, who was the first over-forty runner after all, won a brand-new cellphone.

◄ ►

We stand by the bus, waiting for Beatrice. They've decided to head straight back home to Iten, while I'm staying here in Lewa with Marietta and the children. Little Japhet, our star man, gives me a hug. "When are you coming back to Iten?" he asks.

I shake my head. "I don't know."

Chris, impatient to leave, slides open the minibus door. "Finn, it has been an honor," he says, his voice as smooth as ever. The saga is over, he can get back now to his school, to building his legacy.

Philip shakes my hand and climbs into the bus.

Paul talks to me in a hushed, wistful voice, telling me to greet my family, and to come back to Iten one day.

Beatrice is here now. "Thank you so much," she says, the envelope of cash tucked into the waistband of her tracksuit.

"Look after that money," I tell her. Her life is going to change after this, at least for a while. Everyone is going to want a piece of her prize. "Talk to Godfrey if you need some advice."

She smiles. "I will," she says. "Thank you."

The last one is Godfrey. "Good-bye, Finn," he says quietly, a tear in his eye.

"Godfrey, we couldn't have done this without you. I'll be in touch, I promise."

He nods. "Good-bye" is all he can say. He climbs into the driver's seat and puts the bus in reverse. They all look out, waving.

I wonder if I'll ever see them again. It has been an honor to have known them and run with them. I stand watching as the bus drives off through the dust, bumping along the track, taking them back to Iten, back to the land of runners.

Epilogue

Four months later

It's eerily quiet as we chase like ghosts across the sky, 130 feet up on the Queensboro Bridge. If I could lift my head long enough, I'd see the skyscrapers of Manhattan jutting up along the edge of the East River below me. But I'm focused on the patter of feet, on my breathing. Eventually the steep climb tips and we start running down the other side of the bridge. Making use of the slope, I start snaking my way through the other runners. I went through the halfway point in 1 hour 23 minutes, a half-marathon personal best by over three minutes, and I'm still feeling strong. A sign up on the bridge reads: IF EASIER MEANS TEN MILES TO GO, WELCOME TO EASIER.

Up ahead the sound of the crowd is building. As we come off the bridge, we emerge into sunlight, warm on my neck. A huge cheer goes up from a crowd five-people deep. I feel a surge of energy and can't help smiling. Around the next corner the course turns onto First Avenue, a wide, empty street that seems to stretch on forever, a huge space cut through the middle of everything, opened up for me to run along. People cheering are lining both sides of it, waving flags and handwritten cardboard signs. It's a long way from the silent heat of Lewa.

◄ ►

After returning from Kenya I'm keen to see what I can do in a race at sea level. Toby Tanser manages to get me a place in the New York marathon, running for his Shoe4Africa charity team. But first I have a showdown with my 10K personal best down by the river in Exeter.

The race is flat and I spend most of it running on the heels of two other athletes, feeling comfortable, gliding over the ground, riding light on my toes. As I turn the last corner, a big clock over the finish shows thirty-five minutes, the seconds ticking along to fifty as I cross the line. It is a best time by almost three minutes. In one fell swoop I've moved to a whole new level. I can feel it as I walk around after the race, glowing with satisfaction, shaking hands with the other finishers. Thirty-five minutes. The Kenyan training has paid off after all. I'm now a 35-minute 10K runner. I feel excited as I head off for a warm-down jog. This is just the beginning. Next, a half marathon. Then New York.

But when I wake up the next morning, I can hardly walk. I seem to have injured my thigh muscle.

◄ ►

It's four weeks before I can start training again, so I turn up in New York two months later, on a bright November morning, worried that I'm not in shape. In the days before the race, I head out to Central Park for a few last easy runs. The place is swarming with runners. There are more here than in Iten.

"This city is running crazy," Toby Tanser tells me. He lives in New York, and two nights before the race, he holds a pasta party at his friend's apartment for all the Shoe4Africa team runners. I arrive at the building and look again at the directions. He hasn't given me the apartment number, I realize. It just says eleventh floor. I tell the doorman I'm here for a pasta party.

"Eleventh floor," he says, opening the lift.

There is no apartment number. It's the entire floor. Toby's friend is a famous actor, and his apartment is huge.

In the kitchen a group of Kenyan women are cooking *ugali*. Toby is full of life, hopping around and talking to everyone. I walk into another room and there, among the clinking of glasses and excited New York chatter, are three Kenyan athletes. They're sitting in silence, still wearing their coats and waiting patiently for the *ugali*. I go over to say hello. The man in the middle is Geoffrey Mutai. I tell him I saw him win a cross-country race in Iten back in January. He looks surprised. "How?" he asks me.

"I used to live there," I tell him.

It seems like a long time ago now, even though it was just a few months back. Those long, red trails full of runners, the children laughing and racing along to school. A few days before I left for New York, I called Beatrice to see how she was doing.

"I am good," she said. She sounded happy. I asked her what she had done with her winnings from Lewa. She said she had bought a TV and paid her rent for five months. "The rest I gave to my mother," she said.

Someone comes in and whispers in Geoffrey Mutai's ear. He looks at me. "The *ugali* is ready," he says, getting up. The woman beside him, Caroline Kilel, gets up, too. Both Geoffrey and Caroline were the winners of the Boston Marathon back in the spring. The third Kenyan, another woman, stays where she is. I don't recognize her. She says her name is Caroline Rotich. She's a Kenyan runner, so she must have won something, I suspect.

"What races have you won?" I ask her.

"I won the New York half marathon this year," she says.

But of course.

◄ ►

I decide to wear a watch for the first time in my life and set it to beep every six minutes and forty seconds—the average mile pace for a two-hour fifty-five-minute marathon. That would mean running close to my half-marathon PB twice in a row, but I feel I can do it despite the injury. That half-marathon time predates my Kenya trip. Things are different now.

The first two miles of the race are up and down the expansive Verrazano-Narrows Bridge, downtown Manhattan basking in the sunshine on the horizon. By the second mile I'm already ahead of my schedule, but I feel fine so I decide to go with it. I don't want to be controlled by the watch, I think, wondering why I'm even wearing it. But at each mile I check it again, and at each mile I'm farther ahead of my 2:55 schedule.

All along the course the crowds cheer us. They love it when one of the runners responds, with a high-five or a wave or anything. I'm trying, though, to stay focused on my running. The city's comedians have been out writing signs. One says: WHAT ARE YOU ALL RUNNING FROM? Another says: YOU'VE GOT GREAT STAMINA. CALL ME. 1-834-555-8756. Yet another reads: IN OUR MINDS, YOU'RE ALL KENYANS.

As I truck along at a good pace, far, far ahead, the Kenyans are putting on another show for the world. Geoffrey Mutai, fresh from his *ugali* at Toby Tanser's pasta party, streaks away at the front to win and smash the course record by over two minutes. It completes a stunning year in which every major marathon has been won by a Kenyan in a new course record. If they were good before, they're even better now.

My old friend Emmanuel Mutai, from the One 4 One camp, finishes second, also beating the old course record. I wonder what

Chris is thinking back in Iten. He is no longer the fifth fastest man ever in New York.

In the women's race, Mary Keitany, who once sat shyly talking to me in her cramped living room, sets off like a crazed *matatu* driver, running at a world record pace and pulling ahead of the women's field by over three minutes before being caught and passed right at the end. It's a brave run and wins the hearts of many people watching.

I'm still well under my target time as we head along First Avenue. The huge buildings rising up on either side make me feel tiny, but it's good to have firm ground below my feet, and cool air to breathe. Mindful of how thirsty I got in Lewa, I've been taking plenty of water, and at the eighteen-mile point they hand us all energy gels. I take two.

As we run on, the mile markers keep coming quicker than I'm expecting, but gradually I start to slow. I'm losing my time cushion, the beeps of my watch getting closer to the mile markers. I treat them like reminders to keep pushing. *Come on,* I tell myself, speeding up, passing a few other runners, finding someone at a good pace to draft behind, but trying not to tread on his heels. I'm saving my chant of love until I really need it, but before I realize it, we're in Central Park and nearing the finish. Around the last corner I can't stop the grin beaming across my face. I close my eyes and look to the heavens, holding my arms out. I can't help it. The crowd cheers me, embracing my moment of triumph. I know I've done it. The sub-three-hour marathon is conquered as I cross the line in exactly 2 hours 55 minutes.

And then the emotions begin. I can hardly stand; my calves are in agony. A woman takes my arm, hauling me off to the VIP area by the finish—Toby is a good man to know. It's not much, a few chairs, a box of apples, and some drinks. But the sun is shining. I've just run the New York marathon. Bliss is surging like a drug through my veins. A man standing by the gate like a joyous town crier sums everything up, the reason we do it, the reason I've put everyone through all this, gone so far, pushed so hard, for so long. In his big New York accent, he looks at me struggling to walk, and declares grandly: "Welcome to heaven."

Afterword

A few months later

"Finn." A pause. The phoneline crackles in my ear. "Finn, it's Japhet. Godfrey says there is a problem with the visa."

I'm standing by the window in my living room in Devon, England. Outside, the bare trees shiver in the sunlight. In the kitchen, the children are baking cupcakes. Iten, with its dusty trails and swarms of runners, is becoming a distant memory.

After their performances in the Lewa marathon, Japhet and Beatrice have both received invitations to race in the 2012 Utrecht marathon in the Netherlands. This is a big break for them, the thing every aspiring athlete in Iten dreams of, a race abroad. But first they have to get visas.

Securing all the necessary paperwork to travel to Europe turns out to be a tangled operation worthy of a codename, involving "trusted" customs officers holding on to passports, hurried phone calls from the side of the Uganda highway, and Japhet sleeping on the floor in an empty office in Nairobi Airport with only his jacket as a blanket.

But here I am, two weeks later, waiting for Japhet at the arrivals gate at Schiphol Airport in Amsterdam with Peter, the publisher of the Dutch edition of *Running with the Kenyans*. Beatrice, unfortunately, never got her visa.

"I hope he made it onto the plane," I say to Peter, as we watch lots of Kenyans coming out through the arrivals gates in Amsterdam. Big smiles, smart jackets, gold watches. But there is no sign of Japhet. Next come the Kenya Airways crew. But still no Japhet.

Suddenly Peter is pointing in the air. The Tannoy is announcing his name.

Japhet has been stopped by the customs officers. He has arrived with no luggage—except a small string bag with some tattered running shoes in it—wearing old clothes from the secondhand market in Iten, and holding a letter stating that he is an elite athlete staying at the expensive Houten Hotel in Utrecht. It all looks highly questionable.

Ten minutes later, he emerges, bleary eyed, through the automatic doors, flanked by Peter and a security official. He looks at me and smiles.

"Welcome to Europe," I say.

As we walk back through the airport to Peter's car, he gazes around at everything. "Your country is very beautiful," he says, walking with big, careful steps, taking it all in. It's a cut-glass world of twinkling lights and polished floors, filled with the calm, mellifluous air of western affluence.

"I had trouble on the moving floors," he says, laughing, remembering without fear now his uncertainty, just minutes ago, as he walked through those long passageways, praying that he wouldn't be turned back.

◄ ►

The next morning, the day before the race, I get a call on my hotel room phone. It's the Kenyans. In addition to Japhet, there are two other Kenyans here for the marathon: Viola Kimetto, who won the race a few years before, and Vincent Kipkemoi, the husband of the

2011 Boston marathon winner, Caroline Kilel. We're all going for an easy run together.

We follow the only path from the hotel and find ourselves jogging slowly through a suburban housing area. It's a quiet Sunday morning, the sleepy gray sky still pulled over the city's head like a blanket. The three Kenyans marvel at the neatness of all the houses and gardens, with their sculptured hedges and trees, little trim fences, and tidy lawns. Japhet is grinning. As much as he is loving being here, he is also happy to be with his fellow Kenyans. Together they point out the people walking their dogs. It looks a strange sight suddenly, all these people walking along quietly attached to dogs.

"Some of them even keep the dogs in their houses," Viola tells Japhet, who looks at me to see if it's true.

As we run, we pass a jogger, who grins at us as we go by. But mostly it's quiet, just rows and rows of houses.

"Your country is very beautiful," Japhet tells me again.

◄ ►

"Is he going to run in his jeans?" one of the officials asks me, smirking just a tiny bit as Japhet heads out for a warm-up jog with Vincent half an hour before the race.

A shoe company, Brooks, has agreed to sponsor Japhet for the day, giving him a new pair of shoes from its stand at the marathon expo, and some running gear to race in. The night before, he showed me the shoes he had brought with him from Kenya. They were three sizes too big for him, and worn down so much the soles were smooth. With the rain pouring over the city, it would have been like running in skates.

However, for some reason Brooks didn't give Japhet any track-suit pants, so when the athletes head out for their warm-up, Japhet is still wearing his jeans.

Back at the hotel earlier that morning, the race organizer asked for the athletes' personal bottles to take to the drinks stations. Each of the thirty or so elite athletes handed over a box of plastic bottles filled with tried and tested energy drinks. Japhet looked at me. I'd never done any of this before either, and it hadn't crossed my mind to prepare drinks. All he had was an out-of-date energy gel Godfrey had given him, tucked into the waistband of his shorts.

"There'll be water out on the course," I said.

And so he lines up at the start of the race, surrounded by tall eastern European and Dutch athletes, all with their coaches at their sides giving them last-minute instructions, their drinks waiting out on the course. Japhet has the bemused look of a poor shepherd boy who has just come down from the hills to find two hundred years has somehow passed.

Yet despite everything, the other athletes watch him carefully, for Japhet has one big advantage—he is a Kenyan.

The race starts in driving rain and strong wind. Japhet has never experienced such cold in his life. He lopes off unsteadily behind the pacemakers as I head inside to the athletes' area to watch the race on a big screen.

In the early stages, only the local favorite, Olfert Molenhuis, goes with the pacemaker, with Japhet settling in a second group about twenty meters back. I can see him looking around, buffeted and confused, as though he is trying to remember what to do. Is running still the same in this new world?

After a few miles, he moves to the front of the chasing group, along with Vincent, and the two of them together close the gap on the leaders.

"You are a runner," Vincent told him that morning, as they prepared to leave the hotel. "It is the same in Europe or in Kenya. You just run." It's coming back to him now, it seems.

After a few more miles the television coverage switches to the 10K race, which is happening at the same time, so I go off to visit the marathon expo. On the way back I see one of the other coaches.

"Your guy is not so good," he tells me. "He has dropped back." My heart sinks a little, but I'm not really surprised. Japhet is a novice marathon runner with a best time of 2 hours 28 minutes. The excuses come to me thick and fast. It is colder than he has ever known; he doesn't have any drinks on the course; he has been eating strange food for two days; he slept on the floor in the airport in Nairobi the night before he left. Of course he can't expect to run well.

As I sit back down to watch the end of the race, the camera is following the fourth-place runner, Petr Pechek of the Czech Republic, who runs with his cap tipped forward at such a jaunty angle he looks like a cartoon drunk. The motorbike camera then zooms on down the road in search of the third-place runner. It seems to travel for miles, until up ahead it spies the three leaders running together. As it comes closer, I realize that one of them is Japhet.

He is tucked in closely behind the two towering figures of Molenhuis, the Dutchman, and Aleksandr Babaryka from the Ukraine. He looks calm. His eyes almost seem to be closed as he runs, following the two leaders, sheltering from the wind and the cold.

I can't understand the Dutch television commentary, but I can tell they are talking about Japhet. They are probably trying to work out who he is. The camera pulls up beside him, zooming in to show him fiddling with the drawstring on his shorts. It's tied together loosely in a knot as it was in the shop. He is clearly trying to tighten it but can't.

In the room where I sit, people crowd around to watch the screen as the three runners push on in silence through the gray, drenched suburbs, the drama intensified by the huge physical difference between the two tall, fair-haired Europeans, and the tiny, bucktoothed

Kenyan. The three runners reach 39km together in 2 hours 8 minutes. Just two miles to go. And then it all goes wrong.

As they pass the crowds lining the last few miles of the course, Japhet drops back from the leaders, going slower and slower. His face is now a grimace, his eyes wide, skirting around him.

"I didn't drink any water," he tells me later. "It was too cold." He also complains about the wind and the rain. But more than anything, it was his mind that got lost out there on the cobbled Dutch streets, as the hugeness of his journey came over him, swamping him, sucking the fight out of his legs. He looked bewildered as he ran up the long, straight road to the finish. This was not a man running a race, but a man lost in a strange dream that had ceased to make sense.

In the end he runs the last two miles in 13 minutes, which is about my marathon pace. Two more runners pass him, first the Czech runner with the jaunty hat who was miles behind, and then another runner right on the line. Japhet doesn't even notice. He crosses the line with his arms raised, as though he has won.

◄ ►

Japhet's capitulation over the last two miles costs him €700 (a little less that $900)—the difference in prize money between third and fifth. In the end he wins €300 (roughly $380), enough to keep him going in Iten for six months. But he doesn't seem concerned about the money. Instead, he can't stop grinning.

Later that evening, sitting in the hotel, someone asks Japhet if he is married.

"No," he says. "I am just a boy. I told my father that I have dreams to travel abroad, to run big races. To see other countries." He looks at us, a curtain pulling back in his mind.

"This is my dream," he says. "This, now, is my dream."

◄ ►

The big running event of 2012, of course, is the London Olympics. The Kenyan team arrives in town full of swagger. After their complete domination of the major marathons and the world athletics championships in 2011, the head of Athletics Kenya is outlandishly predicting gold, silver, and bronze for Kenya in every event from 800m up—that's thirty-six medals in the running events alone. It is a piece of bravado that will end up coming back to bite him.

Among the Kenyan team are many of the runners I got to know during my six months in Kenya. First up is Vivian Cheruiyot, whom I first met in the house in Teddington, southwest London. As triple world champion in 2011, she is a strong contender for the gold medal in the first track final, the women's 10,000m. Unfortunately for her, however, the double Olympic champion, Ethiopia's Tirunesh Dibaba, is back on form after two years of injury.

The race soon boils down to a battle between the Ethiopians and Kenyans, but when Dibaba unleashes her legendary long kick for home with a lap to go, Vivian struggles to hang on to her, and gets passed by her teammate as she fades away down the back straight. In the end she has to settle for the bronze medal.

A week later in the 5,000m, Vivian manages to stay close enough to get her revenge and edge past Dibaba on the line, but only for the silver medal. In a race again dominated by Kenya and Ethiopia—they fill the first six places—it is an Ethiopian who once more claims gold.

Things don't fare much better for Kenya in the women's marathon. Mary Keitany, who had me around one afternoon for orange squash in her house just outside Iten, is the clear favorite for gold after retaining her London marathon title with ease a few months earlier, but in the end she fades badly in the rain-sodden streets to finish fourth. Again an Ethiopian claims gold.

Back in Kenya, rumblings of discontent are beginning to surface. Amid reports of resentment at the way Kenya's Olympic committee is running the team—barring some of the coaches from seeing the athletes in the Olympic village—the 1,500m men head out onto the track to do battle. One of them is Nixon Chepseba.

I first met Nixon before his first season racing abroad, just after he broke the local Eldoret track record. His coach was eulogizing about his potential, and he had a certain air of confidence that made him stand out even among all the other successful athletes around him.

However, in 2011, despite finishing the year as the third fastest 1,500m runner in the world, he failed to make the Kenyan team for the world championships, where his teammates went on to win gold and silver.

In 2012 he is more experienced, and he makes it safely onto the Olympic team by finishing second in the national trials. With the three fastest men in the world on their team for London, including Chepseba, this is an event in which Kenya has genuine hopes of achieving a 1-2-3 finish.

But alas, alack. After the Olympics, Kenyans are so disappointed with their team's performance that the government launches a public inquiry. And the race where things go most badly wrong is the men's 1,500m.

Used to running behind pacemakers, Chepseba doesn't seem to know whether to stick or twist. He doesn't have the best sprint finish, but rather than making a decisive move, he hovers around at the front, leading the race at a sedate pace, setting himself up to be passed by almost everyone on the last lap. He ends up finishing in eleventh place, one ahead of his teammate, the now former Olympic champion Asbel Kiprop, who finishes last.

◄ ►

Meanwhile, through all the accusations and conjecture in the newspapers, Brother Colm O'Connell is keeping a low profile back in Iten, dodging calls from the world's media. I speak to him a few days before his prodigy, David Rudisha, steps onto the track for the 800m final.

In 2010 Rudisha broke the world 800m record twice in one week. Then, in 2011, he won his first global title at the world championships.

"There are three things on a global level that you can achieve in athletics," Brother Colm tells me. "Rudisha has two of them. There is one missing. Winning the Olympics, he knows, will give him immortality."

After the Olympics, many people come up to me and tell me that the highlight of the Games was watching David Rudisha win the 800m. "It was almost spiritual," my neighbor tells me days afterward, still shaking his head in disbelief.

With a strong field, Rudisha sets off at the front like a train, churning through the first lap in 49.28 seconds. And then he kicks on. He runs with an elegance and style honed on the football field in front of St. Patrick's High School, running with his teammates in single file, following the rhythm of the athlete in front, back and forth, over and over, all under the watchful eye of Brother Colm. In many ways, Rudisha is the embodiment of Brother Colm's thirty-five years' work coaching athletes in Kenya. Everything he has learned is on display when Rudisha runs. And on a warm evening on August 9, 2012, the world sits and watches the result in complete awe.

Rudisha crosses the line in 1:40:91. It's a new world record. In an Olympic final. Running from the front the entire race. He doesn't need a pacemaker, he is the pacemaker. In fact, seven of the eight runners in the race run personal bests, breaking three national records in the process.

"[Usain] Bolt was good, but Rudisha was magnificent," is the verdict of Lord Coe, the chairman of the 2012 Olympics and a former double Olympic 1,500m champion.

Brother Colm, watching the race on television back in his house in Iten, describes the performance as "exemplary." Speaking to me a few days later, he says: "After the race I felt a sense of relief. It was a just reward for all the months of preparation and sacrifices we had both made."

And what did he do to celebrate?

"I went to Kerio View to have a quiet drink," he says.

◄ ►

The last race of the Olympics is the men's marathon. With the top twenty-five fastest runners in the world in 2011 all coming from Kenya, this should be their crowning glory. Of course, the first problem is picking just three runners from those twenty-five, as each country is only allowed a maximum of three athletes. The Kenyan and world's athletics media is enthralled by the dilemma, with everyone offering a view on who should make the top three.

In the end they plump for Abel Kirui, the world champion; Wilson Kipsang, the leader of Japhet's mwisho wa lami early-morning training group; and Emmanuel Mutai, my onetime training partner.

Controversially, the selectors leave out Patrick Makau, who in 2011 broke the world record, and the 2011 Boston and New York City marathon champion, Geoffrey Mutai.

"In this country, any runner is as good as the other," the head of

Athletics Kenya rather flippantly remarks as the debate rages on.

The big threat is expected to come from the Ethiopians, as usual. But this is the Olympics, and anything can happen.

◄ ►

On that day back in Kaptagat when, from the back of a van, I witnessed Emmanuel Mutai calmly tearing up the road on a 38km training run, the only athlete close to him was a Ugandan called Stephen Kiprotich.

I'd first met him a few weeks earlier at another nearby training camp with Godfrey. It was a quiet day and most of the athletes were sleeping or had wandered off somewhere. Kiprotich sat with his coach, who introduced him to us as "one of the young guys." Godfrey was tickled that they shared the same name, Kiprotich, which means "born when the cows were coming home for milking."

"You know, we Kenyans must watch out for these young Ugandan athletes," Godfrey told me, as Kiprotich grinned shyly. "They are getting very strong."

Godfrey's words turn out to be very prescient, as the Olympics finishes with another surprise defeat for Kenya. And it is the very same Ugandan, Stephen Kiprotich, clinging doggedly to every Kenyan break, who finally gets away to cross the line first.

The medal ceremony for the men's marathon is the centerpiece of the closing ceremony of the Games. Amid all the excitement, noise, and color London can muster, a shy young man from Uganda, flanked on either side by a Kenyan, stands up to collect his gold medal. Kiprotich had left his home and family in Uganda at seventeen to train in Kenya, and now, after six years running with the Kenyans, here he is standing on top of the world. Perhaps I should have stayed a bit longer.

Acknowledgments

My first and biggest thank-you goes to Marietta. In some ways it feels like we wrote this book together. She was a steadying influence throughout, and her sense of adventure, her perseverance, and her kindness were all invaluable.

Secondly, to my wonderful children for taking everything in their stride like three little superheroes.

Also, to my guide and mentor, Godfrey Kiprotich, the most helpful man in the world, a true friend.

To the rest of the Iten Town Harriers, particularly to Chris and Japhet, for all their help and for coming along for the ride.

To Jophie and Alastair for encouraging us to come to Kenya, for looking after us when we first got there, and for lending us the most coveted car in East Africa.

To Ray and Doreen, for their immense hospitality, letting us stay in their wonderful Flea House in Nairobi, and for putting me in touch with Godfrey.

To Anders for all the time spent loafing around in the Kimbia camp. Mama Kibet for the constant supply of rice, beans, and ugali. And to Isaac Arusei for making me feel so welcome.

To Michel Boeting and all the incredible athletes at the One 4 One camp.

To Flora for hand-washing all those clothes and for being such a friend to Ossian.

To Hilda, Brenda, Maureen, Linda, and all the other children of Kapshow in Iten, for their kindness and friendship with Lila, Uma, and Ossian.

To Jeff and Carey, Uhuru, and Apollo for Iten training runs, pasta, and kids playdates.

To Kelly Falconer, a former editor who took the time to point me in the right direction even though she had never met me.

To my agent, Oliver Munson, for seeing the book's potential and taking it on, and for doing such a good job in selling it.

To my co-editors, Ryan Doherty and Sarah Savitt, for sharing my vision and for their skilled pruning of the original manuscript.

To Betty and Robin, for being so supportive right from the beginning.

To my parents, Val and John, for bringing me up with a sense of wonder and adventure.

And to Prem Rawat, for showing me the place from where everything else begins.

Finally, to all the other people who helped me out along the way, especially Stewart and June Vetch at the Muthaiga Club in Nairobi; Chris and Caroline Thouless; Willie and Sue Roberts at the Sirikoi Camp in Lewa; Nancy and Rosie at Lewa; Samani Samwel Indasi and his team of horsemen; Terra Plana; Pieter at the Kerio View; Lornah Kiplagat and Pieter Langerhorst at the HATC; Marguerita North-Lewis; Brother Paul at the Eldoret Golf Club; Geoffrey the kiosk owner, his brother Henry, and the rest of our friendly neighbors in Kapshow, Iten; Alex the night watchman; Ken, Edwin, Raymond, Eliud, and the rest of the Run Fast camp; Tom "Kiprop" Payn; Brother Colm and Ian Kiprono; Phillip Kipchumba and the rest of his training group in Ngong; Tara and Neil; Petra; the Nairobi Waldorf school; the Regency Hotel in Addis Ababa; Tadele Geremew Mulugeta; Mr. and Mrs. William Koila; Simon Biwott; Sunrise Academy in Iten; Braeburn school in Nanyuki; Sarah Watson; Simon the masseur at the One 4 One camp; Tom Ratcliffe; Ricky Simms; Micah Kogo and the other athletes in the house in Teddington; Toby Tanser; Ann and Herb Cook; and my two brothers, Jiva and Govinda.

About the Author

ADHARANAND FINN is an editor at *The Guardian* and a freelance journalist, writing regular features for *The Guardian, The Independent,* and *Runner's World* (UK).

About the Type

This book was set in Scala, a typeface designed by Martin Majoor in 1991. It was originally designed for a music company in the Netherlands and then was published by the international type house FSI FontShop. Its distinctive extended serifs add to the articulation of the letterforms to make it a very readable typeface.